-0. JUL. 19   625.26   P. A. Corley, 2GF

RI   1

625.26

HERTFORDSHIRE LIBRARY SERVICE

This book is due for return on or before the date show
may extend its loan by bringing the book to the lib   r,
once only, by post or telephone, quoting the date o'   n,
the letter and number on the date card, if applicable,   e
information at the top of this label.

RENEWAL   **The loan of books in demand cannot be extended.**
INFORM-
ATION

L.32A

D1339709

-C JUL 1980

W. G. F. THORLEY
C.ENG., F.I.MECH.E

A Breath
of Steam

Volume One

LONDON

IAN ALLAN LTD

First published 1975

ISBN 0 7110 0589 3

All rights reserved. No part of this book may be
reproduced or transmitted in any form or by any
means, electronic or mechanical, including photo-
copying, recording or by any information storage
and retrieval system, without permission from the
Publisher in writing.

© W. G. F. Thorley 1975

Published by Ian Allan Ltd, Shepperton, Surrey
and printed and bound in the United Kingdom,
by R. J. Acford Ltd, Chichester, Sussex

HERTFORDSHIRE
COUNTY LIBRARY

625 · 261
6956145

Contents

Preface

The cult of the locomotive remains unabated. Ten years ago literary pundits were forecasting that the sagas of famous locomotive classes and the associated stories of the people who designed, built and ran them must soon come to an end. That dedicated and somewhat specialised section of the public, ranging from the avid collector of numbers and photographs — known in the business as a gricer — to the professional engineer who makes the mistake of making work his hobby, would, it was said, soon become satiated with the great wealth of fact, anecdote and conjecture about the locomotive which authors of all kinds were pouring out in such profusion.

The pundits were wrong. The last decade has seen an even greater torrent of words and pictures about the locomotive. Encouraged by this evidence of continuing popular interest in the history of railway motive power, I decided to add my humble contribution to this maelstrom of literary effort after a lifetime spent in the service of the LMS and later, British Railways. For 45 years I was associated in one capacity or another with locomotives and the people who had to do with them. If nepotism ever existed to any degree on the Midland and the LMS, it was more than balanced by the opportunity afforded any young man prepared to work, irrespective of his background. In proof of this assertion, I have set down in some detail in this first volume the story of apprenticeship in a motive power depot and of the years immediately following. My only hope is that the reader will find in it a little of the intense interest which I found in enacting my role in some of the scenes portrayed.

Training in the motive power function of the LMS was rigorous but comprehensive. There was a well defined promotional ladder for the man who aspired to become a district or divisional locomotive superintendent and few candidates for these posts escaped the inevitable domestic upheaval every few years in the pursuit of additional and diverse experience. I have tried in successive chapters to give some idea of the great range of technical subjects at which the budding engineer could try his hand with useful and practical results.

Equally important was the acquisition of purely railway operating knowledge for the man who was concerned with the running of locomotives rather more than with the design office and main works procedures. For instance, a knowledge of rules and regulations was an essential qualification for the foreman fitter in charge of a breakdown train, for a shedmaster responsible for the moulding of locomotive cleaners into competent enginemen and for a district superintendent deliberating on the sins of omission or commission of his staff with a view to suitable corrective action.

Most important, however, was the development of management potential. In my early days on the railway there were no schools of transport or staff colleges. Lessons in management were often harsh but essentially practical and acquired within the guide lines of quite a strict code of discipline. In my view they were more effective than much of the sophisticated treatment accorded to management trainees in this day and age.

By offering an admixture of technical matter and personal anecdote, I have endeavoured to provide something for the reader with a general interest in locomotives as well as for the railwaymen like myself who enjoyed the thrill of finding out things in their own way. It would also be a source of satisfaction to me if those members of the numerous preservation societies who are concerned with locomotives find something of use in the book. Faced with the awesome costs of steam traction even for a few weekends a year, they look for every avenue of economy. As a social group they are to be commended and should be assisted in their efforts to portray with such realism the contribution made by our forbears in locomotion to raise the standard and quality of living.

Last but not least, it is my pleasant duty to express grateful acknowledgements to all those in the past who gave me the opportunity to take part in the events related and all those in the present who have helped me to refresh old memories with photographs and discussion. In the first category, the names of Moulang and Rudgard come most readily to mind; there are so many in the second category that it would be quite impracticable to name them all, but I would mention specially A. B. MacLeod, John Edgington and Tim Morrisroe, all of whom have exercised the utmost patience in dealing with my requests for help.

The last word is reserved for the typists whose wish is to remain anonymous, but who consistently performed without demur a first class job of typing about a subject of which they knew very little.

1 Early Days

I was born in 1910 in a small house in the country within 30 yards of a busy four-track section of the Midland Railway and immediately opposite Wellingborough South signalbox. On the farther side of the line were situated the blast furnaces of Thos Butlin & Sons, one of many similar installations which had been built in this area so as to be adjacent to the prolific quantities of iron ore for which this part of Northamptonshire was then famous.

The next signalbox to the north was Wellingborough Junction. From there a loop line about one mile long branched southwards to connect at London Road Junction with the Northampton to Peterborough branch of the London & North Western Railway, which ran due east and passed under the Midland lines at the eastern apex of the triangle thus formed. From my earliest days, I was thus surrounded by the locomotive products of Derby and Crewe.

My father had come to Wellingborough in the mid-1890s to work as a chargehand erector on the blast furnaces then being built by the Wellingborough Iron Company to the north of Wellingborough. Having met my mother, he decided to settle down in the area if he could find work appropriate to his real trade of steam engine fitter. He succeeded in this aim and was appointed to take charge of the operation and maintenance of the newly built local sewage pumping station. This was situated in the triangle of railways described above and comprised twin sets of Tangyes tandem compound condensing engines geared to two-throw horizontal pumps and a battery of Lancashire boilers.

Readers may think it strange that in a book devoted to locomotives and the people associated with them, these pumps have been shewn in Plates 1 and 2. The reason is that it was from this plant, about which I was taught a great deal by my father, that I learned how steam could be safely controlled provided certain fundamental rules were observed: and how maintenance costs could be reduced to an almost unbelievable level, provided that day-to-day care was bestowed on the machinery by conscientious staff year in and year out, thus complementing the benefits of the rugged, simple design and, one suspects, more than ample proportions of much of the equipment when judged by present-day practice. Indicator diagrams were taken at intervals to check the effective use of the steam and Fig 1 shows two which I helped to record in 1924.

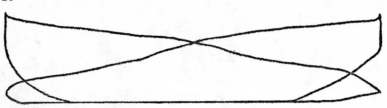

Fig 1a. (*Above*) Indicator diagram taken from HP cylinder, Tangyes tandem compound engine. Fig 1b. (*Below*) Indicator diagram from LP cylinder.

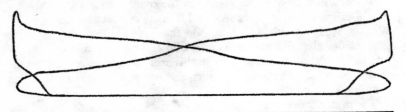

For the interested, the engines were fitted with Meyer's variable expansion valve gear, which was used extensively at one time in steam stationary engine practice. Before this station was closed down in 1966, its machinery had attracted visitors from far and wide and a fine model of it was to be seen in the Model Engineer Exhibition of 1969.

Evidently my father took his work seriously. I still have in my possession text books provided for him by the International Correspondence Schools at Scranton, Pennsylvania, and some examination papers dealing with the care of steam and electrical machines, which he had to send there for correction as this famous institution had no premises in England until well into the first decade of this century. That is what a young man of humble origin and thirsting for more knowledge was prepared to do in those days to enable him to discharge his duties effectively.

Situated in the 'home' triangle was another pumping station to which I had free entry; this was the installation which pumped water from the Isebrook to various locomotive water storage tanks at Wellingborough Loco, the passenger station and Neilson's Sidings. The two sets of pumps were of the Worthington Duplex type, which had no rotating parts (Fig 2) but were arranged with two steam cylinders side by side, the pistons being mounted on rods which were common to the pistons at the 'liquid' end of the pump. The characteristic feature of the Worthington arrangement was the valve motion controlling the admission of steam to the cylinders; this was so designed that one piston acted to give steam to the other, after which it completed its own stroke and waited for its own admission valve to be actuated by the other piston before it made its return stroke. The designed pause of the pistons at the end of each stroke allowed the water

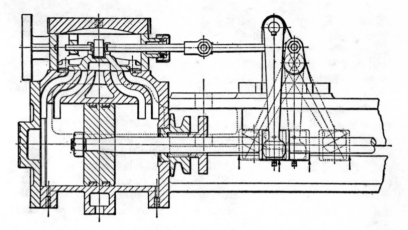

Fig 2. Worthington Duplex steam pump; the opposite side valve gear is shown dotted. *Courtesy Worthington-Simpson Ltd.*

delivery valves to seat quietly and resulted in a smooth delivery flow (Fig 3); also, unlike the system of many types of pump with rotary motion, there was no 'dead centre' and therefore no need for barring round to get the pump to start.

From a tender age I spent a great deal of time with my father at his pumping station. Since both this and my home were excellent vantage points from which to observe the railway scene, I became very familiar with certain aspects of railway operation and acquired the ability to distinguish readily between different types of locomotives and the uses to which they were put.

My earliest recollection of the Midland scene is that of the beautiful Johnson 4–2–2 'Singles' piloting freight trains of the 1916–18 period, many carrying heavy guns and other war supplies. They were frequently stopped, one after the other, at Wellingborough South Up starting signals. In those wartime days there was a constant procession of freight trains on the Midland line to London and the south with the return of balancing empty wagon trains in the down direction. I can recall at this time also the

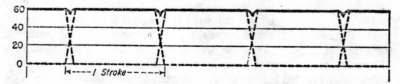

Fig 3. Worthington Duplex steam pump. Thick line shews almost constant delivery pressure. *Courtesy Worthington-Simpson Ltd.*

ubiquitous Kirtley 0-6-0 double-framed locomotives which had the special
appeal of fly cranks whirling round outside the frames, whilst their more
glamorous sisters of the 2-4-0 wheel arrangement were in evidence on
local passenger trains headed by locomotives based on Kettering, Wellingborough, Bedford and Cricklewood and also as pilots of heavy freight
trains. Another class of locomotive to which I became endeared was the
Johnson 0-4-4 tank engines which worked the Higham Ferrers branch
and which included Nos 1246/60 and 1329. Curiously, I have no vivid
recollections of the Midland compounds which then numbered 45, and
15 or 20 of which must have passed my home every day.

Another of these earliest memories is that of lying in bed and listening
to the persistent efforts of an LNW four-cylinder compound coal engine,
struggling to get its train over Wellingborough Junction off the loop line
from the Peterborough branch after standing anything up to two hours at
the signal protecting this junction. The train concerned ran for many
years from Nuneaton to Wellingborough through the night conveying coal
from Griff collieries for remarshalling. Locomotives Nos 18 and 1888,
of LNW Class 23 (rebuilt from LNW Class 30) alternated on the job,
which was a lodging turn, the men and engine returning to Nuneaton
about 1.00 pm the next day with a train of empties. With the light return
load the exhaust of these 2-8-0 compounds was light and sounded muffled,
very different from the noisy efforts of the night before. No 1888 (Plate
6) was converted in 1924 to a two-cylinder simple of the superheated Class
GI (LNW Class 25), whilst No 18 was still compound when scrapped as
LMS No 9602.

These two locomotives were normally the biggest LNW engines which
appeared in this area, for the light passenger trains serving the stations
along the 40 miles of the valley of the River Nene between Northampton
and Peterborough demanded nothing more powerful than a 6ft 6in Precedent or a 6ft 'Waterloo', both of the 2-4-0 type. Looking at my records,
I see that engines of these two classes, bearing names with wide conno-
tations, worked this line for some years in the early 1920s and included
Antelope, Snowdon, Salopian, Glowworm, Speke, Newton, Humphrey Davy,
and *Prosperpine* from the 'Precedent' class, together with *Theorem* and
Wildfire from the smaller wheel class. The regular exception was that the
first passenger train from Northampton to Peterborough (7.40am from
Wellingborough) was almost invariably worked by a 2-4-2, 5ft 6in side
tank. The freight trains were covered by the numerous 18in cylinder,
0-6-0 'Cauliflowers' intermixed with inside cylinder 0-8-0s of mixed
parentage and an occasional four-cylinder compound. The only variation
from this daily pattern was the special treat provided by the sight of a
'Precursor' tender or tank locomotive put on a local pick-up freight after
attention to a heated bearing at Northampton with the object of 'running-
in'.

Thomas Butlin & Sons' blast furnaces and foundries on the north side of the Midland lines completed the engineering environment of my home. Day in day out, year in year out, the exhaust of the huge vertical blowing engine could be heard and the flames billowing from the top of the old open type furnaces could be seen for miles. The real attraction of this plant, however, was the 0–4–0 locomotive which shunted the 50 or so wagons of coal, coke and limestone delivered by the Midland Railway every day. This locomotive was built by Hudswell Clarke in 1894, maker's number 428, and delivered new to Thomas Butlin in February of that year, who numbered it '1' and named it *Edgar* (Plate 8). Coupled wheels were 3ft 0in diameter and cylinders 13in diameter x 18in stroke; it was rebuilt in 1928 and remained in service until December 1954. It was an extremely sturdy machine with which I became very familiar in later years.

To complete the recollection of the railway features of this entrancing triangle of activity it is necessary to mention Wellingborough South signal box, which had a 24-lever frame and was equipped with Midland (rotary) block instruments. Inevitably my curiosity led me to this marvellous vantage point, from where one could look down on a busy scene of movement at any time and also learn some of the intricacies of signalling. Thanks to the signalmen I could work the box by the time I was eleven years old, except that I could not always manage to clear the down fast distant signal, which was nearly a mile from the box. It was in this signal box that I witnessed a long double-headed train of empty wagons fitted with ordinary three-link couplings become uncoupled in mid-length, as distinct from breaking loose. I am still not clear as to how this happens but I learned an early lesson, that of keeping an open mind on apparently impossible occurrences.

In 1922 I won a County Council scholarship to Wellingborough School. As a reward I was taken for my first trip to London over the LNWR route via Northampton to Euston.

There I saw my first 'Claughton' 4–6–0 locomotive, which as it happened was No 2222 the prototype, *Sir Gilbert Claughton*, standing in No 1 platform. It looked an enormous machine, quite the biggest I had seen up to that time. It renewed my enthusiasm for LNW locomotives, which tended to flag when inspired only by the same procession of small, black painted locomotives past my home, month in, month out, in competition with Midland engines of which most types were evident, many of them painted red and mostly well cleaned.

At school, 'half' days were on Wednesday and Saturday afternoons when pupils were expected to avail themselves of the excellent games facilities available, or to be competent marksmen at the rifle ranges, part of the OTC training. I achieved the latter aim, but dodged cricket and football so as to be able to spend the maximum time watching the locomotive scene around Wellingborough, including the little Hudswell Clarke engine at Butlin's furnaces. I had made a peaceful penetration of the furnace premises when about thirteen years old, since many of the employees there knew my father, which provided an open sesame for me. The driver of the Butlin shunter was a somewhat religious but kindly man. In due course I was invited on to the footplate on Saturday afternoons when supervision was least in evidence. I learned to apply the injectors and also became familiar with the motion of a four-wheeled vehicle over rail joints which were not well maintained, and round curves with a radius as small as 42ft; but the really fascinating sessions were when things were quiet and we used to get in a remote siding to study valve and piston events. My tutor would set one crank pin on a centre or angle and invite me to consider the relative position of the other and also the slide valves, with the reversing lever in fore and back gear alternately. Thus I learned to describe the approximate position of both valves for any crank pin and reverser position. At the same time my acquaintance with both Midland engines and enginemen was developing, since I saw both at close quarters when the daily delivery of smelting materials for the furnaces was made about three o'clock in the afternoon. The motive power was either a Midland Class 2F or 3F 0–6–0 or a Class 1F 0–6–0T No 1642. The Midland engine shunted the outgoing empties into a train and it was during these movements that I had my first rides — and drives — on main-line locomotives and this before I was fourteen years old.

In 1924 my father took me to the British Empire Exhibition at Wembley, which had the effect of establishing the conviction in my mind that I wanted to spend the rest of my life with railway locomotives. We travelled on the 7.40am from Wellingborough to St Pancras, behind Kettering 2–4–0 locomotive No 233. Arrived at the exhibition site, a plethora of mechanical engineering exhibits, which included several locomotives, awaited our inspection. There was Churchward's *Caerphilly Castle*, Gresley's *Flying Scotsman*, an LNW *Prince of Wales* built and exhibited by Beardmore & Co and fitted with H. P. M. Beames' version of Walschaerts valve gear and the Reid-Macleod turbine locomotive built by the North British Locomotive Company. And then there were the stands of the railway publishing houses such as the Tothill Press and the Locomotive Publishing Company, of which I had never heard before, displaying literature on many aspects of railways, including motive power. It was an oasis of railway information in a literary desert as far as I was concerned, for in those days, with one notable exception, there was nothing like Ian Allan's *ABC* books to be seen on bookstalls and most railway managements treated requests for information from small boys with scant sympathy. My father bought me *Lectures on the Locomotive* by Dugald Drummond, *Locomotive Management from Cleaning to Driving* by Hodgson & Williams, the current *Railway Year Book* and the *Register of LNWR Locomotives* published by C. Williams of Crewe — the notable exception mentioned above. From this time, too, I became a regular reader of the *Railway Magazine, the Locomotive Magazine and Carriage & Wagon Review*, the *Railway Gazette* and also the *Railway Engineer* until it ceased separate publication. I cannot recall any other single event in my lifetime which opened up such a great storehouse of knowledge in one day!

In retrospect, the years 1925 and 1926 appear to have been spent mainly in preparation for the dreaded matriculation examination to be faced at the end of the 1926 summer term, but every minute which could be spared was devoted to practical lessons on the Hudswell Clarke shunter, the 0-6-0 Midland 2F, 3F and by now, occasional 4F locomotives supplemented by a study of technicalities as far as they were discussed in the railway press of the day, many of which I could not, of course, understand. I did not neglect LNW engines inasmuch as I allocated an occasional 'half' to the LNW London Road station at Wellingborough. There I became a firm devotee of Northampton Driver Emery, who seemed to be rostered principally to the local Northampton–Peterborough pick-up freight trains and who taught me much about locomotives whilst I rode on the footplate during shunting operations at Wellingborough. It was on one of these occasions that I had my first and last ride on a 'Precursor', No 976, *Pacific* which Emery said was 'rather rough at 70mph.'

I began seriously to compile lists of individual engine numbers actually seen, including names, building dates and notes of special features, and there is no doubt that this harmless pastime taught me to be observant. It was made more interesting because I had now available the LNW shed code numbers which was published in the *Register of LNW Locomotives* already mentioned. Unfortunately, the shed label, which was carried in a bracket in the middle of the back edge of the cab roof on LNW locomotives, was frequently missing, whereas on Midland locomotives it was very rare to see the cast iron shed numberplate missing from the smokebox door, and well into the 1930s the name of the shed was painted on the headlamps also. The attitude to details of this sort on the part of the LNW and Midland companies respectively was typical of the difference in their motive power organisations at that time, although I did not appreciate this fact until many years later.

Sometime in 1924 there was an interesting trial centred on Wellingborough locomotive depot, when the Lickey banking engine, 0-10-0 No 2290, came light from Bromsgrove to Wellingborough to take part in comparative trials on coal trains between Neilson's sidings and Brent, a distance of about 60 miles. The event aroused enormous local interest. The lines in and south of Wellingborough were lined with people on the Sunday morning when No 2290, with its own tender replaced by that of Fowler 4F No 3954 performed its allotted task coupled to the dynamometer car and hauling a substantial train of coal — unfortunately I do not know what the load was. The locomotive ran a coupled wheel axle hot when returning from Brent the same evening with a train of empties and that was the last that Wellingborough ever saw of it.

The following Sunday, the dynamometer car and a similar train, the weight of which I again do not know, was hauled over the same route by two

Fowler Class 4F o–6–o locomotives, Nos 3885 and 3922. Double-heading of mineral trains had been normal practice on the Midland main line between Toton and Brent for many years and there is no doubt that Wellingborough enginemen had developed to a high degree the art of working very long trains at a minimum fuel consumption and with maximum operational safety. However that may be, whenever the subject of these trials arose locally for years after, it was averred that engines Nos 3885 and 3922 together burnt less coal on the loaded (up) journey than did 'Big Bertha' by herself. Certainly the drivers of the 4F locomotives would make extra special efforts on this occasion to keep coal consumption to an absolute minimum since the 'big engine' policy was already beginning to take shape; that meant a decrease in double-heading and, therefore, a decrease in the number of jobs for drivers and firemen and their consequent relegation to driving and cleaning duties respectively.

In concluding this introductory chapter, mention must be made of another literary acquisition I made before starting work. The publication in 1926 of Ahrons' *The British Steam Locomotive, 1825–1925* had been advertised some months before with a price reduction for those who ordered in advance and my father had promised me a copy on the assumption that I completed the end of term examinations with satisfactory results. Thus, on August Bank Holiday Saturday, 1926, the postman delivered this wonderful tome devoted entirely to locomotives. I shall never forget the moments of rapture which attended the first look at this book. Nowadays there is such a wealth of literature available on traction of every kind that it seems doubtful if the modern schoolboy suffering from 'railwaymania' can possibly experience the same thrills as we did in those days when given a book like this.

2 The Formative Years

In April 1926, my father wrote to the works managers at Horwich and Crewe Locomotive Works enquiring the conditions under which apprentices to the trade of fitting and turning were accepted therein. The family solicitor had written to the secretary of the Great Western Railway in the previous January, making similar enquiries regarding the practice at Swindon Locomotive Works. Broadly speaking, the conditions were the same at each centre, but whereas the LMSR required a premium of £100 to be paid at the expiration of one month's trial in the shops, after which no portion of this sum would be refunded under any circumstances, the GWR were content to accept the premium in instalments of £10 in advance for each period of six months for five years. The scholastic achievements required by the GW authorities included a credit pass respectively in mathematics, in the English Group, in one foreign language and in one science subject, all at matriculation standard, whereas the LMS appeared to be content with a matriculation or School Leaving Certificate without specifying any particular subjects. In my view, this requirement of the GWR at the very start of a boy's railway career resulted in a far higher proportion of GW apprentices eventually becoming chartered engineers as compared with contemporary LMS apprentices.

All the replies indicated that there were no places immediately available, but Mr Shawcross said that there would be a vacancy at Horwich in early 1927 and that my name would be placed provisionally on his waiting list. It appears that each mechanical engineer at the various centres of the LMSR enjoyed autonomy in the arrangements relating to premium apprentices and there was no central 'clearing house'.

The General Strike which started in May 1926, had the effect of either drastically slowing down or stopping recruitment into the railway industry for a considerable time. I left Wellingborough School in July 1926. Since I had no firm date for starting work anywhere, father decreed that I should go to evening classes (none were held during the day) in engineering subjects at the local technical school; I was to employ the days either in assisting him in his maintenance work at the pumping stations for which he was responsible, or in helping a farmer friend of ours who had a portable power pack consisting of a single-cylinder steam engine mounted on the top of a loco-type boiler and a huge Sanderson tractor of which very few were made. In this period my father taught me how to use a 3½in Drummond centre lathe and read a micrometer.

Nevertheless, this enforced delay in joining the railway was extremely frustrating. So, in the absence of any news of a vacancy at one of the workshops already approached, I took it upon myself in early 1927, to go down to the LMS (ex-Midland) Wellingborough Locomotive Depot — invariably referred to locally as 'The Loco' — and seek audience with the District Locomotive Superintendent in charge of Wellingborough & Kettering depots, one F.C. Anker, with the object of finding out if he had any vacancies for apprentices to the trade of locomotive fitting. Anker was a heavily built man with a florid countenance, who was invariably referred to as Joe Beckett, a contemporary boxing idol; he had earned his soubriquet, it was said, because when he was Assistant Superintendent at Leicester he had knocked down a labourer in the the ashpit to emphasise a point in some discussion they were having.

I remained standing during the interview, for the simple reason that it was not the practice in those days to ask employees or potential employees to sit down on such occasions. Thereby the interviewer put himself at a subtle disadvantage with the interviewed. Mr Anker asked me some elementary questions in arithmetic and general knowledge. He also said that he had asked 'Derby' if he could set on four more apprentices and would let me know if higher authority agreed to his request.

I then informed my father of my precipitate action. It was a painful interview, but he said that having made my bed I could lie on it. He was not impressed when I pointed out that I was going to save him £100 premium plus the difference in the cost of keeping me at home during my apprenticeship, as compared with the cost of keeping me in lodgings, which would have been the case had I gone to one of the main Works.

In due course I was summoned to Derby for a stringent medical examination and given a date to start work at Wellingborough — March 7th, 1927. I reported at 7.55am at foreman fitter 'Teddy' Moore's office in No 1 shed and stood patiently outside until he had distributed the work to some 35, fitters, boilersmiths, tubers and other artizan grades lined up along the shed wall. I soon learned that there was a considerable competition to land a job which would last several days and thus relieve the lucky recipient of the necessity of attending this undignified work queue in the morning. Eventually the foreman bid me accompany him to the fitting shop where I was to commence my training and great adventure with the turner.

In those days, Wellingborough Locomotive Depot consisted of two 24-road round sheds about 250 yards apart where running repairs, standard examinations and boiler washouts were carried out, whilst the shop with four roads was situated roughly halfway between them. Most Midland depots of any size had a shop which was referred to as an 'outstation' shop, although most of them were the responsibility of the local district locomotive superintendent. In these shops, which had been built over the years to relieve the pressure on Derby Works, it was the practice to perform what were known as service repairs to a locomotive; these later became known as intermediate repairs, since they were carried out intermediately between successive major general overhauls in Derby Works.

Quite heavy repairs were carried out in the shop, three of the roads in which were equipped with pits, whilst the fourth led to the wheel lathe; all were served by an overhead crane of 20 tons capacity, operated manually from the decking which covered the main transverse girders of the crane. A locomotive selected by the shopping bureau at Derby for service repairs and which might or might not be a Wellingborough engine, would be propelled by manpower from a small turntable on to a pit. Then a fitter, apprentice and mate would be detailed to do the following work:

Remove wheels for tyre turning.
Strip axleboxes for re-metalling and re-fitting to horns and journals.
Strip valves, pistons and all motion and repair as necessary; this included re-metalling of all coupling rod bushes and eccentric straps, also removal of eccentric sheaves to examine for flaws in axle keyways.
Remove and clean out blast pipe.
Renew safety valves if reported blowing off light; if of the Salter type, they were adjusted.
Examine all boiler fittings.

If boiler cleaning involving the removal of tubes was required, this would be done in one of the sheds either before or after the locomotive was put in the shop, because there was no water there to enable the dirt to be removed effectively from the water spaces. Boiler and firebox repairs as found necessary were carried out in the shop. Occasionally it would be necessary to lift a boiler from the frames to enable the boilersmith to reach firebox stays, which for some reason he could not make steamtight without riveting the outer ends. The fitting of a copper patch in the corner of an inner firebox was to me a real example of the boilersmith's art that was rarely practiced at outstations on the LMSR after the late 1920s. (Fig 4).

This, then, was the environment in which I was conducted on a cold March morning and introduced to Joe Astbury, the turner. He commanded a sizeable area of the shop, where there were situated: a wheel lathe built by Maclea and March about 1875, capable of taking wheels up to 7ft 6in diameter; a large shaping machine; an axlebox boring machine; a $7\frac{1}{2}$in centre lathe; and a 15in centre gap lathe which had a bed about 12ft long, together with one small and one large drilling machine. Like the wheel lathe, the remainder of the machinery was of somewhat ancient origin — some of it, indeed, could have been installed when the shop was built, which was certainly not later than 1883.

All the machines were driven by a line shaft extending from the engine house, which formed an extension of the shop at its south end, into the blacksmith's and coppersmith's shop, which formed a similar extension at

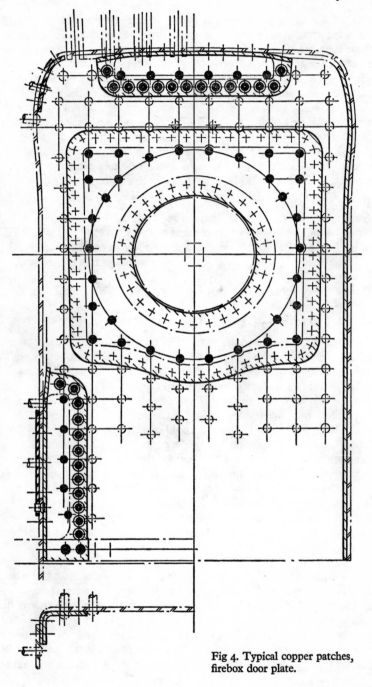

Fig 4. Typical copper patches,
firebox door plate.

its north end. The line shaft had been driven originally by a single-cylinder steam engine of Midland Railway manufacture which incorporated what were obviously some standard locomotive parts. Early in the 1920s, however, this engine and its boiler, both of which remained in working order, had been superseded by a 10hp gas engine, with tube ignition, which functioned until replaced by an electric motor about 1930.

Astbury knew my father. This facilitated my initiation into the society of the shop floor, which for some youngsters proves to be a trying time when they come directly from a public school. In the years immediately following the General Strike, there was still much bitterness amongst railway employees occasioned by the manner in which many of them had been treated by the management upon resumption of work.

Thanks to my unofficial 'off the job' training, principally at the hands of my father, and of which Astbury was aware, I was put on the $7\frac{1}{2}$in centre lathe and given a number of injector top clacks to face up for my first job on my first day. Later in the morning, the firing of the Cornish boiler in the engine house and the working of the associated donkey feed pump was explained to me. The boiler pressure was maintained at about 20lb/sq in for the purpose of heating the adjoining shop by means of steam radiators situated in the pits and at one other point near the machine tools. Fuel consisted of scrap timber from the adjoining wagon repair shops, including some roof sticks from box vans which were being broken up there. I gathered the former were made of ash, steamed and bent to shape, an extremely tough and springy timber which could not be easily broken. It was made clear to me that I was responsible for keeping the shop warm and what the dire consequences for me would be if I failed! In fact, whenever the ambient temperature was below the lower 40s it was impossible to warm the shop adequately. The factory inspector used to hang his thermometer on a scribing block which invariably reposed on the slide rest of the shaping machine when not in use, and wearing a mournful expression, shook his head at the reading which was far below the statutory requirement in the winter months. Yet nothing was ever done to improve the heating. Such working conditions would not be tolerated for even half a shift today.

The work in the machine section of the shop proved congenial and interesting, although its volume fluctuated considerably. It was evident that there was scarcely enough work to occupy fully the available labour force. I learned then that there is nothing more soul-destroying to the average healthy man than to have to pretend that he is busy when it is painfully obvious to the foreman that he is not. The foreman did everything possible to find legitimate work, but the economy had not recovered from the General Strike; locomotive mileage, on which the examination schedule was partly based, was not being generated at the rate on which maintenance resources were calculated; and the volume of work, both in the sheds and shop, was well below normal.

Consequently it was only rarely that all three of the pits in the shop were occupied simultaneously. Nor was there any evidence of a desire to return a locomotive to traffic after service repairs in a target time, since piece work had by this time been discontinued at Wellingborough. Thus a locomotive would often occupy a pit for three or four weeks whilst undergoing service repairs and there was only rarely heavy pressure on the machining facilities.

Astbury therefore had ample time to teach me how to re-profile tyres, bore and face axlebox brasses and plane them for the steel shell, bore eccentric liners and perform a great variety of jobs, including the taper turning and screwcutting of connecting rod big end bolts from bar steel on the 15in and 7½in centre lathes. The variety of special chucks which had been made over the years to accommodate piston rod and valve spindle white metal packings was fascinating. From all I have heard over the years from my contemporaries who served their apprenticeship in one of the main works, I am convinced that I had a far more comprehensive training in the actual manipulation of machine tools in general than ever they enjoyed.

About the beginning of July 1927, a notice was posted in the shed to the effect that any outstation apprentice who wished to enter for the annual examination of mechanical staff for directors' prizes should advise his foreman. Apparently this examination in the subjects of machine drawing, mathematics, heat engines and applied mechanics was held at Derby every year primarily for engineering (privileged) apprentices in the main Derby workshops for whom it was obligatory, whilst outstation trade apprentices were invited to participate on a purely voluntary basis.

The examination, which occupied one full day, was held in the Railway Institute opposite Derby station, under the eagle eye of G. W. Woolliscroft, Superintendent of Apprentices. In view of the fact that I had been in the service about four months and no Wellingborough apprentice appeared ever to have entered for this examination, I sent in my name with considerable misgiving. On the appointed day I duly caught the 6.11am from Wellingborough to Derby, drawing board and T square under my arm, and accompanied by another apprentice, Arthur Beavan, who was four years my senior and shamed into entering by the new boy! In the event he secured the second prize of 20s for new entrants. When dismissed, as was then usual upon reaching the age of 21, he went to work for Vickers Vimy and, I believe, reached high office with that firm.

I attended this examination each year until it was discontinued after the 1931 event. The results were conveyed in the form of a letter to each candidate containing suitable adjurations to continue his efforts in his weakest subjects, and signed personally by Henry Fowler, as Chief Mechanical Engineer in the years 1927/8/9. But in 1930, the year in which I managed to get in the first class and secure the highest marks for heat engines, the signature was that of H.G. Ivatt, who had been appointed Works Superintendent, Derby, in May 1928.

The purpose in mentioning this examination is twofold; firstly, to demonstrate that in those days any young apprentice who was trying to become an engineer, whatever his background, had the channels to bring his aspiration to the notice of his superiors; secondly, to throw another beam of light on the personality of Sir Henry Fowler, who was not too busy to sign personally a letter of encouragement to a humble trade apprentice. He had presented the prizes at Wellingborough Technical Institute in 1924, a ceremony which had been attended by my mother. I remember clearly how she described Sir Henry's speech, in the course of which he had said 'how he loved to see his beautiful red engines running through the countryside'. Perhaps not inspiring talk for embryo engineers, but as a fourteen year old I was thrilled to think that such a man, great in my youthful eyes, loved the sight of his engines as I did.

Two outstanding events roused interest amongst the railwaymen—and indeed most of the inhabitants of Wellingborough—during that summer of 1927. There was the appearance of the first 2-6-0 + 0-6-2 Garratt locomotive for the LMSR, No 4997, from the works of Beyer Peacock at Gorton; and, almost concurrently, the Ljungström turbine-driven condensing locomotive from the same manufacturers, who had built it in 1926 as a private venture, having secured the co-operation of the LMS authorities in carrying out evaluation trials on main running lines.

The secrecy with which innovations of this kind were surrounded is unbelievable today. Nevertheless, some notice had to be given of impending movements and information was passed along the line, so that on the afternoon when the Garratt appeared for the first time at the head of a Toton–Brent coal train, it seemed that every railwayman and a sizeable proportion of other residents lined the railway for a couple of miles to watch its progress. My particular vantage point was Wellingborough North signalbox. I recall how indistinct the exhaust beats sounded, the train having just started from Finedon Road after taking water and getting coal forward. The locomotive, with its 44.5sq ft of grate area, was viewed with apprehension by local firemen who were thankful that only Toton men were involved — so far. Two more of these locomotives appeared that year, but the class very rarely came on to the Wellingborough Loco and then only because an injector had failed or a brick arch had fallen down.

The Ljungström turbine locomotive (Plate 10), which made its debut on the London main line with a train of coaching stock within a few weeks of the first Garratt, did not appear very often in the daylight hours, although it ran tests on night fitted freight trains between London and Sheffield in later months. It seemed to make a considerable amount of smoke when passing Wellingborough at speed. Visiting boiler inspectors brought the story that the locomotive frequently failed with leaking condenser tubes and there was little talk of it amongst shed staff after the early part of 1928.

The other event in 1927 which was to influence greatly the lives of many people, including myself, was the appointment of Harold Rudgard as Assistant to the Superintendent of Motive Power in the Chief General Superintendent's office of the LMSR at Derby, as recorded in the August issue of the *Locomotive Magazine*. Universally known as the 'Colonel', this dynamic character was to become a major figure in the direction of motive power policy and activities in this country until his retirement in 1951. A one-time pupil of S. W. Johnson, he had already been District Locomotive Superintendent at Skipton, Derby and Plaistow before World War I, being appointed to the latter position at the age of 27 after the Midland took over the London, Tilbury & Southend Railway in 1912.

After some 15 months with Astbury and his machines, I was put to work with Fitter Joe Gibson and his mate in the running sheds, where boiler washing and boiler and motion examinations and repairs were carried out. Each apprentice was allocated in turn to a fitter who specialised in a particular aspect of locomotive maintenance, so that he participated in the whole range of work normally carried out at sheds on a locomotive between its successive visits to the chief mechanical engineer's main works. In the case of Wellingborough engines, the CME maintaining works was almost invariably Derby at that time.

I was fortunate to be allocated in the first instance to Gibson, who had served his apprenticeship with the Wellingborough Iron Company and was an extremely competent fitter and turner. Some men are born mechanics and if they combined this quality with a high degree of craftmanship, the scope for using their potential in the field of steam locomotive maintenance was great. Gibson was such a man and, moreover, combined these qualities with the gift of patience and readiness to impart knowledge to a younger man.

At this point it may be of interest to recall the composition of the motive power fleet at Wellingborough in 1927/28. It totalled 94 engines, exclusively of Midland origin, as below:

Class	Wheel arrangement	No allocated
1P	2-4-0	6 Included one double-framed Kirtley engine No 21
1PT	0-4-4	4
1F	0-6-0	1 Double-framed Kirtley engine No 2738
2F	0-6-0	7
3F	0-6-0	33
4F	0-6-0	39
1FT	0-6-0	4

Not, perhaps, a very exciting allocation list, yet it contained sufficient variety to provide ample tutorial scope for learning how to maintain the much bigger and more complicated machines, for the upkeep of which I was destined to become responsible in future years.

For instance, I can say categorically that it was much easier to adjust the bogie axle weights of a Stanier 'Jubilee' locomotive than of a Johnson 0–4–4 tank. Similarly, assembling the inside Walschaerts valve motion of a Fowler Class 7F 0–8–0 locomotive was to prove easy when compared with the Stephenson motion of a double-framed Kirtley engine; in the latter the front half of the eccentric straps were integral with the eccentric rods, which fact frequently elicited pithy comment from the fitting staff. Whilst it is a fact that there were some traps which designers never seemed able to avoid, the illustration mentioned above shewed that designers all the time were improving their products. It was often the continuing demands of the user for more powerful and complex machines within the restricted British loading gauge which militated against easy maintenance.

The principal services worked by Wellingborough engines were local passenger to Northampton, Leicester and the branch to Rushden and Higham Ferrers, the latter being the province of the 0–4–4 tanks, whilst the 2–4–0s coped with the former. The Johnson Class 3F and Fowler Class 4F engines worked double-headed coal trains to London, a few trains to Toton, Staveley and Westhouses on a lodging basis, loaded in the up direction and empty in the down, and one or two trains to points in the Birmingham/Walsall area. Summer excursions to Blackpool were worked by Class 4F engines as far as Belle Vue, and this class also worked occasional specials to east coast resorts situated on the M & GN system.

The maintenance of LMS locomotives was based on a standard schedule of examinations. At Midland depots at any rate these were carried out with scrupulous observance of the stipulated periods or mileages at which different components were examined. The system had been in force on the Midland before grouping, having been introduced by Cecil Paget; it was eventually applied throughout the whole of the LMSR and ultimately British Railways, until the demise of steam. There is little doubt that adherence to its requirements, coupled with the disciplined application of good fitting practices, enabled the Midland to work a heavy traffic with locomotives much less powerful than those of comparable neighbouring railways — although by 1928 it had become evident that good running shed organisation alone could not compensate for deficiencies of power in front-line locomotives without the continuance of costly double-heading.

Briefly, the Midland system of examination provided for the complete or partial dismantling of boilers, boiler fittings and 'stationary' equipment, such as brake gear, on a time basis whilst reciprocating and rotating components were examined on a mileage basis. The principal examination items were:

At 3–5 weeks

Firebox, fusible plugs. Boiler water gauge frames. Carriage warming apparatus. Steam brake. Drip valves in vacuum train pipe.

At 7–9 weeks
Injectors. Vacuum ejectors. Sanding apparatus.

At 9–15 weeks
Safety valves (visual only, but included steam test).

After 5–6,000 miles
Wheels, tyres and axles.
Connecting rod big-ends.
By-pass valves.
Water pick-up apparatus.
Mechanical lubricators.
Flexible oil pipes.

After 10–12,000 miles
Connecting and coupling rods.
Crank axle (built up).
Tender or side tanks
Slide valves.

After 20–24,000 miles
Pistons and piston valves.
Crank axle (solid)
Intermediate drawgear (engine and tender uncoupled).
Tender axlebox oil pads.

In addition, firebox and boiler water spaces together with superheater flue tubes and elements were examined after every occasion of washing out the boiler. The frequency of this operation was dependent upon the quality of the water principally used by a depot's locomotives, and the nature of work performed or the mileage run; a common period was 7–10 working days.

The reference to solid crank axles in the above schedule recalls the substantially greater work load occasioned by defects which occurred in a number of crank axles supplied for some Class 1P 2–4–0 locomotives by a well known Sheffield manufacturer in the early 1920s. Many axles were found to have flaws in the keyways cut in the axle for the reception of the keys for the eccentric sheaves; if these flaws were found at a major overhaul in Derby works, which was usually the case, a dimensioned sketch shewing the direction of the flaw relative to the cross-section of the axle was sent to the owning depot, which was then responsible for monitoring any extension of the flaws that might occur in service. This involved removing the driving wheels from the locomotive at 20–24,000 miles, stripping and thoroughly cleaning the crank axle, and bumping the wheel set against another pair when a thin line of oil would ooze from the fracture. Sometimes the fracture had developed slightly as compared with the sketch and it would then be my job to make an adapted sketch for the records.

Working under the direction of Gibson was easier as compared with other fitters by virtue of the variety of specialised tools which he had devised for specific applications. An example is shewn in Fig 5; it consisted

Fig 5. Sand ejector spanner.

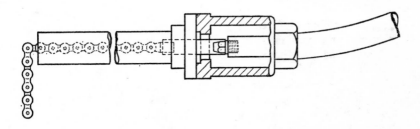

of a thin walled ⅜in box spanner attached to the end of a bicycle chain. This was used to confirm the presence of, and/or tighten up the steam cone of the Gresham & Craven sand ejector without removing the sand pipe extension, which was a tedious and time-consuming process. In fact, by using the tool, a time saving of at least 1½ man hours could be effected on the 7–9 weekly examination of the six sand ejectors on a Class 4F Fowler locomotive.

However, the industrial climate and general shortage of work was such that one did not advertise the merits of time-saving equipment; it was popular neither with one's workmates nor with the Foreman Fitter, whose considerable talent in finding work when there was none was already stretched to the utmost. In consequence, Gibson and I each took advantage of this tool and many others of his devising in our own way. Gibson would disappear mysteriously for a couple of hours 'on a personal job for the boss'; in fact, he was probably tinkering with his own car, an exceptional possession at that time. I could be found in the carpenter's shop, built on one side of No 1 shed, doing my homework for evening classes, for by this time I had embarked on the National Certificate course which entailed three nights a week at the local Technical Institute. There was no such thing as day release for technical education for a trade apprentice in those days even if day educational facilities had been available, which they were not at Wellingborough.

I believe it was in this year, 1928, that an allocation of some brand new Class 3FT 0–6–0 locomotives was made to Wellingborough, being part of an order shared by the Hunslett Engine Company of Leeds. The locomotives were towed 'dead' to Wellingborough with an accompanying wagon containing the motion details. Gibson and I had the job of assembling connecting rods and eccentric straps and rods. We got the impression that the manufacturers had done a first-class job of machining and erection. I have often pondered why the locomotives were not worked in steam from Leeds to Wellingborough, but never discovered the reason. In the early days after their commissioning one was put to work on the branch passenger service to Higham Ferrers during a temporary shortage of o-4-4 engines, but it ran a hot trailing axlebox and they were never used for this purpose again. Yet in another area, the same class was used on Broad Street–Potters Bar trains, which often reached a maximum of 60mph right up to the withdrawal of the service in September 1939. Alas, they still developed many hot axleboxes.

Most of the personalities mentioned in my workaday story so far have been artisans, but I had become much involved with drivers and firemen, not only during working hours in the shed but also at the Sunday morning sessions of the Mutual Improvement Class. This latter institution had been encouraged by the Midland and LMSR managements to the extent of providing accommodation and lecturers, but the organisation and running of the class was undertaken by footplate staff, the charge for the syllabus card being the annual membership subscription. I joined within three months of starting work. I was the only artisan grade to do so, apart from George Renaut, an elderly fitter who had for many years shewn willingness to answer any questions a driver or fireman might address to him. This may sound unexceptional, but in those days the relationship between drivers and artisans was not always cordial. The driver's rate was 90s per week, which easily made him the aristocrat of the railway wages grades. The fitter's top rate was 65s, and it was inevitable that there was feeling between some members of the respective grades.

The mutual improvement classes were usually well attended, being presided over on a Sunday morning in the reading room of the lodging hostel by one Driver Billy Heelin, resplendent in black suit and with gold Albert adorning his stomach. He was not notable for his erudition and was not, according to his regular fireman, an exceptional engineman; but he exercised great authority amongst his fellows and could steer the discussion on an emotive subject—and there were plenty of those—in a manner which, if only he could have seen it, would have been the envy of many a present-day industrial relations officer.

Firemen were expected to prepare themselves for the examination to become a 'passed' fireman (ie, passed to take charge of a locomotive). This examination included the dismantling of one set of motion of a two-cylinder locomotive so that the candidate could demonstrate his knowledge of how to work home on one cylinder if a failure occurred to the opposite side. This part of the examination was perpetuated on the Midland Section of the LMS until the early 1930s, but was eventually discontinued as having become unrealistic and unsuited to the bigger engines then entering service. Whilst it applied, however, the mutual improvement class organized the trial dismantling of an engine on a Sunday morning by the next two firemen due to be passed for driving under the eagle eye of fitter Renaut who was paid 7s 6d by the class and nothing by the company.

Another stalwart of the Mutual Improvement Class was Driver Billy Benbow, a man of considerable girth, afflicted with a speech impediment and blessed with the gift of knowing how to get the maximum amount of work from a locomotive for a given rate of burning coal. He and another driver, George Worker, vied with one another to exact apparently good performances from Fowler Class 4F locomotives, which were never of the most free-steaming variety and at this time were fitted with piston valves having wide rings, which caused uneven liner wear and steam leakage (Fig 6).

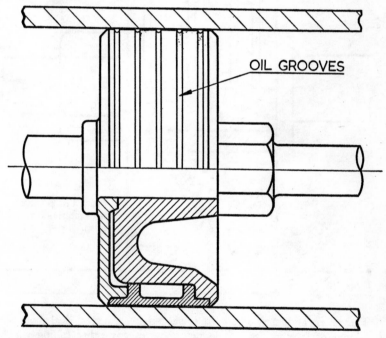

OIL GROOVES

Fig 6. Schmidt wide piston valve ring.

Piston valves were withdrawn at 20-24,000 miles for examination of the spring rings and the liners, but Foreman Fitter Moore would often have them removed before this mileage had been attained on the strength of a verbal report from George Worker. If Benbow came to hear of this (and he usually did!) he did not hesitate to accuse Worker at the Sunday morning forum provided by the MIC of reporting engines unfit which were perfectly capable of doing their booked job! This argument was never satisfactorily concluded until piston valves were fitted with narrow rings, like piston rings, after which liner wear and steam leakage past the valves became relatively infrequent (Fig 7).

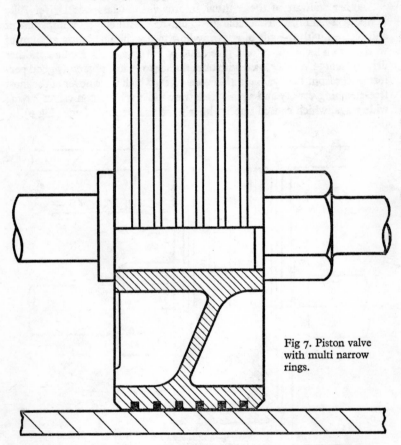

Fig 7. Piston valve with multi narrow rings.

These men, and many others like them, taught me a great deal about the operation of locomotives. I do not know of any other calling which engenders such emotive interest amongst its disciples as does that of steam engine driving. For this fact it is hoped that many generations of Locomotive Superintendents and later, Chief Mechanical Engineers, have been truly thankful. It was the means whereby many unsatisfactory designs were enabled to continue in service, as they could not have done without the interest shewn by their drivers.

In about March 1928, the District Locomotive Superintendent, Mr Anker, was promoted to take charge of the Nottingham district and was succeeded by Mr A. E. Bolderston from Crewe. It was rumoured that Bolderston had not taken readily to the acceptance of Midland shed practices, which by now were being introduced far and wide, and that in consequence he had been sent to Wellingborough to finish his time, which proved to be the case. He was a tall man of upright bearing who never came into the sheds or shop very often. But according to the staff representatives of the local departmental committee (the drivers' 'shop stewards' committee), he was a 'gentleman' who let the various foremen get on with their job without dictatorial interference from him.

Certainly Bolderston took a tolerant view when I came to grief in turning a set of coupled wheel tyres from engine No 3496. This was a Class 3F 0-6-0 undergoing service repairs in the shop. I had actually finished the third wheel set by chamfering the edge of the tyres and left the chamfer tools rubbing lightly against the tyres with the feed disengaged, whilst I moved away to speak to another apprentice. Another younger apprentice appeared on the scene and continued happily on his way after fiddling with the pawl on the automatic feed. I became aware of this only when the belt which drove the lathe from the line shaft began to whistle and slip. The chamfer tool was progressing across the LH tyre and had already sliced off a sizeable cut from the tread about $\frac{1}{2}$in wide. This meant, of course, that the operation had to be continued, not only on this pair, but because all diameters of coupled wheels must be nominally the same, also on the other two pairs already finished, a total of about three days' work.

Fortunately, the tyres were fairly thick, which permitted the removal of more metal, otherwise it would have meant the fitting of new tyres. Quite properly, I was held responsible but when Bolderston visited the shop the next day whilst I was busy retrieving the situation, he did not speak. This reticent man retired about the end of 1929, having earned the respect of Wellingborough staff in the short time during which he held office there.

Towards the end of 1929, I was beginning to realize that I had, to say the least, been a little impetuous in choosing to become a trade apprentice instead of waiting for the promised engineering apprenticeship at a main CME works. For one thing, the LMS practice of the time in using apprentices in lieu of fitters' mates whenever there was a shortage of the latter was not calculated to boost morale. Furthermore, my wage for a 47–hour week was 11s, for which I was quite often doing the work of a fitter's mate, who received about 49s for the same hours.

I could never nurse grievances for very long. So, after some weeks of particularly unpleasant labouring work in smokeboxes during which I felt I was learning very little about the job, I marched into the Foreman Fitter's office one Saturday morning in the early autumn of 1929. I told him bluntly that if he did not cease using me as a fitter's mate I was going to ask to see the Superintendent on the following Monday morning.

If there was one thing which Foreman Fitter Moore detested, it was the possibility of a man complaining to the superintendent. This is understandable and is indeed the mark of a supervisor who treats his men fairly and feels resentment when they are not satisfied with his ruling. Accordingly, Moore told me to report specially to him on Monday morning and he would see that the cause for my grouse was removed.

Well, I asked for it and I got it—'it' being the valve and piston examination on Fowler Class 4F 0–6–0 No 4035. For a mate I was given Charlie Knowles, a holder-up or boilersmith's mate, a genial soul who was extremely likeable but bone idle. Charlie had been 'floating' on the labour market for some weeks following an accident to Jack Horne, his boilersmith partner. Horne had entered the tank of Johnson Class 3F 0–6–0 No 3601 to renew some rivets, taking with him a naked gas jet with a leaky connection to the flexible pipe, as a result of which he collapsed in the tank from coal gas poisoning. He was only removed through the tank filling aperture just in time—and with difficulty, for he was a very heavy man.

No 4035 was notable for the very tight fit of her piston rods in the crossheads, a fact which several fitters had discovered at previous piston examinations. Suffice to say that it took me two whole days to separate the RH piston from its crosshead. No skin was left on the inner sides of the base of my thumbs, because I had to use a 14lb lump hammer to strike the parting wedge, which requires an upward swing in cramped conditions—particularly when one is six feet tall. I shall never know whether Moore deliberately chose this locomotive to quell my ardour to become a fitter quickly or whether it was genuinely the next one due for examination. To my intense relief Jack Horne returned to work on the third day of our partnership and Charlie returned to his mate, full of voluble regrets that he could not stay and see me through! I was allocated another mate, a younger hard working man, and with assistance from several kindly disposed fitters who had had some quiet enjoyment at my expense, I managed to complete the examination in the unofficial but 'expected' time of 47 hours—one working week.

I was never again utilised as a fitter's mate. When employed in the running sheds I worked mostly on my own, and always so when working in the shop, until the completion of my apprenticeship. My guide, mentor and friend, Joe Gibson, came unobtrusively to the rescue when I was given a more than usually difficult job. I remember asking him to check my readings when I was given my first set of slide valves to reset on Johnson Class 3F 0–6–0 No 3580 and how elated I was when he confirmed them as being correct.

I continued to brood, however, on the consequences of my precipitate action in choosing to become a trade apprentice. So I found myself writing in December 1929 to the North British Locomotive Company, The Hunslet Engine Company and Beyer Peacock and Company to enquire if there was any possibility of entering their locomotive drawing offices as a student draughtsman. All three firms sent me a courteous reply indicating that they had a full complement of staff and would have for some time to come.

Thus the year 1929 ended for me on a gloomy note, yet my interest in anything to do with locomotives remained undiminished.

Enter Francis Daniel Moulang, aged 55, of rubicund complexion, rolling gait and southern Ireland ancestry. He succeeded Bolderston as District Locomotive Superintendent at Wellingborough in January, 1930. After more than forty years I still regard the arrival of this man as the greatest turning point in my life.

Moulang served his apprenticeship at the Inchicore works of the Great Southern & Western Railway of Ireland and joined the locomotive drawing office of the Midland Railway at Derby in 1899. He assisted in the design, operation and development of the Midland three-cylinder compound locomotives, actually superintending the making of the patterns for the cylinders of the first five engines of this class and of subsequent MR superheated classes. He had joined the motive power section in the temporary capacity of District Locomotive Superintendent at Toton as a wartime measure in 1916, but never returned to the drawing office, becoming successively District Locomotive Superintendent at York and Buxton before arriving at Wellingborough, which now had Bedford as a sub-depot as well as Kettering.

This strange man with his delightful Irish brogue provided the means whereby I began to realise the depth of my ignorance on so many matters pertaining to locomotives. He was a Whitworth Exhibitioner and could bring a quality of mind and attitude to bear on engineering fundamentals which made everyone in the engineering world whom I had met so far appear rather dull by comparison. This was not to belittle the great skill and knowledge of people like my father and Gibson, who were both highly competent mechanics; but they did not always know *why* they achieved success by doing certain things in certain ways.

I cannot recall the exact circumstances of my first meeting with Moulang. Suffice to say he asked me about my aims, work and progress, which gave me the opportunity to confide my fears of stagnation to someone who, one felt, had a sympathetic appreciation of the aspirations of a young man. His comment was quite brusque and brief. When I told him that I was taking the National Certificate examination in the following April, he said: 'Come and see me when you have passed and I will see what I can do for you'. I did not speak to him again until I received notification in the following August that I had passed the NC examination.

Moulang was as good as his word. Thenceforward I had a training in motive power maintenance and running which was always interesting, often exciting but always directed to the things which mattered. In fact, during the compilation of this narrative, it has been difficult to select the activities to describe, they were so many and varied.

I suppose if I had been able to take a detached view of the relative importance of events at Wellingborough Loco in 1930, the arrival of an allocation from the second batch of 30 Beyer-Garratt locomotives then in course of delivery from the Gorton Foundry of Beyer Peacock & Company would have appeared to be the most significant. Thirteen of these engines were destined for Wellingborough, the remainder at that time being allocated to Toton, from which depot the original three had worked since their debut in 1927.

The later locomotives differed considerably in detail fittings from their three predecessors. One, No 4986, had a rotary coal bunker, designed to lighten the fireman's work whilst another, No 4996, was fitted with a steam coal pusher with the same object in mind. A Davies & Metcalfe exhaust steam injector was substituted for one of the live steam injectors and Anderson's by-pass valves were fitted to the cylinders. With the exception of No 4986, the rotary bunker of which had, of course, to be enclosed, the bunkers of these new locomotives were provided with a heavy sliding tarpaulin operated by steel cables attached to a windlass in the cab. Twenty-five engines were fitted with Parry steam tube cleaners and five with Clyde steam soot blowers. Most of these fittings and other components such as pivot centres, telescopic steam pipe joints and Walschaerts valve gear had not been dealt with at close quarters by the majority of Wellingborough's artisan staff and there was much to discover. It was almost impossible to get a drawing of anything, except of proprietary fittings, the manufacturers of which were only too pleased to send literature relating to their products in an effort to secure fair treatment for them. The situation afforded a wonderful opportunity for a 19 year old to show that he could make a contribution by collecting information about the new locomotives from every possible source. This I did, supplementing it with my own observations as the locomotives entered service and began to aggregate mileage.

When a new locomotive was introduced, it was usually the boiler that presented the initial difficulties to the running shed staff. The Garratts were no exception. The injector delivery clack boxes were mounted on steel pads rivetted to the firebox back plate instead of being attached direct to the back plate, which was normal LMS practice. Several failures occurred due to serious leakage between the mounting pad and the back plate and in every case the blow was located at a point on the periphery of the pad adjacent to a longitudinal stay nut. It was surmised that this nut had been fitted prior to the caulking of the pad and that the latter process had been hampered in consequence, resulting in leakage. When the asbestos mattresses—another innovation—were removed and the pads thoroughly recaulked, no further trouble was experienced.

Trouble was also experienced in traffic due to the collapse of the drop grates fitted to facilitate fire cleaning. Burning of the frame of the drop portion of the grate used to occur resulting in the whole assembly falling into the ashpan (Fig 8).

It was considered that the warping and burning of the drop portion was due to it getting literally engulfed by live fire at disposal operations

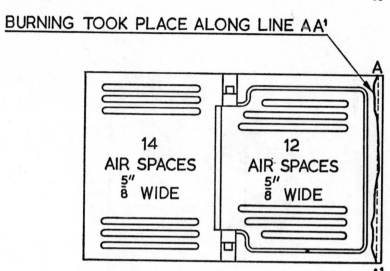

Fig 8. Drop grate Beyer-Garratt locomotive.

and a definite sequence of fire-dropping operations was introduced which effected considerable improvement.

The burning of the ferrule fitted to protect the firebox end of the super-heater tubes (Fig 9) took place at a greater rate than had ever been experienced with the Class 4F Fowler 0–6–0 locomotives. This was indicative of the severe conditions in the firebox which obtained when working trains of 1,500 tons between Toton, Wellingborough and Brent. Firehole deflector plates also burnt away rapidly compared with any previous experience. Another component which suffered by burning was the tip of the steam cone of the soot blowers if it was left protruding—incorrectly—into the firebox after use; here again a training campaign was mounted which helped to some extent.

The most crippling defect which arose in the working of the Garratts was the incidence of heated coupled wheel axleboxes, which had inadequate bearing area to sustain the loads imposed upon them. Every one of Wellingborough's 13 Garratts ran at least one hot coupled axle during the first 18 months of their life. When they first arrived at the depot the hydraulic wheel drop had not been installed and on one locomotive it was necessary to uncouple the front unit, where the heated bearing was situated, from the boiler unit and lift the former separately under the shear legs.

The separation of the units proved to be a difficult job in the absence of a drawing and a lack of knowledge of the arrangements on the part of the fitters concerned. Confusion also existed amongst enginemen as to how

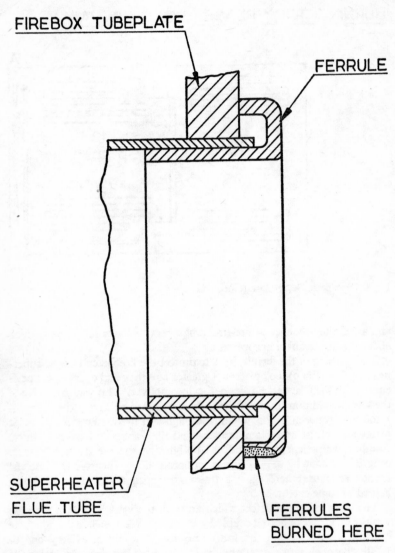

Fig 9. Burning of superheater flue tube ferrules, Garratt locomotives.

they should designate a particular axlebox, since no All-Line instructions had been issued. On at least one occasion the wrong pair of wheels was taken out, firstly because the location of the affected pair had been incorrectly described and secondly because the latter showed no external signs of heating, which is often the case if the white metal does not fuse completely. Accordingly I wrote privately to Beyer Peacock and asked how they designated the position of axles on Garratt locomotives. Their reply formed the basis of an instruction to enginemen which was duly posted (Fig 10).

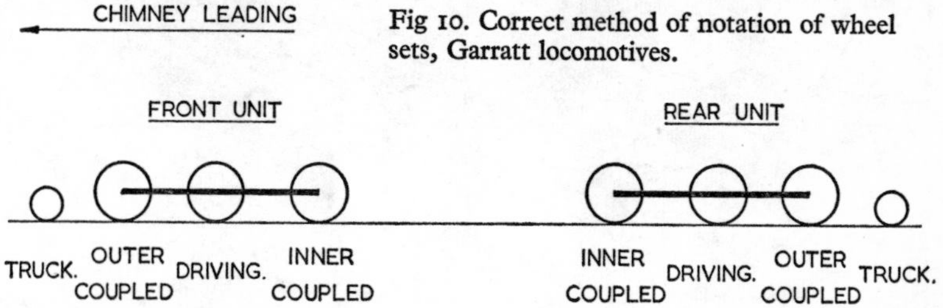

CHIMNEY LEADING ←

Fig 10. Correct method of notation of wheel sets, Garratt locomotives.

FRONT UNIT   REAR UNIT

TRUCK. OUTER COUPLED   DRIVING.   INNER COUPLED   INNER COUPLED   DRIVING.   OUTER COUPLED   TRUCK.

The results of the researches into axlebox design had not been published —indeed, many were not completed at this time. Thus there was no guide to using staff and as existed in later years in the form of, for instance, E. S. Cox's classic contribution to the proceedings of the Institution of Locomotive Engineers in 1944.* In the light of later knowledge, much time-wasting conjecture was aimed at showing that water splashed from the pick-up gear on the leading unit was responsible for some of the heating, or that the worsted underkeep pads had disintegrated and caused the lubrication to break down. Experiments in devising a means of minimising the splash when water was picked up from track troughs made some months earlier at Hathern troughs near Loughborough had indicated that the fitting of a deflector in advance of the scoop could help in picking up more water and minimising splash and therefore wastage. In fact, the Garratts were so fitted (Fig 11).

Another fundamental weakness which became apparent with increasing mileage was the liability of the main frames to fracture at the corners of the coupled wheel horn gaps. It was said that the thickness of the main frames had been kept to a minimum with the object of weight reduction, but the latter aim was certainly never achieved since I believe that every locomotive of the class had huge frame patches fitted at some time in their life, enveloping the coupled wheel horn gaps and thereby increasing total weight. Another particularly vulnerable area appeared to be the inner end of the trailing unit, where fractures originated in the top sandbox bolt holes and spread upwards and downwards.

During the first winter at Wellingborough, the Garratts must have

* *Locomotive Axleboxes* — E. S. Cox (*Proceedings*, Inst Loco Engs. (Paper No 447, 1944)).

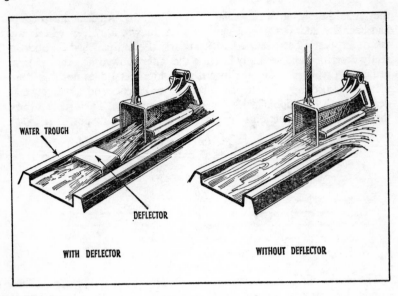

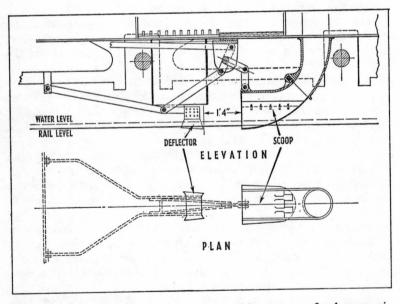

Fig 11. Arrangement of deflector fitted to water pick-up gear as fitted to experimental tender tank. The same arrangement was fitted to the LMS Garratt locomotives.

caused an appreciable increase in the consumption of domestic coal, since there was nowhere where these locomotives could be stabled under cover. Consequently huge, open fire baskets had to be positioned, one at each of the four corners of the locomotive to protect the cylinder castings, with two smaller fire devils, one at each side of the cab, to protect the injectors. Despite this, a fitting which was often damaged by frost due to its isolated and unprotected position behind the cab was the box which housed the water indicator gear and which was itself full of water. A glance at the picture of a Garratt locomotive shews how this fitting was really out on a limb (Plate 14).

Another unusual trap for the unwary lurked in the simple process of taking up the brakes, should the fitter omit to adjust the gear on *both* units. It was common for a driver to report that brakes wanted adjusting on the leading *or* trailing unit, but not both, and more than one unthinking fitter adjusted the reported unit only. Since only one brake shaft, suspended from the boiler unit, operated the pull rods on both units, it was, of course, necessary to adjust the brakes on both units simultaneously. Failure to do so led on one occasion to a near-runaway between Souldrop and Sharnbrook with an up coal train, and to a few instances of flats on tyres due to uneven distribution of the total braking effort.

When brick arches on the Garratts began to deteriorate to the point of requiring renewal, I was detailed to make drawings for the carpenter so that he could construct some suitable 'centres'; this was the term given to the wooden frames on which the arch was built between the sides of the firebox, which rested on the tubeplate at its front edge. I then accompanied the tuber and his mate in the construction of the first arch, which consisted of no fewer than 144 bricks. Subsequent arches were made to this pattern, since I never saw an official drawing for this component until many years afterwards when very large individual firebricks came into use. The arrangements for LMS Garratt locomotives were as in Fig 12. From this it will be seen that the number of bricks had been reduced to 27, with correspondingly fewer joints to fail and less time required to erect.

I was also 'OC' the Clyde & Parry soot blowers, the tarpaulins over the bunkers, the rotary bunker on No 4986, the coal pusher on No 4996 and a number of minor items. By the early part of 1931 I had collected sufficient data to enable me to compile a thesis and enter it in a competition for the Durham Bursary awarded by the Junior Institution of Engineers. I entitled my effort *Some interesting points in the maintenance and working of Garratt locomotives.* Whilst I can see its defects now only too well, it gave me some excellent practice in the marshalling of information and presentation of facts, even if some of the conclusions were wrong!

Before leaving this section of my recollections on Garratts, I may mention one 'mystery' concerning them which continued to be debated years after the last had been consigned to the scrap heap. But this mystery

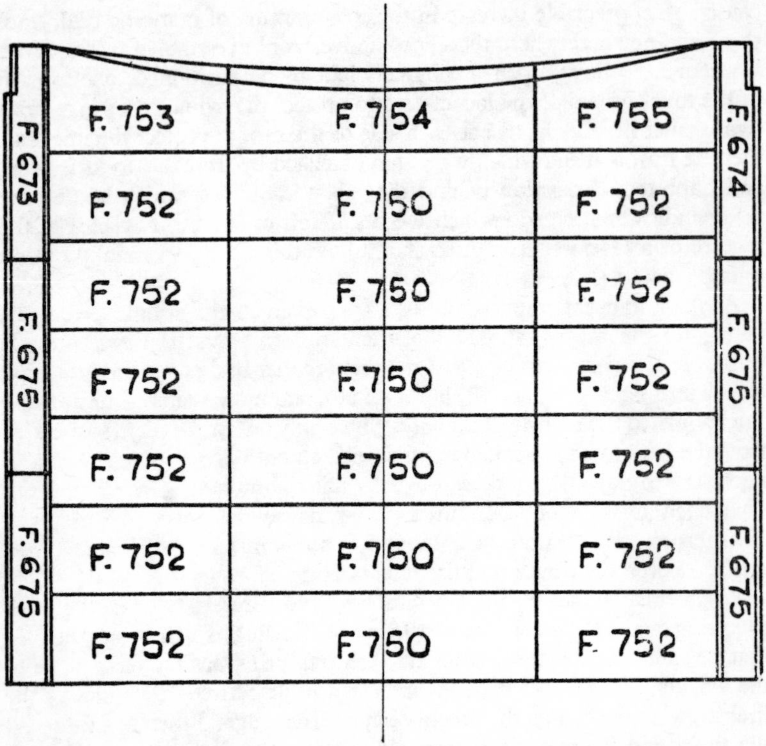

F. 673	F. 753	F. 754	F. 755	F. 674
	F. 752	F. 750	F. 752	
F. 675	F. 752	F. 750	F. 752	F. 675
	F. 752	F. 750	F. 752	
	F. 752	F. 750	F. 752	
F. 675	F. 752	F. 750	F. 752	F. 675
	F. 752	F. 750	F. 752	

Fig 12. Later type of brick arch consisting of only 27 bricks for LMS Garratt locomotives. The original arch had 144 bricks.

was solved—at any rate to the satisfaction of Wellingborough Loco apprentices—in this year of grace, 1931.

Right from the appearance of the first of these locomotives in 1927, it had been a matter of considerable speculation amongst all interested staff as to why, when the locomotive had started from rest and travelled a short distance under fairly heavy load, the exhaust from two two-cylinder uncoupled engines with cranks at 90 deg and exhausting into the same blast pipe, appeared at the chimney as four evenly spaced beats per revolution of the driving wheels. Watching the relative motion of the cranks of the separate engine units and trying to co-ordinate their movement with the aural indications from the chimney did not give any accurate idea of what was happening. The occasion, already mentioned, when it had been necessary to uncouple the front unit of a Garratt locomotive from the boiler unit to enable it to be lifted separately, presented an opportunity to pursue the matter farther.

During the work of reassembly the wheels of the rear unit were positioned so that when the engine was ready to move again under its own steam, the relative crank positions of the two units ought to produce eight equally-spaced exhaust beats per revolution. Being a new engine the tyre thicknesses were virtually the same throughout both units; nevertheless all coupled wheels were calipered to confirm uniformity of diameter. The locomotive was now moved under its own steam, slowly and without load. And lo! eight distinct exhaust pulses were seen and heard at the chimney.

Opinion amongst the onlookers was that the beats were not quite evenly spaced, which is not surprising when it is remembered that the cylinders of the front unit were about 20ft from the blast pipe, whereas the corresponding distance for the rear unit was about 50ft.

The next step in the investigation was to start the engine, apply the brake and open the regulator wide with full cut-off and run it up the loco yard. Within 150 yards, the aural indication was four beats per revolution only, although the exhaust was not clear cut. When stopped, still with full regulator and continued brake application, the cranks of the two engines had abandoned their careful setting and slipping must have occurred, although it had not been apparent.

The result of the next test was more informative. The locomotive was again run with a good regulator opening and restrained by the brake. The consensus of opinion of observers was that the four regular and heavy exhaust beats now heard corresponded with the exhaust events of the front unit; so the conclusion was reached that this front engine had the major influence on exhaust indications at the chimney when the locomotive was working under heavy load conditions. I looked at the relative crank positions of these locomotives scores of times over the years and rarely saw them in phase to give regular exhaust beats. It would be inconceivable, when account is taken of the incidence of track curvature, differences in the rate of tread wear of coupled wheels and different degrees of slipping of the latter which most certainly took place, for cranks to phase for any length of time so as to produce a clear-cut four-beat exhaust at the chimney, which was the result of the simultaneous arrival at the blast pipe of the separate exhausts from the two units.

I formed the opinion that the long exhaust pipe from the rear unit acted as a kind of receiver: and that when the exhaust from the front unit, with its superior pressure and speed, traversed and left the blast pipe, it induced a quantity of steam from this 'receiver' to go with it. The two exhausts appeared as one except at starting, when the time lag was sufficient for both to be aurally and visually apparent provided the crank positions were such as to permit this. In later years, I noticed what when the six-cylinder LNER Garratt No 69999 was working on the Lickey incline, the aural indication from her chimney was invariably six regular beats per revolution.

In 1950, that well-known connoisseur of locomotive riding, Edward H.

Livesay, writing in *The Engineer*, mentioned the phenomenon on the LMS Garratts and quoted no less an authority than André Chapelon as being equally mystified after the latter had ridden on the 4-4-4-4 locomotives of the Baltimore and Ohio Railroad, which also had two independent driving units. Since both Messrs Chapelon and Livesay propounded theories which I did not support I wrote at length to *The Engineer* describing the tests as above. The letter was published, but neither of these gentlemen pursued the matter further as far as I knew.

At 20 years of age, hardly a day passed in a running shed without some novel incident. Since I possessed the only drawing board and tee square in the place, I was invariably given the job of making any sketches relating to failures. A few of the new Fowler Class 7F 0-8-0 locomotives had been allocated to Wellingborough and these also provided much novel and interesting work in the early months of their working.

There was still a number of Fowler Class 4F 0-6-0 locomotives at the depot. They were mediocre in performance, their salvation lying in the fact that they were well maintained and driven. It was my job to assist Jack Cope, a fitter from Derby Erecting Shop, to change piston valve liners when worn to the extent of permitting noticeable steam leakage before the advent of the narrow rings, as already related. This work ceased at running sheds once the valves were equipped with multi narrow rings and liner wear was greatly reduced thereby.

I mention this work because it is indicative of the jealousy with which the foremen of the various shops at Derby guarded their working empires. They hotly contended that only their very own specialised staff were able to do certain work, which in their view could not possibly be carried out by mere shed staff. In fact, up to 1929, the steel ferrules which protected the copper superheater flue tubes at the firebox end were changed at many sheds by a tuber sent from Derby Works!

Another example of this professional jealousy, in this case, perhaps, attended, by more reason, was afforded by the failure of an engine of the Claughton class at Bedford. A few of these engines had been allocated to Leeds and Kentish Town for work on the Midland section and this one, which I believe was No 6017, shed a portion of its ph outside valve gear when passing Bedford at speed on the up fast line (the detached portion landed in the yard of Bedford Gas Works). The valve gear was stripped at Bedford depot and fitter Billy Grace, a young man from Derby Erecting Shop, was sent to fit new valves and gear; I was detailed to work with him. As there had been a major disturbance of the gear it was necessary to reset the valves, which was of absorbing interest to me since it was the first occasion I had seen piston valves set by equalising the lead when operated by Walschaerts gear.

Two other infrequent failures relating to Fowler Class 4F locomotives occurred about this time; one involved a broken driving crankpin on No 3851 (Fig 13). The failure was typical; the original fracture had spread

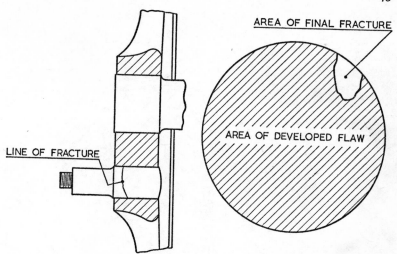

Fig 13. Broken driving crank pin, Fowler Class 4F locomotive.

right across the cross section of the pin until the final tear took place over quite a small area. We did not know much about the metallurgical aspects of fractures at running sheds, but the examining fitters knew what signs to look for. Personally, I found that the paper given to the Institution of Mechanical Engineers by L. W. Schuster, the chief engineer of a famous engineering insurance company, in April 1933* gave me nearly all the information I ever needed subsequently to determine the nature and quite often probable cause of a particular type of fracture; in most cases metallurgical examination confirmed the initial judgments.

The other failure was that of a driving wheel tyre on Class 4F No 3873 which fractured and opened about $\frac{3}{8}$in; a cleaner named Ted Rudd found it by feeling the gap as he was wiping the outer face of the tyre and was awarded 10s, I think, for his vigilance. I have a note that the tyre was $2\frac{1}{2}$in thick, a long way from the scrapping thickness of $1\frac{7}{8}$in; it is most probable that defective material was the cause, although I never heard this confirmed.

Hot coupled axleboxes were fairly frequent on Class 4F locomotives. Whilst, in the light of present day knowledge, there were design defects which would have been difficult and costly to eradicate, occasionally simple errors of fitting could cause a costly bearing failure. The sketch, Fig 14, shews an example of this; an adaptor was screwed into the top of the axlebox and in turn an angled casting was screwed into the adaptor, the former receiving the coned end of the lubricating oil supply pipe.

* The Investigation of the Mechanical Breakdown of Prime Movers and Boiler Plant by L. W. Schuster. Proceedings of the Institution of Mechanical Engineers; Volume 124, 1933.

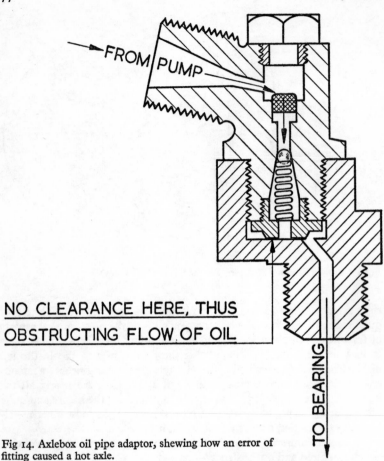

Fig 14. Axlebox oil pipe adaptor, shewing how an error of fitting caused a hot axle.

In the case under notice, the angled casting had been screwed into the adaptor so that the bottom face was bearing hard on the latter, thus obstructing the flow of oil to the bearing.

The Class 7F 0–8–0 locomotives, being very much of the same family tree, often displayed the same weaknesses as their elder sisters. But it was a distinct novelty when No 9579 failed at Corby with a whistle that persisted in discharging steam at full blast, disturbing all and sundry in the middle of the night, despite the efforts of the enginemen to wrap rags around it to muffle its importunate cacophony. The whistle valve stem was pushed off its seat by a double-faced 'hammer' which pivoted about one of two pins according to whether the right- or left-hand chain was pulled in the cab. Owing to constant contact between the hammer and the valve stem, the latter became burred over and finally an especially vigorous tug by a crew member caused it to stick in the main body casting of the whistle, permitting an uninterrupted supply of steam to the whistle bell (Fig 15).

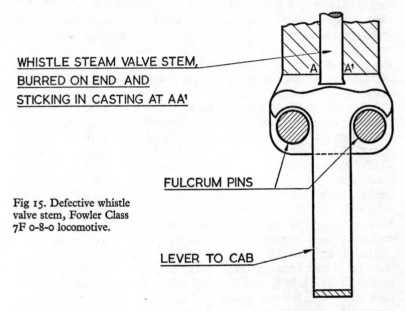

WHISTLE STEAM VALVE STEM,
BURRED ON END AND
STICKING IN CASTING AT AA'

FULCRUM PINS

Fig 15. Defective whistle valve stem, Fowler Class 7F 0-8-0 locomotive.

LEVER TO CAB

Closely related events of this nature often occur within a short space of time. Two weeks after No 9579 had provided the local newspapers with their lead story of the week, Johnson Class 3P 4–4–0 No 716 came on the shed to turn after working a local passenger train from St Pancras and the driver came to report that he could not move the whistle handle when he was about to move from No 2 shed turntable. On this locomotive, the whistle valve was of the plug type and operated by the rotary movement of a handle attached to an extension of the valve spindle, which passed through a hole in the front cab sheet.

Close examination revealed that the whistle valve spindle extension was bearing heavily on the bottom arc of the aperture in the cab front sheet. This could mean only one thing: that the whole boiler had somehow slipped down relatively to the cab. In fact, when the firebox lagging was removed it was found that the ph expansion bracket which, with a similar bracket on the lh side, carried the boiler in the frames had fractured along the whole of its length in the right-angled bend, thus allowing the boiler to slip down and slightly sideways. The final fracture had no doubt taken place when the locomotive bumped on to the turntable.

Class 4P three-cylinder compound locomotives were only occasional visitors at Wellingborough and almost invariably their incursion into the depot was because something on them had failed. I find I have recorded two such instances; No 1035, of Kentish Town, failed with a broken steam blower pipe which rendered it unsafe for further working because of danger of blow-back from the firebox to the footplate when the regulator had to be closed; whilst No 1018, of Trafford Park, failed with a vacuum train pipe broken at the point where it entered a screwed wrought iron connecting socket. In the first instance, the blower pipe had simply worn wafer thin and eventually burst; in the second case the vacuum pipe broke because it was insufficiently stayed and vibration had caused it to fracture at a point of maximum stress in the threaded portion, where it entered the socket.

In late 1930 a message was received at the depot one afternoon to the effect that a passenger train from Northampton Castle had been stopped at Wellingborough London Road Junction's starting signal and could not restart. The signal was situated immediately north of the river bridge which formed the summit of the steeply inclined ¼ mile gradient extending northwards from London Road Junction. The bridge also spanned the local riverside 'boulevard' so I was despatched on my motor cycle to the scene of frustration to be greeted by Wellingborough driver Harry Porter. He was in charge of none other than the famous No 5031 *Hardwicke*, that stalwart of the 'Precedents' which figured in the 1895 race to Scotland.

Alas! I doubt whether any of the passengers in the three coaches of the train would have been impressed at that time by the exploits of the locomotive 36 years before, since they had already been standing for half-an-hour within three minutes' ride of their destination. Harry Porter was also fuming, the trouble being that he could not release the brake on the engine although the vacuum gauge was showing 21in Hg. This engine was fitted with a vacuum-controlled steam brake very similar to the arrangement used almost universally on Midland engines, whereby inward movement of the vacuum piston in the driver's brake valve caused a corresponding inward movement of the steam plug which admitted steam to the brake cylinder through the medium of a controlling bar. On Midland engines, this bar was in a vertical plane and the brake valve was well away from the boiler; but on the 'Precedents' and many other LNW classes, it worked in a horizontal plane directly over the boiler front in a very hot, dry atmosphere. These two features caused the steam plug to stick just off its face, admitting sufficient steam to the brake cylinder to prevent movement of the wheels from a dead start. I had heard of this trouble, but Porter had neither experienced nor heard of it. His language was rich and pungent as I mounted to the footplate and gave the offending plug a smart tap with the palm of my hand, after which we heard the brake release.

On another occasion Class 1P Johnson 0-4-4T No 1246, which had been fitted a few months earlier with vacuum-operated push and pull gear, refused to budge from the sidings at Wellingborough with the second train of the day thence to Higham Ferrers—a short run of only 9 miles there and back, but a very important one since the return trip always conveyed a substantial number of first-class passengers from Higham & Rushden to connect with the 8.40am from Wellingborough to London, as well as a host of schoolboys for Wellingborough School. I was despatched to the station to see what the trouble was.

Arrived at the offending engine, which was coupled to its two coaches ready to leave with chimney leading to Higham Ferrers, I ascertained from the driver that he could get the standard 21in Hg of vacuum in the train pipe, but could not get any steam into the cylinders when he opened the main regulator valve in the boiler. In other words, his brake was off, but he could not get any tractive effort at all.

It is convenient to refer to Fig 16 in explaining the reason for his dilemma. The vacuum-controlled regulator was widely used on LMS push-pull units and necessitated the use of two vacuum pipes running the length of the train, each terminating on its dummy plug in the usual way. One pipe was the normal vacuum main train pipe; the other was the regulator vacuum pipe which was connected into the main train pipe by means of a choke 'A'. The regulator vacuum pipe was coupled to the underside of a control piston in cylinder 'B' mounted on the lh outside of the smokebox; this piston in turn was connected through suitable leverage to a supplementary steam valve 'C' and two balancing pistons, the latter valve being arranged in the main steam pipe from the boiler to the steam chest.

There was a plain driver's disc valve in the cab of the locomotive and also in the driving compartment of the leading coach of the set. When these were in the 'open' position, they were closed to atmosphere, which allowed a vacuum to exist in the regulator train pipe and thus under the control piston in cylinder 'B'. As the top side of the control piston was open to atmospheric pressure via small holes drilled in the cylinder cover, the piston was forced down and opened the supplementary steam valve 'C', thus admitting steam to the cylinders. When either of the driver's disc valves was in the 'shut' position they were open to atmosphere, the vacuum in the regulator train pipe was destroyed and steam valve 'C' was closed.

On the morning of the rumpus, I checked that the main regulator valve on the locomotive was open and that the driver's disc valves were also in the open position, but the train did not move. I walked to the front buffer beam of the engine and standing in the four foot bent down to listen for any leakage which might account for the trouble. In bending, I rested my hand inadvertently on the regulator vacuum pipe coupling head, which was resting on its dummy plug. Immediately I heard the slide valves give their characteristic bang as they came on to the port faces under the pressure of boiler steam and I moved out of the four foot quicker, I think, than ever before or since. What had happened was that the regulator train pipe was not seating properly on its dummy plug until assisted by the weight of my hand; after that vacuum was created, and the supplementary steam valve was opened — to some effect!

In theory, when driving from the coach the driver was supposed to be

48

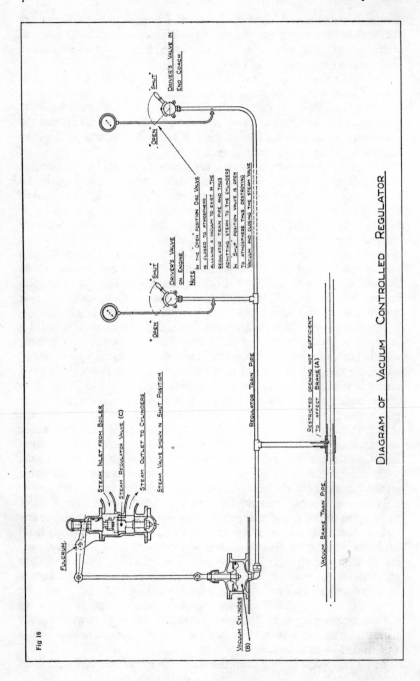

Fig 16

DIAGRAM OF VACUUM CONTROLLED REGULATOR

able to vary the amount of steam being admitted to the cylinders through supplementary valve 'C' by varying the amount of vacuum in the regulator train pipe through manipulation of the disc valve. But the piston in control cylinder 'B' at that time consisted of a leather ring clamped between two plates and it was very difficult to adjust the pressure of the clamping nuts to give just the right pressure on the wall of the cylinder. If the nuts were tightened too much, the piston stuck; if the nuts were not tightened enough, air was drawn past the piston, which would not then operate the supplementary steam valve. As a result, it became the irregular practice for the driver to eschew the use of the disc valves, leaving them both in the open position, and when driving from the coach, to rely on the fireman to operate the main regulator valve in the usual way.

Henry Longfellow's translation in *Retribution* of von Logaus's proverb, 'Though the mills of God grind slowly, yet they grind exceeding small' was never more apposite than when applied to irregular practices connected with locomotives. Sooner or later, disaster or potential disaster occurs and Wellingborough's push-and-pull train was to be no exception. It had just arrived in Wellingborough Station about 7.15pm, coaches leading; the driver, George Bollard, alighted from the driving compartment and proceeded to the toilets on the down slow platform; the fireman, who was making his first trip on a push-pull locomotive, descended from the engine footplate to position the headlamps for the return journey. With both men absent for valid reasons, the train moved briskly away unattended in a northerly direction and eventually came to rest near Finedon Station—only some three miles distant since, fortunately, an injector was working and the boiler pressure soon fell.

The fireman had apparently not understood clearly from Bollard that he required him to close the main regulator when running into a station—and indeed the rules required him to leave it open. When Bollard left the driving compartment, he had returned his disc valve to 'open' in preparation for returning to the engine footplate. When the vacuum in the regulator train pipe rose under the influence of the small ejector, the supplementary steam valve opened and the unit moved off. Stories were current of George Bollard appearing on the platform hastily adjusting his dress and of the fireman frantically chasing the engine and yelling to it to stop.

George Bollard and his sons Charlie and Bernard were all drivers of the best type at Wellingborough and part of a family which was very highly respected in the town. This fact would most certainly have stood George in good stead when he was summoned to Derby the next morning to face the 'Colonel' (Rudgard), who had on his desk all the national press which had featured the lurid story. Rudgard took a merciful view, the punishment was light and Wellingborough and the world at large gradually forgot the nine-day wonder.

Looking back, in my view the events related above would not have happened if the apparatus had been more reliable, although the whole project got off to a bad start. A locomotive inspector named Shirley from Nottingham had been sent to train Wellingborough enginemen in the working of pull-and-push trains. On the first day of operation Shirley, driver 'Tricky' Shaw, the fireman and myself were on the engine when it backed on to the train in the sidings at Wellingborough Station preparatory to working the first train, Class 1P Johnson 0-4-4T leading chimney first, up the branch to Higham Ferrers. I had been instructed to accompany the first two or three double trips in case any adjustment was required to the wire which ran in a conduit along the roof of the coaches and terminated at one end in a 'pull-down' handle in the driving compartment of the driving trailer, the other end being connected to the whistle valve on the locomotive. In the event, we found that whoever had last uncoupled the train from a P&P locomotive had apparently omitted to uncouple the whistle wire; I had about ten minutes to 'acquire' some copper wire from an adjacent signal lineman's cabin, splice the whistle wire and couple it up.

We departed just on time. On arrival at Higham, the inspector instructed the fireman to open the main regulator valve on receipt of the right-away signal and thereafter leave it open. Both the fireman and I were somewhat disconcerted when steam was not shut off at the usual place for the Rushden stop and when the brakes were applied, the fireman closed the main regulator, thinking that he had misunderstood Shirley's instructions. When approaching Irchester Junction, after the Rushden stop, again steam was not shut off at the usual location preparatory to reducing speed to the permitted 10mph over the junction, although an early brake application was made. Again the fireman closed the main regulator, reopening it after traversing the junction.

Approaching Wellingborough station, we did not hesitate to close the main regulator at the usual location and a normal stop was made. Shirley and the driver hurried from the coach to the locomotive and enquired with some acerbity as to what we (the fireman and I) were playing at. We asked the reciprocal question in equally pungent terms and described what had happened, whereupon Shirley turned and examined the connections between engine and coaches—only to find that the regulator train pipe had never been coupled; consequently the supply of steam to the cylinders could not be controlled from the driving trailer. Since the oversight did none of us any credit, we agreed to profit by the incident but not to broadcast its details, only warning others in a general way.

On another occasion I accompanied the train to Higham Ferrers one afternoon because the regulator vacuum control piston had been reported passing air, thus preventing the supplementary steam valve from opening. There was about 1¼ hours booked wait before returning to Wellingborough, so I removed the vacuum cylinder cover and tightened the clamping nuts of the piston in order to squeeze the leather out on to the cylinder walls. After reassembly, I operated the vacuum disc valve in the cab and was dismayed to find that the piston was almost immovable and steam thus prevented from reaching the steam chest. As it was now within ten minutes of train departure time, I removed the cylinder cover again very quickly and eased the clamping nuts; but the damage was done, the leather did not retract and was still very tight in the cylinder.

The fireman helped me to lever the piston out of the cylinder whilst the driver went to an adjacent tannery to borrow a file. With this I eased the fit of the leather so that it required a slight pressure to enter the cylinder, reassembled the gear and we left one minute late.

On another occasion leakage of air past the piston arose when the set was in service. On this trip there was no time to disassemble anything. After ordering a substitute engine to be available at Wellingborough, I rode on the footframing at the side of the smokebox and held the supplementary steam valve off its seat with a tommy bar for the five miles from Higham to Wellingborough, thus avoiding any delay. It was a silly thing to do: but who cares at twenty years of age?

One other anecdote must bring this chronicle of the Higham branch to a close. I had gone up again on the same train with the lengthy standing time at Higham one afternoon in the autumn of 1931 to perform the standard examinations in the driving compartment of the coach, a chore which occupied about five minutes. At the end of the terminal platform at Higham Ferrers was an enormous walnut tree and soon the enginemen and myself were using every means to 'scrump' as many walnuts as we could. Returning to the locomotive about ten minutes before departure time, we found the fire had gone out! We set to and collected oily waste and oil from the station lamp room, plus scrap sleepers which, mercifully, were stacked on the platform, and quickly got a fire going from the embers. Steam pressure was high enough to create vacuum and aided by the 1 in 100 falling gradient from Higham to Rushden we managed to lose very little time. We were eventually right on time at Wellingborough with no questions asked.

In later years the LMS type of pull-and-push apparatus was much improved by replacing the piston in the vacuum control cylinder with a flexible diaphragm so that sticking was eliminated. For longer trains of four to five or even more coaches a 'quick start' feature enabled the vacuum in the regulator train pipe to be created much more quickly. The whistle wire along the top of the coaches was replaced by a vacuum horn.

Not all the incidents which provided those moments of drama to enliven the daily scene occurred outside the depot, however. During an unusually busy period in the summer of 1931, I was sent into the shop to assist the turner to overtake a backlog of work and had occasion to put the pistons of Class 3F No 3601 into the lathe to check them for bending and to polish the rods. This was normal Wellingborough practice at a valve and piston examination. The piston head and its rod were mounted between the centres (Fig 17) and driven by a pin which projected from the catchplate screwed on to the mandrel and engaged with a hollow hexagonal

Fig 17. Piston head with
carrier on nut, Johnson
Class 3F No 3601.

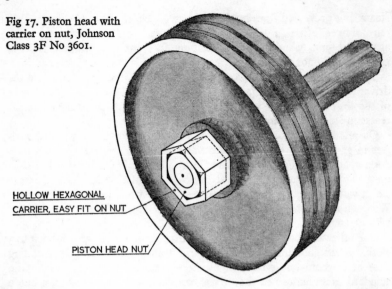

HOLLOW HEXAGONAL
CARRIER, EASY FIT ON NUT

PISTON HEAD NUT

carrier; the latter was a loose fit on the piston nut, being placed thereon as the piston was loaded into the lathe. This was necessary because the corners of the nut were not far enough from the axis of the rod to engage with the driving pin.

I polished the rods and checked them for truth. I lowered the second assembly to the shop floor and removed the chain slings from the piston and left it in an upright position ready for barrowing to the engine. It was replaced in the cylinder by Fitter Bill Ash, who put a rope sling round the piston head nut to lift the piston and rod into the cylinder; he also replaced the cylinder cover and for the next three weeks the locomotive stood waiting some other material which had been sent for repairs to Derby.

During this three weeks, search was made on several occasions for the lathe carrier, which seemed to have disappeared. It did not reappear until No 3601, repairs now completed and in steam, moved from the pit on to the turntable, a movement which was accompanied by a loud bang and a cloud of steam. Portions of the left front cylinder cover lay on the brickwork surrounding the turntable, although the corresponding piston appeared to be intact. Closer examination revealed the missing lathe carrier still in position on the nut of the piston head where I had left it. It was such a good fit on the nut that it simply made the latter look a bit bigger and it had not been noticed by Ash when he lifted the piston into the cylinder. Unfortunately, it was too big to enter the recess cast into the cylinder cover into which the piston head nut passed at the end of the forward stroke. Thereafter the carrier was painted white to remind the unwary of its presence.

This episode served as a timely reminder that good practices pay. Almost in the same week a piston for one of the new Hunslet-built Class 3FT locomotives was returned from Derby works, where it had been sent because of a suspected defect in the rod end. It was returned with a new rod and when the assembly was replaced and coupled up to the crosshead the fitter 'pinched' the engine over the centres to establish that the new piston had the necessary clearance at the end of the stroke. It had not, as was forcibly demonstrated when the piston struck the front cylinder cover, fortunately without breaking it; Derby had fitted a piston rod which was ⅝in too long.

Mention of the turntable recalls another mishap of this period when a Fowler Class 4F 0–6–0 No 3906 moved off the pit into the well of the turntable, as the table itself had not been set for the movement. The engine was being prepared for service by driver Archie Perkins, who decided to move it to facilitate access to an oiling point in the motion. Unfortunately the steam pressure was too low to provide sufficient braking power to stop the locomotive from rolling gently into the turntable well, catching one end of the table itself as it did so. This prevented more than the leading coupled wheels becoming derailed and the principal damage sustained by the engine was a broken piston tail rod sleeve.

It was the effect on the driver which lingered most in my memory. He was a good driver and yet was so ashamed of his failure to 'set' the table before moving the engine, as required by standing orders, that he went into the messroom and sobbed bitterly. Because he was a good man, his punishment was light and in later years I endeavoured at all times to review *all* the factors surrounding a disciplinary charge.

I had myself been dealt with in a lenient manner some months before when arraigned on the heinous charge of altering the design of a locomotive without permission of the Chief Mechanical Engineer. It came about in this way. Early in the life of the then new Class ǀ3FT 0–6–0 locomotives, some of the drivers in the shunting links had equipped themselves with a supplementary regulator handle, made of approximately 3/16in plate, which clamped on to the regulator handle proper and enabled a driver to operate the regulator without having to bring his head inside the cab; this was a valuable asset when shunting. The blacksmith, Harold Roe, a stout ally, and I decided to produce a more sophisticated affair with a wood-faced handle and wing nuts which could be fixed to or removed from the regulator handle proper in moments (Fig 18). I approached a driver friend in the shunting link with the first one; and from that moment we were in business! The blacksmith bent the handles to shape and I polished them and fitted the wooden hand pieces and wing nuts. We did not accept money for these favours, one of which found its way into the locker of almost every shunting driver, but we both smoked and cigarettes were the exchange medium.

I never knew to what extent the authorities were aware of our nefarious

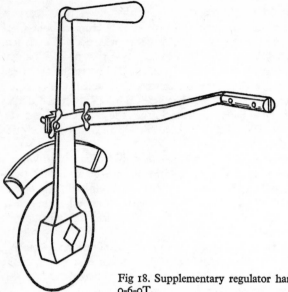

Fig 18. Supplementary regulator handle LMS Class 3F 0-6-0T.

activities. But when an article appeared in the October 1930 issue of *The Locomotive* from the pen of one David L. Smith which, among other things, criticised the arrangement of regulator handles on LMS shunting tanks, I could not resist an impulse to send a sketch of our supplementary handle to the editor with a description of its use and virtues. It was published in the next (November, 1930) issue. Retribution was swift. The description had mentioned a 'Wellingborough reader' and a month after publication, the offending page from *The Locomotive* was displayed on the shed notice board alongside an invitation from the superintendent to let him hear from anyone who knew anything about the magazine article or supplementary regulator handles. Naturally the blacksmith and I kept mum, but after a week Moulang sent for me. 'Now Thorley', he said, 'I know perfectly well this is your doing'. He went on that Colonel Rudgard, who had spotted the item in *The Locomotive* and sent it to Moulang from Derby, was annoyed that it had not been submitted as a staff suggestion. Moulang suggested I should do this immediately, at the same time delivering himself of a few observations on the iniquities of pseudo-locomotive designers who had not yet learned to obey authority. Eventually the locomotives were fitted, when shopped, with a permanently fixed supplementary handle which was not nearly as effective as ours. When received at Wellingborough, they were condemned by the drivers, who continued to use the unauthorised version.

This rebuff to my impatience for improved design and desire to broadcast details for the benefit of mankind did not inhibit me from further literary adventures. In the March 27th, 1931 issue of *Mechanical World and*

Engineering Record I had an article over my own name on *The Examination of Locomotives*. I believe I received the magnificent sum of 30s for this effort, which represented nearly two weeks' wages from the railway. It was in fact my pecuniary needs which were the incentive. There was virtually no overtime or Sunday duty and the occasional Sunday out with the breakdown gang to clear up the mess resulting from an incident during the week often nearly doubled my take-home pay.

The first occasion on which I enjoyed this great privilege, as a non-member of the regular breakdown gang, was when a long freight train from Bristol to Somers Town via Gloucester, Broom Junction, Stratford-on-Avon and Olney broke loose between the latter place and Ravenstone Wood Junction, where the SMJ line joined the MR branch from Northampton to Bedford. This branch was known to enginemen as the 'The Mounts', owing to its violently undulating contours with gradients which were not long but severe. Great skill was required to handle a loose-coupled freight train safely to Oakley Junction, just north of Bedford, where the branch joined the main line to London. On the occasion under notice, I believe the train broke loose in the dark hours either on or shortly after Ravenstone Wood Junction, but the driver did not become aware of this until approaching Olney, which was in the bottom of a dip.

When he realised that his train was not complete, the driver applied his brake. Whereupon the rear portion overtook the front portion and a considerable wreckage resulted, a number of wagons being precipitated into the River Ouse (Plate 17). The contents of the wagons were valuable, large quantities of tobacco, cloth and other consumable goods were strewn about the scene. Immediately a wagon was eased out from a pile of wreckage, an inspector of the Goods Department pounced on it to examine and catalogue its load in the greatest detail, thereafter arranging its transhipment by the quickest and most expeditious means. I was very impressed with the zeal displayed by these inspectors in protecting customers' goods and reducing claims, which would otherwise be made on the railway company. Another practice of those days which regrettably is no longer universally observed was the sheeting over of immobilised vehicles, which had to be put on the lineside to await suitable wagons on which they could be loaded for transit to a main works for repairs or scrapping. It is not good psychology to expose badly damaged vehicles to the imaginative gaze of passengers as they passed them, often in slow procession because of track repairs also necessitated by the incident.

My job on these early breakdown expeditions was to station myself on the crane superstructure and relay the foreman's signals to Harry Knibbs, the regular crane driver. Although he was a grade 3 Fitter, 'Knibby' skilfully avoided any hard work in the shed most of the time by suggesting to the Foreman Fitter that there were a number of chains and slings which wanted looking at in the breakdown vans, or that the acetylene flares wanted checking or the crane gears greasing. When he was unfortunate enough to be allocated a set of Garratt brake blocks to change or was designated to free a tender water pick-up apparatus which had seized, I had often helped him since he was very portly and sweated profusely. Now that we were mates on the crane, I began to get back some of the bread which I had cast previously on the waters. I learned a great deal from him about the care and manipulation of this 15 ton Cowan Sheldon crane of ancient lineage but sturdy performance. As a result of the interest shewn, Moulang decreed that all apprentices should learn to drive the crane before they completed their apprenticeship, a decree which stood me in excellent stead in later years.

It was another breakdown job which enabled me to show that I needed money and was prepared to work for it. Two heavy girders required for a bridge renewal programme were being conveyed from the Butterley Company's works in Derbyshire to a point on the LTS line on flat wagons designed for this purpose. They were marshalled at the end of an ordinary freight train next to the brakevan in which was riding a loading inspector from the Goods Department; he was to watch for any sign of movement of the girders on the wagons during transit. The train was recessed at Wellingborough, where the inspector found that one of the girders had moved. So he proceeded to the Control Office to request the attendance of the Wellingborough breakdown crane to reposition the load. The control staff contended, however, that as the load had already travelled more than half the distance to destination and had only shifted two or three inches anyway, there was no need to reload: moreover, since the girders were required on site the following weekend, to detain them for crane attention might well jeopardise the work of renewal.

The inspector fell prey to these specious arguments and the train carried on to a point about ½ mile north of Luton station. Here one of the girders shifted well and truly, taking itself, its own and two or three adjacent wagons together with the brakevan down the embankment, which at that point bordered a small recreation ground. Wellingborough and Kentish Town cranes were summoned to clear the mess from the running lines and the girders and vehicles were left down the bank, sheeted over, to be dealt with on the following Sunday.

The Foreman Fitter asked me if I wanted to go. When I replied in the affirmative and with alacrity, he said he would arrange for me to be called with the rest of the gang at 4.30am on Sunday morning, as an early start was to be made. Awakening at 6.00am the next morning and having heard nothing of the caller-up or my own alarm clock, I dashed down to the 'Loco' on my bicycle, then my only means of conveyance, only to have the awful truth confirmed—the caller-up had missed me and they had gone without me! Wellingborough Control Office could offer no comfort in the shape of anything on wheels going towards Luton for at least two hours, so I pedalled off and covered the 35 miles to the scene of the mishap in about 2½ hours. I was greeted with cheers on arrival and ordered by Moulang to get breakfast in the mess van, then take up my supernumerary position on the crane, which I did until the job was completed at about 10.00pm.

About this time I was invited to give a lecture to the MIC on combustion. This was well received and thus encouraged I undertook to talk about diesel-powered locomotives on my next lecturing venture, as isolated examples of these were beginning to appear in various parts of the country. Few examples of diesel prime movers were then readily available for inspection so I obtained a 10hp Wolseley car engine off a scrap heap, cleaned it in the bosh and sectioned the cylinders on the shaping machine to provide a model sufficiently realistic to demonstrate the principles of an internal combustion engine irrespective of whether the fuel was petrol or oil. Ultimately the model was held at Derby available for loan to any of the thirty or so improvement classes on the Midland Division.

Not all activities and aspects of training were concerned with locomotives. Some time after Moulang took office at Wellingborough, District Locomotive Superintendents were made responsible for the maintenance of the majority of outdoor machinery in their districts, an organisational change which coincided with the initial implementation of a policy of modernising equipment and methods at LMS motive power depots. The ambit of surveillance exercised by the locomotive superintendent was considerably increased and now included items such as locomotive feed water softening and lineside treatment plants, coaling and ash loading plants, booster pumps for increasing the pressure of shed water supplies to improve boiler washing out, and hydraulic wheel drops as well as goods shed cranes, capstans and water mains. A softening plant was installed at Wellingborough with the object of improving the water obtained from the Isebrook, which contained calcium and magnesium salts, by a precipitation process using lime, soda and sodium aluminate.

The installation of mechanical coaling and ash loading plants at about the same time provided experience of a different kind of machinery. The coaling plant was of the type which incorporated an underground bunker, filled by rotating a full wagon through about 125 deg and from which coal was fed on to a bucket conveyor which elevated it to a sufficiently high level to enable it to be gravity-fed to the locomotive tender or bunker.

On one memorable occasion an outdoor machinery fitter, Charlie Brooks, was making some adjustment to the wire rope which revolved the wagon tippler cradle. To enable him to turn the gears and thus the rope drum by hand, he had wedged the solenoid-operated brake for the drum in the off position. The adjustment completed, he put a loaded wagon on the cradle and set the machinery in motion to empty its contents, forgetting meanwhile to remove the wedge from the brake gear. When the current was automatically cut off upon the wagon reaching the limit of the tipping position, the brake naturally failed to operate and the cradle with wagon ran back at speed, accompanied by a noise from the gears which brought people running from far and near. The only damage was a slight flattening of some

of the strands of the wire-hoisting rope; these got trapped between mating
gear teeth when it continued to unwind from the drum, since there was
still no brake available to stop the latter when the cradle reached its position level with the track.

Moulang was always intensely interested in any measures which might
result in the more economical use of fuel. On an occasion when a quantity
of asphaltic bitumen lay in the loco yard preparatory to repairs to some road
surfaces, he devised some experiments to see if smokebox 'char' could be
used to raise steam in locomotive boilers after washout, using the bitumen,
made suitably viscous by heating, as a binding agent to make what were,
in effect, briquettes of 'char'. I used the hydraulic press to make the briquettes by compressing a mixture of 'char' and melted bitumen in a scrap
connecting rod big end bush. When ejected from it the briquette resembled
a Stilton cheese in shape, which after cooling could be handled into a
firebox without disintegrating. When about 5 cwts had been made in this
laborious way, an attempt was made to raise steam in a Class 3FT locomotive, No 16636, using the then 'standard' firelighter, a supply of which
was made by the steamraisers every Saturday morning from scrap sleepers
and nails. A proportion of coal was fed on to the firelighters first to ensure
ignition and the briquettes were fed on to the caol.

This experiment failed because there was virtually no volatile material
left in the 'char', which simply glowed a dull red without appearing to give
off any useful heat. I found later that about 1911 the GCR had experimen-
ted with a mixture of 75 per cent coal and 25 per cent smokebox 'char'
residue of a South Yorkshire coal on an Atlantic type locomotive in actual
service. The locomotive was fitted with a Galloway Hill grate in which
atomised steam jets were discharged under the firebed to assist combustion
and the diameter of the blast pipe orifice was increased to avoid the 'char'
being lifted straight through the flue tubes. The results, however, were no
more satisfactory than those from my experiment.

As a matter of historical interest, a Galloway Hill furnace was fitted to an
MR Class 1FT No 1850 at Swansea in 1913, but with the different object
of improving the combustion of a Welsh coal of a vitreous nature which
clinkered easily. The use of the patent grate did, in fact, succeed in this
object but I cannot trace that there was any extension of the experiment on
the MR except the fitting of a similar furnace to Class 3P No 762; one may
suppose that the case for further expenditure on what must have been a
costly deviation from the standard grate arrangement could not be supported on financial grounds, a situation which has befallen countless
attempts to improve the overall thermal efficiency of the steam locomotive.
Perusal of the test reports throws an interesting side light on the motive
power used for fairly lengthy runs in those days. We read, for instance, that
No 1854 (Plate 18) worked the 8.30am passenger train the 80 miles from
Swansea to Hereford in February 1913, load 6 = 73 tons to Talyllyn
and 7 = 81 tons thence to Hereford, reached at 12.20pm. Not a bad

effort for a 40 ton locomotive, judged by the standards of the latter days of steam.

The characteristics and performance of lubricating oil was another subject which constantly engaged Moulang's attention. At the time, two blends of lubricating oil were in use for trimming fed bearings, known as Texas and 'G' respectively. Moulang schemed out a series of static experiments, in connection with which I constructed a simple machine which could be driven from the line shaft in the shop. It comprised a spindle running on roller bearings with two steel 'journals' keyed on to it; the latter carried blocks of white metal to simulate bearings, which were machined to fit the journals and which were provided with a slot to carry a lever from which depended variable weights. In this way the bearing pressure per unit of projected bearing area could be arranged to correspond with that of different locomotive bearings, but the peripheral speed of the journal was constant as there was only one fast and one loose pulley mounted on the spindle. The speed was arranged to correspond with the axle journal of the standard 3,500 gallon tender at 30mph, since it was the heating of tender axlebox bearings of Class 4F 0–6–0 locomotives which was causing concern at the time. The experimental journals were lubricated by small felt pads supplied with oil lifted from a reservoir by worsted strands on the capillary principle. The distance of the oil in the reservoir from the underside of the journals could be varied easily. Arrangements could also be made for the journals to run in an oil bath to simulate flood lubrication.

The results were extremely interesting and of real practical use; maximum temperatures at which the bearings would run indefinitely without serious heating were measured by high reading thermometers ('borrowed' from a long-suffering Technical Institute), inserted in suitable pockets drilled in the white metal blocks. Of particular interest was the influence of the depth of oil in the reservoir on the load which could be maintained at constant temperature by the respective oils under test when using pad lubrication, and also the effect of the ambient temperature, which rose to 93degF during some of the tests. The latter were supplemented by road tests on a locomotive, to be described later.

Moulang would invariably suggest some modification or extension of an investigation. His comments on the results contained an element of debunking, if necessary, but always words of encouragement and advice.

One reads so much today as to how apprentices of varying potential should be trained. In my view one ingredient is often lacking from the training programme—the personal and regular interest of a supervisor of sufficient status, but not too remote from the daily scene. Moulang possessed the art of dispensing wisdom by practical demonstration. When the first of the Wellingborough Class 7F 0–8–0 Fowler locomotives became due for its first valve and piston examination, it was found that the valve spindles proper were secured by flat tapered cotters inside a moving hollow sleeve which took the place of the valve spindle crosshead usually associated with Walschaerts valve gear and piston valves (Fig 19). Through the sleeve was drilled a $\frac{3}{4}$in diameter hole; into this projected the tapered end of the valve spindle, which a fitter spent two days trying to move from its seating in the sleeve by driving a wedge behind it.

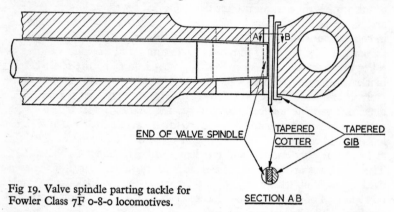

END OF VALVE SPINDLE   TAPERED COTTER   TAPERED GIB

Fig 19. Valve spindle parting tackle for
Fowler Class 7F 0-8-0 locomotives.   SECTION A B

Moulang, having been informed of the difficulty by the foreman fitter, quickly appraised the situation. He pointed out that the mating surfaces of the cotter and the flat surface of the gib were not absolutely smooth. He then instructed me to draw file the gib and cotter and polish them with emery paper to a mirror like finish. When assembled in the hole in the sleeve, a smart tap with a hand hammer on the head of the wedge was sufficient to break immediately the joint with the valve spindle proper.

In this business of training, Moulang did not omit exercises which steered one's thoughts on to managerial topics. Since the commencement of my apprenticeship I had assisted the foreman fitter in the maintenance of locally held records pertaining to locomotives, since he did not at that time boast his own clerk, known as a shop officeman. The Midland Railway had developed a system of individual records for every locomotive which, if properly maintained and used in conjunction with the soundly-based system of reporting defects by drivers also in force, provided a running history of the locomotive from the cradle to the grave. The system had been promulgated throughout the LMS after grouping, though it was adopted with varying degrees of enthusiasm or resignation by the constituent companies. In addition, in 1927 a repair costing scheme applicable to every locomotive had been introduced; this required the work done at motive power depots to be coded in the same way as in the main works according to a sub-division of engine and tender when a 'heavy' or a 'light' repair was carried out.

Not many 'heavy' category repairs were carried out at motive power depots, but 'light' repairs were fairly common. A 'light' repair covered, for example, reprofiling of wheel tyres and refitting of axleboxes to journals;

or renewal of piston valve liners; or removal of 50 or more boiler tubes on the same occasion. Although there were other combinations and types of component repairs which together constituted a 'light' repair, the three items mentioned above were those arising most frequently at running sheds. Their execution occasioned not a little paper work in the Foreman Fitter's office. Many a locomotive has had only 49 tubes removed in order to avoid raising the necessary documentation. If the number became 50 or more, Foreman Fitter Moore would go to extraordinary lengths to avoid a given repair acquiring 'light' status—that is, until he found that I could complete all his paper work in about an hour a day, getting thoroughly familiar with all the systems of documentation in the process. Purely running repairs, together with standard scheduled examinations, were at this time coded under two blanket numbers, 19 for engine and 20 for tender.

Whatever the criticisms levelled against such a comprehensive costing system it enabled the really 'bad' locomotives, from point of view of cost, to be quickly identified and scrapped. The benefit was not just to the company's finances; people in charge of motive power depots welcomed the rapid withdrawal of locomotives with repair characteristics which disrupted any sort of planned shed maintenance programme and whose continued existence necessitated, in the aggregate, the retention of huge stocks of stores for ancient locomotives of so many different classes. When one reflects that at the 1923 grouping the LMSR possessed 10,316 locomotives of 393 different types and that by the end of 1931 the stock had been reduced to 9,032, comprising 261 types, one begins to realise the sort of problems besetting the locomotive chiefs of the day and to appreciate the relative simplicity and effectiveness of the administrative systems used by the LMS to point the way to rationalisation of the fleet—and this without the help of the management consultants so fashionable in the present day and age. In place of the latter was the decisive influence of Sir Josiah (later Lord) Stamp, President of the Executive and his personal conviction that the statistics were necessary. He was supported in their creation by the managerial skill of W. V. (later Sir William) Wood, Vice-President for finance and service departments.

The material used in effecting locomotive repairs at sheds was also charged to individual engines, apart from certain items in bulk, like split cotters. Nothing could be obtained from the stores without the appropriate demand note, which also had to be endorsed with the foreman's signature before presentation to the storekeeper for items such as files and the more expensive hand tools. Add to all this information the figures of coal issued to and mileage run by, each locomotive and there was very little that could not be ascertained within a few minutes in meaningful terms about the cost aspects of any locomotive on the system.

Costs were not, of course, the only criterion by which the performance of individual locomotives and classes was judged. Another most important feature of running shed organisation was the casualty reporting system. This required the completion of an engine casualty report if three or more minutes were lost in running due to mechanical defect; or if an engine failed, after being fired, to get on its train to time through any defect which should have been found by the examining fitter or preparing driver; or was due to a concealed defect; or, in the event of fusible plugs being 'dropped' whether time had been lost or not (it usually had!). A further category of incidents which was reportable even though no time had been lost included heated axle bearings and connecting rod big and little ends; and, strangely, defects which rendered a locomotive unable to return to its owning depot on its booked train because there was insufficient time to carry out repairs at the foreign depot where it had failed. In my recollection very few ex-MR depots reported the last category of incidents to Divisional headquarters at Derby unless there was a hate campaign on at the time between two depots, which did arise occasionally. In addition, the system involved the submission of reports when time was lost due to inferior coal, mismanagement by enginemen, shortage of water, overloading, slipping, weather conditions, shortage of coal, priming and—last but not least from the public's point of view—steam heating irregularities.

Reference to the facsimile of the front of the principal report form (Fig 20) will show that the information to be rendered was pretty comprehensive and usually led to a firm conclusion being entered on the back of the form (Fig 21). In my view, the prominence given to the entry 'Staff at fault' was unfortunate, since there were too many District Superintendents who were prone to blame staff without really examining in depth all the circumstances surrounding a casualty. Thus they did not form a properly balanced judgment before invoking the disciplinary scheme by framing charges against fitters or drivers which could not be supported subsequently.

Francis Moulang did not err in this way. When I had completed my part of the work by entering appropriate details on the report form for the foreman fitter, the latter and Moulang would confer as to the conclusion and necessity for any sequential action. I would sometimes be summoned to these parleys and be invited to express an opinion. My view was never dismissed without Moulang explaining why and often insisting on a series of experiments and observations on the engineering aspects of a case before finally entering a conclusion.

In the early part of 1931 Moulang had said to me: 'The next time the Colonel pays us a visit, I will ask him to have a look at you'. Mention of the 'Colonel' in motive power circles—and here I include drivers, fitters, senior clerks and many other grades—brought only one individual to mind. That was Harold Rudgard, gazetted Lt-Colonel, Land Forces in 1925 after a distinguished army career in the Sherwood Foresters and later in command of various railway workshops in France in World War I. As previously mentioned, he had been a pupil of Samuel Waite Johnson at

E.R.O. 47987

London Midland and Scottish Railway Company

CAUSE, OR EXPLANATION OF CASUALTY AND CONCLUSION.

Engine No............ Date.............19...... Delay............ hrs.........mins.

NATURE OF CASUALTY............

CAUSE OR EXPLANATION:—

....

STAFF:—

At fault............

Recommendation

Signed............
District Loco. Supt. or Running Shed Foreman.

Date............

Superintendent of Motive Power.

E.R.O. 47987

L M S Shed............ Date............19......

ENGINE CASUALTY REPORT

Shed............ Engine No............ Class............ Date............19......
Driver............ Fireman............ No............ Stationed at............
Shed............ Class............ from............ to............
Driver............ Fireman............ Stationed at............
Train............ m............ from............ and............ Load { Regulation............
Delay....... Hrs.......Mins. { Actual............
Nature of casualty............
Cause of casualty............
Part at fault............ Last Heavy Repair in C.M.E. Shops.
Date last renewed............ Date.— Shop.—
Date last examined (Daily)............ By whom............ Shed............
    "   "   (Standard) By whom............ Shed............
Has this part been reported on } By whom............ Shed............
any of the six previous trips } Date............
If so state:—What was done............ Date............ Shed............
By whom............

Particulars of the six previous trips:—

Date	Driver	Mileage	From	To	Time Casualty Occurred
1					
2					
3					
4					
5					
6					

Engine { gave train up } at............ to............
       { exchanged } for............ Engine No............
Dist. Loco. Supt.'s or Running Shed Foreman's Remarks and Summary of Driver's Report:—

....

Signed............
District Loco. Supt. or Running Shed Foreman
(over

Divisional Superintendent of............

Fig 20. (*Left*) Front of engine casualty report form. Fig 21. (*Above*)
Back of engine casualty report form.

Derby, a fact of which he was very proud. Because his pre-war appoint-
ments had been widely separated geographically, he was known personally
to several thousand men over a wide area, many of whom had served with
him in the armed forces. In 1931 he was still assistant to J. E. Anderson,
superintendent of motive power of the LMS and an officer with considerable influence on all aspects of locomotive policy.

It was not until August 1931, that the anticipated visit took place, an
impending occasion the imminence of which could not fail to be recognised
by every member of the staff. Engine pits and shed floors and windows had
a special clean, fitters' cupboards were vetted for excess tools and sponge
cloths and the coaling and ash plants together with the shed yard generally
were cleared of coal spillage and ashes. Actually, Wellingborough 'Loco'
was always kept reasonably clean, but an extra investment in spit and
polish on these occasions was well worth the effort involved if only to
avoid the unpleasant consequences if Rudgard's intense dislike of dirt and
untidiness in any form was aroused. This was a lesson which I learned
early and applied throughout the years I spent at motive power depots.

On the morning of *the* day, I was warned to hold myself in readiness to
be summoned to the presence of the mighty after the midday meal break,
during which I went home specially to don a clean collar and overalls. In
due course I was ushered into Moulang's office, in whose chair presided the
'Colonel'. He was a short, dapper but stocky man of military appearance
who proceeded to bombard me with a number of personal questions
followed by some of a technical nature, three of which I can remember
clearly to this day. They were:

(1) What is the relationship between the height of blast pipe and the
grate area?
(2) How would you determine the thickness of the flange of a pair of
inside connecting rod big end brasses?
(3) How does an injector work?

I can also remember approximately my answers. To the first question I
replied that, in general, the smaller the grate the higher the blast pipe,
particularly on saturated engines. The second evoked the response that
the thickness of flange was determined largely by the total available space
between the axleboxes on the crank axle and the width between the crank
webs. The third question was easy meat. I had been lecturing on injectors
to the MIC a week or so previously and proceeded to blind my peers with
science by describing in some detail how the kinetic energy of the steam
from the boiler was transformed into pressure energy at the delivery clack
after being condensed by the feed water as the mixture passed through the
various cones of the injector. All good stuff, which seemed to discourage
any more questions of a theoretical nature for Rudgard's next question was
essentially practical.

What, he asked, did I know about the relative performances of the steam-actuated coal pusher on Garratt No 4996 and the rotary bunker on No 4986? I replied that the pusher was only effective after the weight of coal remaining in the bunker had been reduced to about 4½ tons, any amount above this being beyond the capacity of the single operating cylinder. On the other hand, I said that the rotary bunker was very effective in bringing the coal forward, but that I had heard some drivers mention that it revolved on its own when the locomotive was travelling at about 40mph (about the highest speed which a Garratt reached in normal service) with a train of 100 empties between Elstree and Radlett; and that firemen turning round for the next spell of firing were disconcerted when occasionally they found the bunker upside down. Rudgard asked Moulang whether he had heard of this. When the latter replied in the negative, the Colonel directed me to go and find a main-line driver who had handled No 4986 and send him into the office.

To my joy I found Billy Heelin, the MIC chairman, signing on duty in the drivers' lobby. Explaining quickly what it was all about, I sent him into the presence, knowing well that he would confirm my statements with pungent comments of his own, since he was the first one who had mentioned to me the misbehaviour of the bunker and also one who could exercise considerable fluency in the use of adjectival embellishments to any story he recounted. He emerged with the air of having told 'them' something and said that I was to re-enter the office. This I did, whereupon the Colonel disclosed that he had decided that I should have a spell on the footplate of Garratt locomotives working between Wellingborough and Brent and that he required me to report not only on the coal trimming arrangements on locomotives Nos 4986 and 4996, but also on the soot blowers, the Class 'H' exhaust injectors fitted to all the last batch of 30 locomotives and on their steaming propensities and general performance. I was to be very careful not to get hurt, etc, etc.

It is impossible to describe my elation at this pronouncement. In those days, official permission for anyone to ride on the footplate, other than those such as instructors and inspectors whose duties necessitated their presence there, was not easily obtained and granting of the concession was the prerogative of but a few senior motive power officers. Pupils and premium apprentices either enjoyed or endured during their training, according to their inclinations and dispositions, six weeks on the footplate, commencing on shunting duties and finishing on express passenger locomotives. Prior to about 1930, they undertook fully a fireman's duties, but I believe as a result of union pressure following some rumblings from elderly top link drivers to the effect that they were too old to drive *and* fire, the students were relegated to third place on the footplate, they were expected to perform the fireman's duties in the preparation of an engine for service, its firing in service as far as their experience and skill permitted, and the disposal duties before stabling.

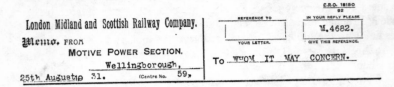

E.R.O. 18180
92

London Midland and Scottish Railway Company.

Memo. FROM

MOTIVE POWER SECTION.

Wellingborough,

25th August19 31.   (Centre No.   59$_{"}$

REFERENCE TO

IN YOUR REPLY PLEASE

M.4682.

YOUR LETTER.

GIVE THIS REFERENCE.

To   W^OM IT MAY CONCERN.

The bearer, W.G.F. Thorley is hereby authorized to ride on the footplate between Wellingborough and Brent.

F.D. Moulang

District Locomotive Superinten
-dent.

Fig 22. Author's first footplate permit.

The great majority of these budding engineers did, in fact, take to firing with zest and some acquired considerable skill; a few did not relish this phase of their training, which required a high degree of physical fitness, was uncomfortable, dirty and had to be performed at any hours of the day or night. Whilst my mission was not to fire locomotives, I knew that my driver and firemen friends would ensure that I had plenty of opportunity to do so when not engaged in recording observations. Further, no time limit had been set on my itinerant activities, indeed by the skilful inclusion of a number of additional subjects not included in the remit given to me by the Colonel and encouraged by a twinkle in Moulang's eye when he gave me my footplate 'pass' (Fig 22) my particular brand of footplate training lasted not six weeks, but six thrilling months.

3 Graft, Grime and Glamour

Not many enginemen of the steam era would admit openly to any feelings of glamour about their calling. Yet, the turnover of staff in the grades of driver, fireman and engine cleaner was practically nil in the years before the 1939–45 war. Wastage only became a significant factor in railway administration after the war, when there was on offer a wide variety of jobs carrying higher wages and better conditions than those in railway operating, and moreover when social change was developing.

Deep down, most enginemen did like their job despite the irksome conditions resulting from shift work, lodging away from home, weather conditions and a dozen other considerations attending life on the footplate which have to be experienced before they can be appreciated. Even at Wellingborough, the majority of whose locomotives worked heavy mineral trains carrying no attractive mileage bonuses, there was little open outcry when the first Garratt locomotives arrived with 44·5sq ft of grate area, compared with the modest 23·6sq ft of the Class 7F 0–8–0 or the 21·1sq ft of the Class 4F 0–6–0 Fowler engines. I did once hear a fireman protest when he came on duty and unexpectedly found a Garratt marked to his train. A relieving superintendent who happened to be in the running foreman's office and overheard him say he would not work it told him he had better sign off duty again and go home. The fireman changed his mind and I never heard of a similar incident.

Yet the working of a 1,400 tons coal train from Toton to Brent or from Wellingborough to Brent, returning on 100 empties within an eight-hour shift was a really tough job. In the summer months when the running was good, a fireman who had already fired a Garratt from Wellingborough to Brent and back with about 7 tons of coal was expected to empty the smokebox and clean the fire if his engine arrived on Wellingborough ashpit before about 7hr 40min was up. In practice, the running foreman would often relieve men on arrival if relief was available and not insist on observing the letter of the agreement. Nevertheless the authorities must have become sufficiently apprehensive that they were approaching the physical endurance limits of one fireman in this class of duty to spend a lot of money in fitting rotary bunkers to 29 locomotives less than two years old, following the successful operation of the prototype on No 4986.

The running of this engine was the first item to engage my attention after being awarded freedom of the footplate. I concentrated on the alleged tendency of the bunker to rotate when half-empty at 40–45mph. It is of interest to examine the arrangement of the bunker, because the design was characterised by rugged simplicity throughout. Plate 14 shows the 9 tons capacity bunker in position whilst Plate 20 shows the operating mechanism revealed with bunker removed. The bunker itself had the shape of a conic frustum, the larger-diameter end resting on rollers (clearly visible in the photograph), whilst the rear, small-diameter end was carried by a spigot which rotated in a bearing bracket mounted on top of the rear-unit water tank. Mounted over the main frames of the rear unit was a two cylinder piston valve engine with no reversing gear, which imparted motion to a worm mounted on a cross-shaft. This worm engaged with what was, in effect, a huge worm wheel in the form of a cast steel toothed ring which encircled the bunker at its forward end, its protective shield being visible in Plate 20. Motion of the bunker engine in either direction caused the bunker to rotate. Because the axis of the latter was inclined towards the foot-plate, the coal was brought forward towards the shovelling plate, the aperture into which the latter was fitted being closed by a steel hatch during the movement. The piston valves of the bunker engine were arranged without lap or lead, and the valves were made so as to just cover the steam ports. By using a three-way cock to control the supply of steam from the boilers to the cylinders, reversal of the engine could be effected by rever-sing the direction of the steam, the exhaust side becoming the inlet and vice versa. This resulted in inefficient use of steam, of course, but that was not important since the total amount of steam required to operate the bunker on the heaviest duty was negligible. These little engines were no trouble whatsoever and neither required nor received any attention other than oiling.

My first trip from Wellingborough to Brent on No 4986 was uneventful. On arrival at Brent up sidings, it was usual for the engine to be detached and run round the semi-circular loop which passed under and to the down side of the main lines on to the ashpits opposite Cricklewood Loco; here it would be taken over by a relief crew of Cricklewood men, who would clean the fire and throw coal forward ready for the return working of the standard train of 100 empty wagons to Wellingborough. Meanwhile the Wellingborough men thus relieved would 'take to' another engine, already serviced, attach to their train and depart for home, all within the space of about 45min. On this occasion, no relief engine was available and we awaited the servicing of No 4986, which operation occupied less time than usual, thanks to the rotary bunker.

Sure enough, when we were between Elstree and Radlett at a mean speed of 43mph, the bunker commenced to revolve slowly. It could only be checked by setting the three-way cock so that a mere breath of steam was admitted to the bunker engine, sufficient to prevent further movement of the bunker. I spent next day making a sketch of a catch designed to effect positive locking of the bunker in the correct position for firing and submitted it to Moulang, who sent it to Rudgard. No 4986 and all subsequent bunker conversions to the rotary principle were fitted with a catch of similar, but not the same design as mine; it was produced, I presume, by the locomotive drawing office at Derby.

Having confirmed the reports on the vagaries of the rotary bunker, I next arranged a trip on Garratt No 4996. Again I found that the drivers' complaints that the coal pusher was ineffective until more than half of the full complement of nine tons of coal had been used, were fully justified. I reported accordingly. Ultimately the pusher was replaced by a rotary bunker, so that it became standard in this respect with the other 29 locomotives in the second batch.

It is, perhaps, unfortunate that the design of the pusher was not developed. Although the rotary bunker was undoubtedly effective, the latter's first cost was higher than that of the coal pusher; it required additional labour and about 130 per cent more time to open the hatch doors and refill the coal space as compared with the conventional bunker, or with the bunker fitted with the coal pusher. Further, any developments in coal pushers made at this time would have been available for application in later years to LMS Pacific-type locomotives and may have thus improved the performance of the steam pushers with which many of them were fitted.

On the initial trips I made in discharging the remit given to me by Rudgard, I soon became aware of the truth of the maxim that anything good will sell itself: and that no amount of adjuration or, in extreme cases, near-coercion by management will persuade men to make use of something from which they see no benefit and more likely a disadvantage to themselves. Locomotive enginemen are no exception in this respect. Indeed, because they perform a highly responsible task with little direct supervision, they tend to become rugged individualists with scant regard for equipment which does not fulfil the claims made for it. In my youthful judgment, the two proprietary makes of soot blower fitted to the second batch of 30 Garratts came in this category. All designs then current appeared to work on the same principle, that of discharging a jet of steam, expanded from boiler pressure, so that it impinged on practically the whole area of the firebox tubeplate and in theory prevented the formation of deposits at the tube ends; it also cleaned in turn each zone of tubes which it encountered. Standard instructions required the soot blowers to be used when the engine was working heavily at late cut-offs in open country, so that the maximum amount of soot would be drawn through the tubes and distributed over green pastures rather than suburbia's washing.

The trouble was that the soot blower was fed by a 2in diameter pipe and valve of corresponding size. If the latter was opened with the engine working heavily, the boiler pressure fell quicker than the barometer when a typhoon is impending, and this just at a time when every bit of tractive effort was needed. Consequently the blowers were neither liked nor used regularly; their moving parts seized up and eventually they joined that valiant limbo of devices designed to promote thermal efficiency but which probably never did so to the degree predicted by their advocates, principally the manufacturers.

Anything which could have materially improved the steaming of the Garratts after their initial gilt had worn off would have been welcomed by those who toiled upon them. As a class they were not in the top twenty for free-steaming propensities. As so often happens when a new class is introduced upon the success of which many professional reputations may depend, the use of good quality coal was mandatory and the engines were the subject of attention from some eminent headquarters locomotive inspectors who did not normally condescend to overmuch concern with the working of mineral trains. In the early 1930s an additional grade of supervisor appeared in the shape of firing instructors, one of whom, named Frank Way, was allocated to Wellingborough.

Way had been a driver on the Somerset & Dorset Joint Railway and was characterised by a very smart appearance, invariably enhanced by a smart bow tie whether he was on or off the footplate. His first appearance at the shed elicited some pithy comment amongst enginemen as to how he would fire on a *real* main line with some *real* locomotives. To his eternal credit, and despite his age and portly figure, Way demonstrated good firing methods on the Garratts. He hung his coat in the commodious cab and applied himself to the fire for an hour on end, never departing from his own precept of 'little and often' and rarely exceeding more than eight shovelsful at one firing. Neither was he averse to facing the Mutual Improvement Class on Sunday morning and defending the principles of good firing in debate which occasionally became heated.

I recall the occasion when Teddy Allen, an experienced and popular fireman, startled the class by flat disagreement with Mr Way's 'little and often' methods. He could, he said, maintain a higher degree of superheat by first getting a hot fire all over the grate before leaving Neilson's sidings at Wellingborough, then firing continuously about 30 cwt of coal into the box whilst his 1,400 tons train accelerated over the $3\frac{1}{2}$ miles to Irchester Junction; there, he claimed, he could close the firehole doors and not re-open them before reaching Harlington, some 25 miles distant, thus having negotiated the bogey of Souldrop Summit (albeit at the lower level of the goods line but in tunnel) and already more than halfway up the long pull from Bedford to Leagrave. Thereafter, he said, he would only fire twice more to Brent sidings.

Way digested this statement with imperturbable good humour. But before he could answer, another top link fireman, 'Jock' Burroughs, described how he fired at a rate not exceeding eight shovelsful increments and regularly arrived at Brent with no more than 3in thickness of fire anywhere on the grate. I quickly confirmed this, having ridden with Burroughs a few days previously and noted his agile movements when distributing coal into the back corners of the wide Garratt grate.

Under Way's skilful guidance that Sunday morning session ended with the 'little and often' brigade gaining a discernible victory over the advocates of heavy firing. It is a pity that this particular argument was not subjected to the light shed by properly instrumented tests employing alternately the two methods of firing, particularly with regard to the respective degrees of superheat obtained and maintained over different sections of the route. There was always a number of firemen who, if for no other reason than a disinclination to acknowledge their physical limitations, would seek the easiest way *to them* of firing a large locomotive, not because they scorned authority's desire to achieve minimum fuel consumption.

Several firemen complained of considerable discomfort in the region of the rectum after a spell on Garratt locomotives, alleged to be due to the intense heat to which their posteriors were subjected when they turned to the bunker shovelling plate. Fireman Allen mentioned above, affected a unique sartorial style during the summer months when on Garratt locomotives; it consisted of a period bathing costume worn under his uniform overalls and shirt, which he removed before going into action with the shovel. I had a great deal of sympathy for all of them. Although blessed myself with a healthy physique and a frame of generous proportions, I never cared much for the kind of exertion which generates bodily heat; my sympathy did not often assume the practical form of insisting on taking the shovel from a fireman, either then or in later years. *Chacon à son goût!* My preference was for devising means of lightening physical burdens by the application of engineering science whenever possible. I hasten to add that my philosophy has never caused me to belittle the remarkable feats of skill, intelligently exercised by firemen since the dawn of railways and so faithfully recorded by the notable and enthusiastic laymen who have been granted permission to ride on the footplate from time to time.

After the Garratts had been in service about two years hauling mineral trains between Toton, Wellingborough and Brent, a substantial acceleration of freight trains in general was effected. Enginemen took several weeks to accustom themselves to it. When the engines were originally introduced, the load for a Garratt between Wellingborough and Brent was 90 loaded wagons of 10 tons capacity plus a 10 or 20 tons brakevan, and the running time was of the order of 3hr 40min for the 60 miles. This may not be regarded as very ambitious from the point of view of the overall average speed achieved, but it has to be remembered that the train was loose-coupled throughout; and the sole brake power was that provided on the locomotive itself, supplemented by any braking effort the guard could coax from his hand brake in the brakevan. The guards became very skilful in employing the very limited brake power at their command, since by applying it when the train was on several adverse and favourable gradients simultaneously and also negotiating curvature, for instance, on the slow lines through Bedford Station between Bedford North Junction and Kempston Road Junction—they could do much to avoid buffings shocks to the brakevan and themselves by keeping taut as many couplings as they could.

The accelerated workings involved a reduction in the load from 90 to 87 loaded wagons and some 40 minutes in the running time between Wellingborough and Brent: the actual figure varied slightly as between individual trains. The first two days of operation of the new schedules were chaotic as men struggled to observe the new timings. On the Tuesday evening Rudgard 'phoned Moulang and instructed him to send me on the 11.10am Wellingborough–Brent the next day to see if it was possible to eliminate the stop for water at Luton. The nominal water capacity of a Garratt was 4,500 gallons and with the opportunity of picking up about 1,000gallons at Oakley troughs, 11 miles from Wellingborough, it was possible to reach Hendon safely provided there were no undue delays en route.

One of the snags militating against sound judgments on the water situation on a Garratt, however, was the water gauge itself, situated behind the back panel of the cab on the fireman's (rh) side; it was float-operated from the rear tank, which was connected by a large diameter levelling pipe to the front tank. Thus if the engine was chimney leading on a down gradient, the gauge showed *less* water in the tank than there actually was; conversely when the engine was chimney leading uphill a false sense of security was engendered as the gauge could show 1,000 gallons *more* water than there actually was. Apart from this vagary, the gauges themselves were inaccurate even when the locomotive was standing on the level, probably due to the number of joints in the operating mechanism.

I decided that the only way to present a report which was worth anything was to measure the depth of water directly in the front tank when the locomotive was moving on a level gradient as per gradient board. This meant calibrating the tanks beforehand. I did it the same evening, so that next morning I was equipped with a slender iron dipstick marked off in inches and gallons which I could insert in the front tank filling hole; this was easily accessible from the platform over the front unit pivot centre immediately in front of the smokebox.

Next morning arrived heralded by strong, blustering wind and rain. Garratt No 4988 was marked to the 11.10am Brent, the driver being Teddy Robinson with his regular fireman, Albert Butcher. Robinson was a stolid, slow-thinking man, pleasant enough but always grateful to anyone who would relieve him of the responsibility for a decision. Butcher was a tall man of smart appearance who rarely complained of the extra work entailed in coping with his mate's heavy-handed driving techniques, but who, like other firemen linked with drivers who were not fully master of their job, cheerfully resigned himself to making the best of things until a change for better or worse at the annual reshuffle when engine crews were freshly paired.

I explained to Robinson that he was required to try to run to Brent without stopping for water at Luton and that in order that he could have a reliable estimate of the water remaining before Luton, I would ride on the platform in front of the smokebox. I would signal to him with a wave of the hand if my dipstick reading on the 1 in 940 grade just beyond Leagrave indicated that there was no necessity to stop at Luton. He assented readily. It was typical of the man that he never enquired as to what minimum amount of water would suffice for the achievement of this aim. He did, however, call attention to a 15mph temporary speed restriction over Milton viaduct, situated between the foot of Sharnbrook bank and Oakley troughs; this might well prevent the complete replenishment of the locomotive tanks over the troughs due to insufficient speed. Robinson promised, however, that he would try to 'pick up' the train as quickly as possible after the slack (which only applied to the locomotive), so as to secure the highest possible speed over the troughs. Whereupon we backed down to Finedon Road and attached to the now reduced maximum load of 87 wagons of coal and one 20 tons brakevan, total weight approximately 1,470 tons.

The journey was uneventful to Oakley troughs, although I had begun to regret that my concern for accuracy had landed me on the platform in front of the smokebox, particularly when the front unit slipped just before reaching the summit at the south end of the 1 mile 100 yards long Sharnbrook tunnel; as a result I was bombarded with unburnt fuel and engulfed in exhaust steam. Robinson observed strictly the 15mph restriction over Milton viaduct. He had extended the couplings and begun to accelerate the train so that the mean speed over the $\frac{1}{4}$ mile long troughs was about 19·5mph, enabling about 1,300 gallons to be picked up but not overflowing the tank, although I had requested the fireman to leave the scoop down for the whole length of the trough. I was quite elated at this result, since there was a widely-held belief at Wellingborough that it was not possible to pick up water at less than 25mph. I had, however, read the paper by Chambers, Chief Draughtsman in the Locomotive Drawing Office at Derby entitled *Improvements in Water Pick-up Gear* delivered to the Institution of Locomotive Engineers in March 1931, which indicated that water could be picked up effectively at lower speeds than this, now confirmed by my own observations.

We continued to Leagrave, where I ascertained that there was 2ft 4in depth of water in the leading unit tank. So I signalled to Robinson that all was well for passing Luton at 'speed', right away to Brent. Then the rot set in.

We were brought nearly to a stand by signals at Harpenden North and then Mill Hill distant was reversed in our faces. We shunted there for 20 minutes, detaching two consecutive vehicles with hot axleboxes, spotted by a signalman en route. We rolled slowly into Brent and came to rest with scarcely 500 gallons of water left, which is not a lot when one considers the size of the boiler. Butcher was filling the latter approaching Brent with the live steam injector, which blew off when we came to a stand. I mounted the footplate and needed no assurances from either man that they had done their utmost to keep time until the fortuitous delays. The footplate was dirty, indicative of the fact that Butcher, who was normally a man of meticulous cleanliness on or off the footplate, had had a full-time job making sufficient steam to cope with the new timings and a driver who had not yet learned to benefit from the differences in performance of the valve gear of the Garratts as compared with the Class 4F 0-6-0 locomotives, small though they may have been. Needless to say, I reported to Moulang that with a full load it would not be wise to omit the Luton stop as a regular arrangement, since the margin remaining at Brent was too small if there were any significant delays en route—of which in fact, there were many during the winter months.

Moulang asked how I had found it possible to quote such accurate water readings throughout the trip. That obliged me to disclose where on the locomotive I had ridden. He promptly forbade me to ride there again.

Three days later I accompanied Driver George Worker (of piston valve fame) and fireman Burroughs on Garratt No 4989 working the 1.40pm mineral train from Wellingborough to Brent. Again the load was 87 loaded wagons and 20 tons brakevan, but it included a number of lightly-loaded wagons of goods. It was apparent as soon as we got the whole of the train on the move at Finedon Road that it was a much lighter train than No 4988 had worked three days previously. Furthermore this train was booked main line from Sharnbrook to Kempston Road Junction, south of Bedford Station, so that the tortuous route through the latter was avoided and there was an uninterrupted approach to Oakley troughs where, according to gauge, 1,500 gallons was picked up.

The tank gauge showed 2,000 gallons on the almost level stretch south of Leagrave. Thus there was no anxiety about omitting the Luton water stop on this trip, despite the fact that the tank gauge showed a nil reading from Radlett to Brent (although on arrival there on time I could still measure 11in of water in the front tank.) Unlike Robinson on No 4988, Driver Worker knew from the general performance of the locomotive, the 'feel' of the load and all the other factors of which a good driver becomes aware almost without realising it, that he was not going to be short of water. He certainly needed no confirmatory evidence from me, which had I proferred it, would nevertheless have been received with courtesy. He had made the working of this 1,300 tons train look easy, his fireman was not overtired and no risks had been taken; but Worker agreed that it would be unwise to omit the Luton water stop regularly in view of the varied exigencies which frequently occurred in this type of traffic working.

The Class H exhaust steam injectors fitted to the Garratts did not assist in the maintenance of steady steaming conditions; their delivery capacity could not be regulated to meet the demand for steam without frequent shutting off and reapplication, with accompanying loss of water at the overflow. Consequently enginemen tended to use the live steam injector during heavy hauls of fairly long duration, eg Bedford to Leagrave, 56min, during which time the live steam injector would be working almost without interruption on a full load train. All the efforts of the representatives of official policies who had to deal directly with enginemen such as inspectors and instructors could not ensure the exclusive employment of the exhaust injector in these circumstances, despite the publicity given for the figures of water and—most important to the firemen—fuel savings obtained by its use, claimed to be of the order of 10 and 8 per cent respectively. What happened, in fact, was that the exhaust injector was used on the undulating portions of the route, eg Luton to Brent, on which the injector in current use, whether exhaust or live steam, would in any case have to be shut off and reapplied several times due to the highly fluctuating steam demand. Thus the exhaust injector was not used in the very circumstances in which it could best demonstrate its capability of saving fuel and water as compared with the live steam injector. It was not popular with maintenance staff due to its erratic behaviour and, in my view, never justified the extent to which it was applied right up to the demise of steam. I did my utmost in my capacity as MIC lecturer, both in these early days and in later years, to 'sell' the advantages of this relatively expensive instrument; but whilst one could convince some of the enginemen some of the time, they were too intelligent a group of men to convince all of them all the time of the advantages to the railway company and to themselves of a piece of heat conservation apparatus which did not measure up to its live steam counter-part in ease of application and reliability.

Exhaust injectors were like a lot of other pieces of machinery which, when operating as designed are very good; but if their reliability is not high, they eventually fall into disuse. Another factor which may have militated against their wholehearted 'adoption' by the men most concerned was the fact that the live steam injector fitted to the Garratts was a verti-cally-arranged flooded injector of very high reliability; it rarely required any attention apart from the cleaning of the moving and delivery cones. It had been fitted to large numbers of Midland engines for many years; if men's affection for it was to be enticed in the direction of another injector, the latter had to be *very* good.

After some two years of running, the steaming performance of most of the Garratts was beginning to fall off. After the usual tests and plumbing of the blast pipe with the chimney had been carried out, and in the absence of any other indication as to what remedial action should be taken, Moulang decided to decrease the diameter of the blast pipe orifice to $5\frac{1}{2}$in—I believe it was originally $5\frac{3}{4}$in. I made several trips on engines so altered and there is no doubt that there was a notable improvement in steaming; but equally there was without doubt a corresponding increase in fuel consumption. By this time, however, the whole class had been fitted with rotary bunkers and I never knew a fireman who would not cheerfully feed a few more shovelfuls of coal per mile over the grate if by so doing he could produce all the steam required and avoid the ignominy of losing time through shortage of steam. Most firemen were apprehensive of censure by their drivers, with whom they usually spent a substantial portion of their leisure time when lodging away from home. Plenty of steam meant good relations on and off duty.

Of the scores of steam locomotive types on which I have ridden, I found the Garratts the most comfortable, although the highest speed I ever recorded was 53mph when working light engine. The cab was commodious and as it was mounted on the boiler unit, which was itself slung between the front and rear unit pivot centres, it was virtually isolated from the vibration arising from axleboxes knocking in the horns, and to an extent was free of some of the modes of oscillation to which the cab of the rigid wheelbase locomotive was prone. In their early days nearly all the engines suffered flats on tyre treads for reasons already explained, plus the additional one that the locomotives traversed long sections operated under permissive block regulations; if the initial speed at the commencement of a down grade, with its unknown conditions ahead, was too high, a few of the minority of less capable drivers were prone to apply the powerful steam brake and leave it applied irrespective of whether the wheels picked up or not. The reaction of Foreman Fitter Moore to this was 'They put the flats there, they can wear 'em out' (or words to that effect); as this one defect *did* make the cabs rattle, Moore regarded it as a deterrent likely to make the drivers more careful in future.

Long, heavy, double-headed mineral trains had been a feature of the Midland Railway main line connecting the Notts and Derbyshire coalfields with London since the early part of the century. They had engendered train-handling techniques the exercise of which required considerable skill and a first-class knowledge of gradients on the part of enginemen. The use of Garratt locomotives placed an even greater burden on the driver, since their brake power was much less than that of two Class 4F 0-6-0 locomotives. Moreover there was no means to exploit the odd vacuum-fitted wagon which occasionally appeared in mineral trains, since only the original three Garratts of 1927, Nos 4997–4999 inclusive and one of the later batch, No 4984, were able to operate a vacuum brake. The last-mentioned engine was vacuum fitted specially some years after it first entered service to enable it to work experimentally some coaching stock at relatively high speed, but later it reverted to steam brake only.

The descent of long falling gradients with a Garratt and full load commenced, therefore, at very low speeds, which was held so that the kinetic energy of the train did not build up to a figure which the locomotive brake could not contain. For instance, when breasting the summit in Sharnbrook tunnel the driver would note the increase in tempo of the exhaust beats, reduce the regulator opening and shut it completely when a slight increase in speed indicated that sufficient of the front portion of the train was over the 'hump' for it to pull over the remainder by gravity. At this juncture the fireman would apply the hand brake steadily to get the waggon buffers gently together without precipitating the guard through his van window at the other end of 87 wagons; thereafter the driver would use the steam brake to control the speed, which averaged 20–22mph on the section Wymington–Oakley Junction.

Skill was needed to tighten couplings without snatch when gently applying steam again. A number of traffic control staff never seemed able to grasp the necessity for such caution when a driver was being questioned regarding alleged loss of time and cited a distant signal at caution as the reason. 'Ah', they said, 'but the distant was cleared long before you got to it'. The fact is that if the driver of a heavy loose-coupled unfitted train sights an adverse distant signal when running under power on the level or slightly uphill or downhill, he has usually little alternative but to close the regulator, whereupon the couplings will slacken; when the distant is cleared steam cannot at once be reapplied fully so as to avoid loss of speed without danger of rupturing couplings, pulling out a wagon headstock or injuring the guard. A momentarily adverse distant which would not cause any significant loss of time to a fully-fitted fast train, may cost five minutes delay to a lengthy, loose-coupled, unfitted train. One cannot help reflecting that some of the most notable compilers of train running logs of the past (and of the present, for that matter) cannot have fully realised the implications of an adverse distant for an unfitted train when they impugned its hapless driver for delaying one on which they were just about to witness a record. Likewise the pundits who expected the driver to keep a breath of steam circulating through the steam chests and cylinders of the locomotive braking an unfitted train whilst coasting downhill; exhortations to do just this were numerous and official, but I do not recall ever seeing a locomotive inspector or anyone else give a practical demonstration as to how it was to be done with safety.

Intermingled with the jobs in links involved in Garratt workings were some rostered to be worked by Class 7F 0–8–0 Fowler locomotives, nicknamed 'Austin Sevens' after a popular car of the period. The load for one of these locomotives from Wellingborough to Brent was 56 loaded wagons and brakevan on the accelerated timings, which they handled well when new, although the Class H exhaust injectors were no more satisfactory than on the Garratts. Northwards they hauled iron ore trains to Staveley and it was on one of these that Moulang staged an acceleration test with Class 7F No 9501 starting a train of iron ore from rest at Kettering Station to Glendon South Junction, about $2\frac{1}{2}$ miles mostly rising at 1 in 160. I accompanied him on the footplate and we got away in fine style to the astonishment of some platelayers who rarely saw an engine worked to the limit of its capacity in this location. The object of the exercise was to check the validity of Ribeiro's train resistance charts, which I had seen advertised in, and acquired from, *The Locomotive*. Unfortunately I did not keep the details of this run, except some calculations which compared the performance of a Class 7F with that of Class 4P 4–4–0 No 990 fitted with so-called Deeley's valve gear which Moulang had worked out many years before when in the drawing office. According to these the ihp of No 9501 which could be maintained would be limited by the boiler capacity to about 840 at 20mph.

Another investigation was undertaken to convince a gentleman named Hampton, the District Controller at Bletchley, that his frequent letters of complaint to Moulang concerning the timekeeping of Bedford (St Johns) to Bletchley P & P trains, alleging time lost by locomotive, were not justified. These motor trains, as they were labelled in the working timetable, consisted of a 31 ton vestibule coach and a Class 1P Johnson 0-4-4T engine, either No 1260 or No 1272 provided by Bedford.

Seven of the twelve intermediate stations or halts between Bedford and Bletchley had no platforms at the usual level and to enable passengers to board and alight from the coach a pair of retractable steps formed part of the coach's equipment. When drawn out they were, of course, foul of the structure gauge. A valve was opened in the vacuum train pipe by means of linkage attached to the steps, thus destroying the vacuum and effectively preventing movement of the train until the steps had been fully retracted back into the coach, like a kangaroo retrieving its young; if the steps were not pushed back with considerable force, the valve did not fully close and the aged guard had to descend again, pull out the steps and bang them home with even greater force.

The train was strengthened on Saturdays by the addition of another coach and on one or two trips by a van as well. The booked time of 43 minutes allowed for a train which stopped at all intermediate stations and halts in the sixteen miles between Bedford and Bletchley did not, at first consideration, appear to be exacting or impracticable, until a closer look at the working book revealed some requirements almost impossible to meet. For instance, two minutes, including station times, was allowed for the $\frac{3}{4}$ mile between Wootton Broadmead and Kempston Hardwick, during which time 21in Hg of vacuum had to be re-created after the steps had been pushed in and before the train could start; this left only $1\frac{1}{2}$ minutes to start, accelerate, decelerate and stop $\frac{3}{4}$ mile away at a halt not much longer than a billiard table. When the recognised time of $\frac{1}{2}$ minute for station duties was all required, the time for running the $\frac{3}{4}$ mile became one minute. In fact on Saturdays, there was always an increase in the number of elderly ladies of stately mien and matronly proportions who had to negotiate the coach steps twice in order to shop in Bletchley, and station duties then occupied more than 30 seconds.

My job on a foggy Saturday morning in November was to ride on the engine of the motor train, commencing with the 11.00am Bedford–Bletchley and remain with it on all successive trips throught the day until arrival at Bedford at 8.13pm. During this time I was to keep a strict log of times to the nearest second of every significant phase of the operating pattern, having first synchronised my watch with the standard time shown by Bedford (Midland Road) Telegraph Office. Locomotives and crews were changed twice during the period of observation and I changed footplates as necessary. We got off to a bad start, not leaving Bedford until 11.02am, because it was the anniversary of Armistice Day and instructions then current required drivers to observe the two-minutes silence if it was practicable to do so.

After two or three double trips with two coaches it became obvious that adherence to the times shown in the WTT could not possibly be maintained on the Saturday service. The delays became cumulative, since the terminal times were too tight and a late arrival at Bletchley or Bedford often meant a late start for the next trip. I kept the log as accurately as I knew how, but I have never ceased to envy those gentlemen whose writings in the popular railway press suggest an almost superhuman gift for reading the split second-hand on a watch and recording the reading whilst observing simultaneously the next operation to be timed amidst the noise and activity of the footplate of a locomotive in motion. On the occasion under notice the speed probably never rose above 40mph on an all-stations train; how the pundits managed to achieve such implied accuracy at 100mph and over, I shall never know.

Suffice it to say that the collated results of my humble efforts were sufficient to convince Mr Hampton that a more realistic WTT for this section would have to be introduced if an improvement in timekeeping was to be effected, together with a complete overhaul of the station clocks at Bletchley. The latter not only showed gross variations among themselves according to the platform on which they were situated, but enjoyed no concord with the one at Bedford St Johns or with standard time per telegraph office. Moulang made great play on this feature when writing to Hampton, who was effectively silenced from then on—with not even a note of reproach concerning the incident on the last trip made that day, when the driver had to set back after overruning in a fog the tiny platform at Wootton Pillinge, which was not illuminated. Altogether the exercise proved a salutary lesson for me on how to fight battles by first getting the facts right.

Mention was made in a previous chapter of tests to determine certain characteristics of lubricating oil. *Inter die*, they investigated suitability to sustain given unit bearing pressures and also to retain for long periods the necessary qualities to enable journals to be fed by the principle of capillary attraction, the oil being fed by worsted strands suspended in the axlebox oilwell to a felt pad in contact with the journal. The last exercise in this, my first series of experiences 'on the road', was to determine the length of time and mileage that the axleboxes of a standard LMS 3,500 gallons tender would run without replenishing after the initial filling when new underkeep oil pads had been fitted. For this purpose, tender No 3435 attached to Fowler Class 4F 0–6–0 No 4333 was selected. The axlebox inspection doors were sealed with a strip of tin in which was stamped an instruction to the effect that no oil should be added unless a journal was found to be running warm; meanwhile the locomotive was confined to Wellingborough–London mineral workings so that its performance could be monitored regularly.

Not entirely unanticipated was the variation in opinion amongst enginemen as to the degree of heating which a journal could attain before being described as 'warm' or 'hot'. Enginemen did not carry thermometers with them and a degree of heating which one man would dismiss as insignificant would alarm another man and wreck the experiment. Accordingly, I drew once more on the thermometry equipment of a long-suffering Technical Institute. I now made a series of trips with No 4333 to determine the temperatures at which tender journals were running and the rate at which the oil level was falling in the underkeeps. After the first month's working, involving 15 trips to London and back and some 1,875 miles running during which the axleboxes remained sealed, the readings of temperature and depth of oil in the underkeeps were as under:

Table I
Depth and temperature of oil in axlebox underkeeps

Engine: No 4333, Tender No 3435
Train: 10.05am, Wellingborough–Brent

Journal	left leading		right leading		left middle		right middle		left trailing		right trailing		
	Depth of oil inches	Temperature °F	Depth of oil inches	Temperature °F	Depth of oil inches	Temperature °F	Depth of oil inches	Temperature °F	Depth of oil inches	Temperature °F	Depth of oil inches	Temperature °F	Atmospheric Temperature °F
At Wellingborough	$\frac{3}{4}$	57	1	57	$\frac{7}{8}$	57	1	57	1	57	$\frac{7}{8}$	57	57
Luton	$\frac{3}{4}$	75	1	77	$\frac{7}{8}$	75	1	70	1	75	1	71·5	68
Brent	$\frac{7}{8}$	77	$\frac{15}{16}$	73·5	$1\frac{1}{16}$	77	$1\frac{1}{8}$	72·5	1	77	$\frac{7}{8}$	75	64·5

It will be noticed that the depth of oil in some of the underkeeps was greater at Brent than at the commencement of the trip at Wellingborough. First thoughts were that some water had entered the underkeeps when picking up at Oakley troughs, but there was no trace of it at Brent. There was a remarkable similarity in the final temperatures recorded.

Preservationists worried about the price of oil may like to note that the tender ran another three weeks and 1,000 miles before any more oil was added to the underkeeps, and then only because the engine was required to work to Staveley at short notice one day and the Foreman Fitter was anxious that it should not be reported running warm away from home. This brought the experiment to a conclusion with no permanent benefit, mainly because of the administrative difficulty of training thousands of enginemen not to panic and flood the underkeep with oil at the slightest sign of a 'warm' journal. It was not all that many years previously that drivers had been fined for permitting bearings to run hot. Thus it was hardly surprising that liberal application of oil was frequently made to a suspect bearing at the first sign of the smallest increase in temperature, irrespective of the fact that very often oil applied in this way did nothing to alleviate the condition of the bearing.

Experiments designed to find means of improving the delivery of oil in the correct quantities to the various bearing surfaces of a locomotive were many and varied in these days when search was being made for every economy. Worsted trimming feeds were very good in regulating the flow of oil provided they were kept clean or renewed fairly frequently. Since many of the older preserved locomotives are fitted with them, the sketch (Fig 23) may be of interest to those charged with the maintenance of trimmings and observance of economies in the use of lubricating oil on preserved locomotives.

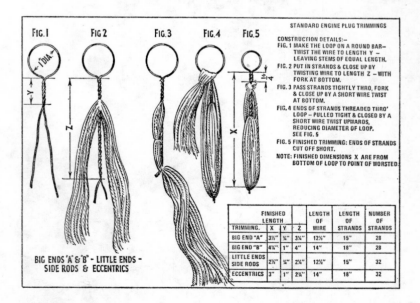

STANDARD ENGINE PLUG TRIMMINGS

CONSTRUCTION DETAILS:-
FIG. 1 MAKE THE LOOP ON A ROUND BAR-TWIST THE WIRE TO LENGTH Y – LEAVING STEMS OF EQUAL LENGTH.
FIG. 2 PUT IN STRANDS & CLOSE UP BY TWISTING WIRE TO LENGTH Z – WITH FORK AT BOTTOM.
FIG. 3 PASS STRANDS TIGHTLY THRO, FORK & CLOSE UP BY A SHORT WIRE TWIST AT BOTTOM.
FIG. 4 ENDS OF STRANDS THREADED THRO' LOOP – PULLED TIGHT & CLOSED BY A SHORT WIRE TWIST UPWARDS, REDUCING DIAMETER OF LOOP. SEE FIG. 5
FIG. 5 FINISHED TRIMMING: ENDS OF STRANDS CUT OFF SHORT.
NOTE: FINISHED DIMENSIONS X ARE FROM BOTTOM OF LOOP TO POINT OF WORSTED.

BIG ENDS 'A' & 'B' - LITTLE ENDS - SIDE RODS & ECCENTRICS

TRIMMING.	FINISHED LENGTH			LENGTH OF WIRE	LENGTH OF STRANDS	NUMBER OF STRANDS
	X	Y	Z			
BIG END "A"	3½"	¾"	3¼"	12½"	15"	28
BIG END "B"	4¼"	1"	4"	14"	18"	28
LITTLE ENDS SIDE RODS	2½"	¾"	2¼"	12½"	15"	32
ECCENTRICS	3"	1"	2¾"	14"	18"	32

Fig 23. Some plug and tail trimmings for MR locomotives.

A fireman taking the examination before being passed for driving duties was required to make representative worsted trimmings. I recall seeing one man on holiday at Yarmouth practising the manufacture of them whilst sunning himself on the beach in preparation for what would probably be the most important event of his working career during the ensuing week— the examination for driving.

4 Winter of Discontent

My 21st birthday was due in November 1931. On that day I expected to be liberated from the bond of apprenticeship at the princely wage of about 21s 3d per week, and either be sacked or elevated to the grade of improver fitter at 51s per week. My dismay was acute, therefore, when I in mid-October 1931, asked the chief clerk my probable fate and was informed that my apprenticeship would not expire until March 7th, 1932, five years from the date of its commencement. My parents had no piece of paper which indicated that a five-year period of apprenticeship was mandatory, irrespective of age on entry.

So, for the first time since joining the railway, I experienced a sense of grievance. Not only was I prevented from earning more money on the railway: I could not leave its service without disclosing that I had failed to serve the full five years apprenticeship, which in those days was regarded as the minimum time in which the skills of a trade could be acquired. The logic of that theory was lost on a young man of 21, who tended to see his continued bondage as simply the machination of staff clerks, over-zealous in pursuit of economies for their masters.

Moulang was sympathetic but could not help, since the Staff Office at Derby was all powerful in these matters. He did, however, promise to continue my training on the lines of that suitable for an engineer as compared with that of a tradesman; and in this, as in all matters, he was as good as his word. He pointed out also that even at the end of the five years' stint there could be no guarantee of continued employment; I would be well advised to be prepared for dismissal in March 1932 and to be investigating the prospect of alternative employment meanwhile.

I obtained the name of a City firm of employment specialists in accountancy and engineering and was duly enrolled on its waiting list as a potential employee. I remained on the list for more than two years, but the only job ever offered for consideration was with the Assam Company in the country of that name, which I declined after learning something of the climatic conditions. I wrote to numerous well-known engineering firms when I learned of any expansion plans from the technical press, and had an advertisement inserted in *The Engineer*, costing half a week's wages, drawing attention to the invaluable assistance which would soon be available to the highest bidder. But alas! no potential employer realised what an opportunity he was missing, except that I had an interview in the Cunard

offices at Liverpool and two years later—or too late—was offered the post of
fourth engineer on the *Scythia*.

Seeing in the technical press that competitive examinations were to be
held for commissions in the Stores Branch of the RAF in some 3–4 months'
time, I forwarded my application. By the same post I enrolled as a pupil of
a well-known correspondence school on a 'crash' general knowledge course
to prepare myself for the worst the Air Ministry could produce in the way
of examination papers, samples of which were available from previous
competitions.

The examination at the then RAF headquarters in Adastral House at the
bottom of Kingsway was scheduled to occupy two days. The first was
occupied by an orally conducted interview; only the candidates who
survived this hurdle took the written examination the next day. Thirty-six
young hopefuls striving for a total of five commissions attended the ordeal.
By the time a sealed note was handed to me informing me that I was *not*
among the successful ones, more than twenty had received missives in
similar terms.

In due course, on March 7th, 1932 I was informed in a letter from Moulang that the Chief General Superintendent required him to give me notice
to leave the service on March 14th, one week after the completion of my
apprenticeship. Although expected, the feeling of being written off the
books after five years of hard work as of no more account than a casual
labourer was not one to promote any sense of achievement or devoted
loyalty to the firm, although one pretended to be light-hearted about it. As
so often happens, however, when all looked black the unexpected happened;
I received another note signed by Moulang, dated March 10th, which read
thus: 'I have seen Mr (J. E.) Anderson, the Superintendent of Motive
Power, and suitably pointed out to him that if your services are dispensed
with, the Company may lose advantage of the special training you have had on
footplate work, etc and it is agreed for the notice dated March 7th to be withdrawn'. In handing me this note personally, and with great glee, Moulang
said, 'There you are, Thorley, pin this note to the one giving you notice
last week and you will have a better reference than any I could give you'.

Years later, in 1947, I met John Eccles, the then senior staff officer in the
motive power section of the Chief Operating Manager's department. He
told me that he had always remembered my name as he understood that I
was the only apprentice fitter at a running shed retained in the service of the
LMSR in the capacity of improver fitter after completing an apprenticeship in 1932. I have never been able to confirm this statement by reference
to records, but it may well be true; it was a widespread practice to discharge all those who had completed their apprenticeships, not only on the
railway but also in industry, with the opportunity of returning as vacancies
occurred. But vacancies were then few; I knew several tradesmen who
accepted jobs as porters at busy stations in the summer in order to preserve
unbroken service—and for a tradesman that is a bitter pill to swallow.

5 Consolidation

Elevation to the grade of Improver Fitter brought satisfaction infinitely more exhilarating than the addition of some 30s to the basic wage. The latter was welcome and, in my view, overdue; but the feeling of being officially considered capable of undertaking responsibility and decision-making in the business of maintaining locomotives was at that time worth more.

Not that March 1932 was a time to rest on one's oars in the belief that the spectre of unemployment had passed. Although Moulang had persuaded Anderson to overrule the staff functionaries and retain me in the service, he advised me not to assume that the reprieve was indefinite. Accordingly I continued to look for alternative employment in any sphere in which I could use to the best advantage the training already undertaken.

Meanwhile Moulang sent me to Bedford with another fitter to carry out the first valve and piston examinations on the second batch of Beyer-Garratt locomotives since new. The examinations became due at the same time as No 1 shed at Wellingborough was out of service for turntable repairs and thus pit accommodation was severely limited: hence the decision to carry out the work in the small, straight, two-road shed immediately adjacent to the station at Bedford, in which was also housed a wheel drop capable of dealing with a complete bogie. Moulang suggested that I should keep a record of the time taken for each item of the examination as it might assist him in arguing for the retention of staff in the future.

A superficial consideration of the relative depot maintenance costs of a 2-6-0- + 0-6-2 Garratt locomotive as compared with the two Class 4F 0-6-0 locomotives which it displaced might lead to the supposition that the Garratt would cost less. But even that early in their lives it was becoming apparent that standard examinations of Garratt locomotives cost considerably more than two 0-6-0s already many years older, mainly because of the additional 'work arising' in the case of the former. The outer coupled wheel crankpins of the Garratts were fitted with split brasses retained by wedge cotters similar to the leading coupled wheels of the 'Royal Scot' and Class 4 2-6-4T parallel boiler engines. Wear of the brasses was rapid in the outer radius into which the flange of the crankpin pressed heavily when the locomotive negotiated a fairly tight curve; this necessitated renewal of the white metal lining of the brasses at fairly frequent intervals. The work involved in the relining with white metal and subsequent machining of four crossheads was greater than the corresponding operation on eight slide blocks of the o–6–o locomotives.

There were three external main steam pipe glands to be kept in steam-tight condition, which implied regular renewal of the special fibre packing provided for this purpose. Although the engine of the rotary bunker required no attention, the various fastenings and hinges of the bunker doors kept the blacksmith busy and maintenance of firegrates and brick arches ensured a regular modicum of overtime for the artisan grades concerned, whilst the presence of exhaust injectors nullified any saving which might otherwise have been expected from having to maintain only two injectors on one Garratt locomotive as compared with four on two o–6–o locomotives.

I have no precise figures to quote, but I am convinced that a substantial portion of the indisputable saving of the cost of a driver and fireman, only achieved when a Garratt was hauling a full load train, was absorbed by the additional running maintenance costs incurred. One was led to conclude then that there was only a limited field in this country for relatively very powerful locomotives, a conclusion which is still valid today.

During this spell of work at Bedford, I continued to take every opportunity to gain footplate experience, by riding on the engine of the 8.05am passenger from Wellingborough to Bedford, the same engine having worked the 4.25am newspaper train from St Pancras as far as Leicester the same morning. At this time it was invariably a 'Claughton' 4–6–0 fitted with a tender from a withdrawn Robinson 2–8–0 former WD locomotive, 50 of which had been acquired by the LNWR after World War I. I fired most mornings. It seemed a long way from the tender shovelling plate to the firehole door and it was then a long way to throw the coal. I also operated the water scoop over Oakley troughs and discovered how difficult it can be to withdraw the scoop at speed, particularly if it has not been eased back slightly *after* having been lowered initially and before entering the water.

Return to Wellingborough in the late afternoon was on a Fowler Class 2P 4–4–0 rebuild, provided by Bedford, whose allocation then included five of these engines, Nos 549–553. They were easy to fire and once the whole grate area had been well covered, a number of subsequent firings could be effected without lowering the bottom flap of the firehole door; in this way the crew were protected to some extent from the heat of the fire and less cold air was drawn directly into the tubes.

After two months of pleasant work at Bedford, I was advised by Moulang that George Renaut, the fitter at Wellingborough already mentioned was to retire in June and that I was to fill the vacancy. At the same time, he pointed out that there was no guarantee of the position being retained indefinitely; indeed, considerable pressure was already beginning to be brought to bear on District officers to make reductions in staff costs due to the continued decline in traffic. He reiterated that it was in my own interest to take every opportunity of comparing the cost of shed maintenance of the new and bigger engines coming into service with that of the larger numbers of smaller engines displaced, as it would enable him to discuss the staff elements of maintenance costs on a factual basis.

With Renaut's retirement came an invitation from the MIC to take his place when firemen practised the dismantling of one side of a locomotive: also to deliver the annual lecture on injectors, another of Renaut's regular commitments.

About this time, Wellingborough and Northampton classes combined to do honour to a Southern Railway driver named Oliver from Nine Elms who had already had published several books, under the pseudonym of Socrates, dealing with many practical aspects of locomotive design and methods of handling. The Labour Hall at Wellingborough was packed with an enthusiastic crowd of enginemen for this event.

Inevitably the discussion centred on the relative merits of short or long cut-off working. Oliver stressed that two things contribute to good locomotive performance viz, boiler efficiency and cylinder efficiency; one had to find for oneself the ideal method of working for each class of engine and not accept without question that short cut-off working was invariably the correct practice to adopt.

Interest in the art of handling locomotives was also fostered by the Railway Locomotivemen's Craft Guild which operated under the aegis of the Manchester Education Committee. Membership of the Guild comprised at this time nearly 1,000 enginemen members together with 72 District Locomotive Superintendents, Inspectors and Running Shed Foremen. A major contribution to the success of this movement was the fact that the Manchester College of Technology had for some years conducted courses on practical locomotive management supported by suppliers of railway equipment and stores. They were shrewd enough to realise that the Guild provided a platform for their representatives to promote understanding of the purpose and best means of using their wares to the men whose opinion, expressed after experience in ordinary everyday running conditions, could spell its success or failure.

Although in receipt of only 51s per week as compared with the fitter's top rate of 65s per week, an improver fitter undertook exactly the same range of duties as his more mature colleagues. When working in the shed I had my fair share of the less pleasant work, such as resetting blast pipes, renewing superheater element joints, examining equipment in tender tanks and changing bearing springs and brake blocks. Outside I continued *ad hoc* investigations to satisfy whenever possible Moulang's passion for including hard facts in his replies to some of the more pompous letters received from Derby headquarters, which were initialled on behalf of the Superintendent of Motive Power by some budding engineer newly released from one of the main workshops.

Coal consumption was always an evergreen topic for recrimination by high authority. They tended to forget occasionally that, despite a well-organised coal office with its own inspectorate for monitoring the quality of supplies, sheds did sometimes receive consignments of dubious value for locomotive use when seams were getting thin. During one prolonged argument with his peers, Moulang decided to make a practical test, which I carried out, to determine the consumptions of the same locomotive on the same duties and with the same loads using Ollerton and Sherwood coals respectively. The locomotive chosen was No 1230, an ex-S & D 0-4-4T, No 52, sent to Wellingborough when the LMS absorbed the S & D stock in 1930. On each test, it worked every motor train trip from Wellingborough to Higham Ferrers and return, commencing with the 10.55am departure from and ending with the 10.50pm arrival at, Wellingborough. This involved a total of 10 round trips, equal to 92·6 miles, including a little shunting in stabling the train at the end of the day's work. Ollerton coal was used on the first test, which was repeated three days later with Sherwood coal. I rode on the engine on every trip noting boiler pressure, method of working and water consumption, of which I made a direct measurement after each trip as the Whitaker patent tank contents gauge was not sufficiently accurate for the purpose of the test. The results are tabulated below (Table II) for the interest of preservationists since some interesting features of branch working are revealed therein.

Table II
Comparative tests, Ollerton and Sherwood Coals

Engine: No 1230
Weight in working order: 49 tons 10cwt
Weight of train: 2 coaches = 56 tons for 19 trips = 87·97 miles
5 coaches = 126 tons for 1 trip = 4·63 miles

	Test No 1	*Test No 2*
Coal supplied	Ollerton	Sherwood
Coal used, (including 5cwt for lighting up), cwt	38	33·5
Water used, gallons	2,520	2,352
Coal per mile, lb	45.96	40·52
Water per mile, gallons	27·2	25·4
Water used per lb of coal, lb	5·92	6·27
Ash in fire and ashpan after test, lb	172	178
Large clinker, lb	2	17
Smokebox 'char', lb	26	31
Duration of test, hours	11·5	11·5
Running time, hours	3·61	3·73
Weather conditions	Fine, moderate wind	Fine, moderate wind
Ambient temperature, average during test, °F	48	47·6

At first glance, the 'coal per mile' figures appear very high for such a light train until it is realised that for a locomotive duty extending over $11\frac{1}{2}$ hours, the locomotive was in motion for less than 4 hours. In these circumstances the standby losses assume great significance and are one of the reasons why so many short branches were so uneconomic in operation. Tests of this kind were sufficient, however, to indicate relative coal consumptions and clinker-forming propensities; they helped to decide the allocation of the great variety of coals offered for locomotive purposes. The relatively high water consumption per mile recorded with engine No 1230 may be compared with those obtaining with engines of very similar design and dimensions when employed on more onerous duties more than 20 years earlier, working trains of 140 tons (excluding weight of engine which was 53 tons 4cwt in working order) from Luton to Moorgate and return; here the terminal margins were very much shorter. In table III are shown the figures for three locomotives on their respective duties.

Table III
Water consumptions, Class 1P 0–4–4T locomotives

Engine No	Origin	Trailing load tons	Route	Miles per trip	Water used mile, gal
1230	Johnson, Derby for S & D	56	Wellingborough– Higham Ferrers	4·63	27·2
1320	Johnson, Derby for MR	140	Luton– Moorgate	32·25	19·2
1373	Johnson, Derby for MR	140	Luton– Moorgate	32·25	26·5

The figures relating to locomotives Nos 1320 and 1373 were culled from test records compiled by Moulang in 1912 after difficulty had been experienced by some drivers in getting from Luton to Moorgate without stopping for water, although it was usual to stop at Harpenden in the down direction. The locomotives were fitted with condensing apparatus, use of which would have virtually no effect on water consumption in the up direction, as the grade from Kentish Town to Moorgate is ruling down through the tunnel section; thus very little water would be used and not much condensing would take place. What is particularly interesting is the degree to which the traffic potential of these locomotives was utilised when they were the biggest of their kind available, and to realise how necessary it must have been to encourage good enginemanship to maintain an acceptable service, even for those days. A parallel performance of the Johnson 0–4–4 tanks was to be seen on the Leeds–Bradford section of the LMR, where it was not uncommon for these diminutive engines to head trains of 8–9 coaches well into the late 1920s.

Table III emphasises that to quote water (or coal) consumption on a *ton mile* basis without revealing what the engine is doing between successive trips can be grossly misleading; it could not be used to construct a working time-table without knowledge of the context in which the figures were generated.

Another outdoor job which had become a regular assignment arose from the fact that Wellingborough did not possess a locomotive weighing machine. The nearest convenient one for the Garratt depots, Wellingborough and Toton, was situated at the west side of Derby No 4 Shed, where engines were weighed after undergoing repairs in the main works. Heated coupled axlebox bearings had continued to bedevil the Garratts ever since their début. Many of them ran hot again after refitting and when en route to Derby for weighing, the latter being a mandatory procedure for these engines.

In an attempt to reduce the aggravating incidence of repetitive heating, Moulang instructed me to ride with all the larger locomotives on trial trips after attention to heated bearings, and also to witness the weighing of Garratt locomotives at the conclusion of their trial trip of 63 miles from Wellingborough. With the aid of a thermometer, I became reasonably adept in judging whether to go forward with a bearing which was warming up early in the run or whether to return home and partially lower the wheels again to examine the bearing more thoroughly; even this latter procedure was much cheaper than allowing the white metal to fuse, with the possibility of damage to the journal.

Sometimes a bearing which had given no sign of heating to a serious degree in the early miles of a trial would deteriorate rapidly at a later stage. Class 4P 4-4-0 compound No 1005 (the first Deeley compound originally numbered 1000) afforded an example of this trap for the unwary on her trial trip after attention to the trailing coupled axleboxes.

We went slowly to Kettering where all appeared well. While the crew turned the locomotive I arranged with Control a fast line 45mph path to Bedford.

In common with the pure Midland compounds No 1005 was not equip-ped with mechanical lubrication to the axleboxes; the trailing coupled bearings were fed by worsted tail trimmings from oil feed boxes situated on the footplate. At Sharnbrook summit, up to which point we had not exceeded 40mph, I removed the trimming from the delivery tube of the lh oil box in order to flush the bearing with oil direct from a feeder. I was greeted with a puff of smoke, a sure indication that a serious degree of overheating had already occurred. We carried on at the same pace to Bedford, where the lh trailing axlebox was found to be fairly hot. I had to admit failure and return with the engine to Wellingborough for further attention.

Another failure, not entirely unexpected, concerned Fowler Class 7F 0-8-0 No 9552, which had given continual trouble with heating of the rh driving axlebox ever since it was allocated to Wellingborough as an almost new engine. All the axleboxes had been trammelled for correct distance between centres, the horn blocks had been checked for accuracy of their linear dimensions and for parallelism, the wheels had been sent to Crewe main works more than once for journal skimming and special examination, and Foreman Fitter Moore had by this time exhausted not only his patience but also all the known avenues of investigation usually applied in a persistent case of heating. After the sixth reassembling of the engine after refitting of the offending axlebox, the foreman fitter instructed me to accompany it on the Wellingborough–Kettering–Bedford–Wellingborough circuit and endeavour to produce a clear result, one way or another.

We ran the 15 miles of the Wellingborough–Bedford section in 22 minutes, which was quite enough in the circumstances for a locomotive with 4ft 8½in diameter wheels and no guiding truck. Alas! at Bedford the same axlebox was again very hot. It was of the manganese bronze variety, cast with deep pockets in the top, presumably to reduce weight and cost. I filled two of the pockets with water and boiled two eggs therein for my breakfast before returning to Wellingborough. The engine was proposed and accepted for a casual repair in the main works in an attempt to remove the cause of heating, but my recollection is that it continued to run hot at intervals for the rest of its days. Indeed the 'Austin Sevens' were a notable —or notorious—class in this respect: No 9552 must have been the classic of them all.

Quite a few 'Austin Sevens' suffered another defect which puzzled shed staff when the symptoms first showed. This was a fracture in the wall of the steam chest, the symptom of which was a blow in the smokebox at first thought to be a defective blast pipe joint, until it was shown to be continuous with the regulator opened and the engine stationary. We had no drawings of any kind for these locomotives at Wellingborough. Eventually we located the position of the fracture by lowering a periscope into the caverns of the cylinder casting, an artifice also used by the boilersmiths when examining some boilers for dirt when the draughtsman had forgotten that light travels only in straight lines and had neglected to provide inspection doors or plugs in the right places. I make no apology for my sketch (Fig 24), which was the best guess I could devise to convey to the Shopping Bureau at Derby where we thought the trouble lay as the main works, of course, had the job of rectification. Moulang attributed the defect to insufficient thickness of metal of the steam chest wall, which in his view should nowhere have been less than ⅜in; he recollected that when involved in the design of the Midland compounds, he drew a cross-section of the cylinder castings at ½in intervals throughout their length to ensure adequate wall thickness everywhere in the casting.

One minor design defect which was rectified locally related to the method of suspending brake hangers on Beyer-Garratt locomotives. The top pins had pear-shaped heads drilled with a circular hole, through which passed a ⅝in bolt to secure the pin to the brake hanger bracket in the

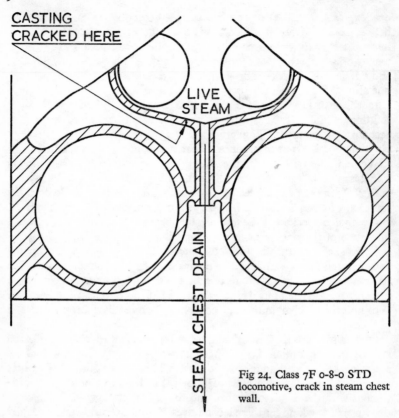

CASTING
CRACKED HERE

LIVE
STEAM

STEAM CHEST DRAIN

Fig 24. Class 7F 0-8-0 STD
locomotive, crack in steam chest
wall.

driving and inner coupled positions and to the main frame in the outer
coupled position; there space was limited, so a ⅝ in stud was substituted for
the bolt. In practice, it was difficult to prevent the stud working out of the
main frame. After three outer coupled brake hangers had collapsed on to
the permanent way, I suggested to Moulang that the hole in the head of the
pin should be filed to a square shape and the existing studs and bolts
replaced by new ones with square shanks (Fig 25). Moulang agreed. For
my enthusiasm I was awarded the job of carrying out the modification to
Wellingborough's allocation of 13 Garratts. By the time I had filed 156
holes from round to square, I vowed to make no more suggestions which
could involve me in repetitive work of this kind! This anecdote, however,
is a reminder of the way in which safety fastenings of all kinds tend to look
foolproof on the drawing board; yet when they are subjected to dynamic
forces of quite limited movement, they quickly become loose and fail to
fulfil their designed purpose.

Some types of failure provide scope for speculation as to how they
occur; Class 4F No 4333, the tender axleboxes of which had been the

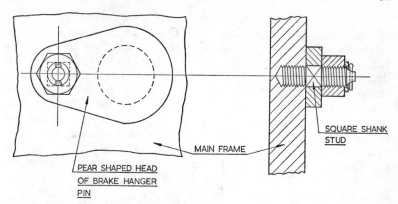

Fig 25. Improved fastening for brake hanger top pins, Garratt locomotives. It did not prove to be the complete answer.

subject of the oil tests, provided such an instance. A chisel, which had by some mysterious and undiscovered means found its way into the front exhaust passages of the lh steam chest, became wedged between the steam chest front cover and the piston valve front head, breaking a large portion out of the periphery of the latter (Fig 26). The same week a large portion of

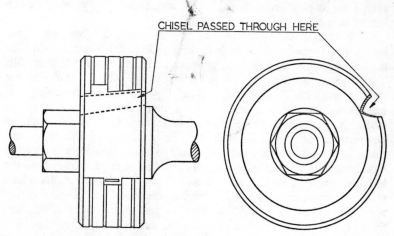

Fig 26. The piston valve which passed a chisel.

one of the piston valve liners which carried two heads for the double exhaust arrangement of Garratt No 4973 broke away for no apparent reason. This was followed by the incursion of Class 6 4–6–0 No 6399 *Fury* at the depot.

After *Fury* had undergone modification following the bursting of a high pressure water tube, part of the 'wall' of the firebox, near Carstairs in early 1930, when the Superheater Co's representative was killed and the railway fireman seriously injured, it ran further trials involving use of the dynamometer car and production of indicator diagrams. The trials were conducted on Sundays from Derby on the main line to London. I do not know whether it was the intention to project them beyond Wellingborough, but the first one certainly terminated there when the feed pump which fed the high pressure drum failed in the vicinity. On the following day, Frank S. Pepper visited the depot to examine the offending pump; he was experimental draughtsman in the locomotive drawing office at Derby and seasoned in the wiles of the locomotive, as he had been on the footplate when the fatality occurred at Carstairs.

I was scraping a regulator valve at a nearby bench when Pepper, an extremely agile man, jumped from the footframing at the side of the boiler to the floor. In so doing he caught the ring on the third finger of his right hand in a split pin securing one of the joint pins of the indicator gear, stripping the flesh down to the second joint. The coppersmith rendered first aid, but Pepper declined the assistance of the wheeled litter which was the pride of the shed and suitably accompanied made his way to the cottage hospital, where the finger was amputated under a local anaesthetic. By this time the engine was beginning to earn an unenviable reputation; quite apart from its poor performance, it was viewed with a wary eye by all who had to do with it.

On its next trial, which was to terminate at Wellingborough, I was brought on specially to uncouple the engine from the tender should it be found impossible to turn both together in No 1 shed's 55ft turntable. Total wheelbase of No 6399 was 52ft 9¼in, but the difficulty was to balance the load on a table of an old design. I did, however, succeed in turning it in one piece. It was then recoupled to the dynamometer car ready for return to Derby, under the eye of Herbert Chambers, the Chief Locomotive Draughtsman at Derby. He chatted cordially about this highly unconventional locomotive, about which I had read so much. Suddenly there was a loud bang. Except the driver, we all moved away more quickly from the locomotive than, I suspect, we had moved away from anything for a long time. The first thought of the driver, a phlegmatic individual, was that another tube had burst; but nothing blew past the newly fitted balanced firedoor, which was contrived so as to close automatically if pressure built up in the firebox. By this time, seeing clouds of steam issuing from between the engine and tender *under* the footplate, we realised that it was only the intermediate steam heating hosepipe which had burst!

The same symptoms of decline in the traffics of the main-line railways, and all the accompanying stringent financial measures, were apparent from the late 1920s to the outbreak of war in 1939 equally as much as in recent years. But in those days nationalisation was to the man in the street just a gimmick of the ideologist; and the popular press did not offer so much gratuitous advice to railway managements as they have done since national-isation became a fact. I have never been able to appreciate masses of statis-tics, but a simple table such as that below appealed:

	1924 = 100	
	1929	1932
Total receipts	95	75
Total expenditure	95	80
Net revenue	98	57
No of passengers	86	76
Passenger receipts	87	73
Tonnage of goods	94	74
Goods receipts	97	75

This sort of information, contained in an article in *The Economist*, told its own startling story. It enabled one to appreciate some of the radical chan-ges which began to take effect in LMS locomotive depots in 1932. One of the most discernible to artisan staff was the introduction of a revised locomotive examination schedule, which stipulated that moving parts were to run considerably greater mileages between successive examina-tions.

Connecting rod big ends were now examined at 10–12,000 instead of 5–6,000 miles, piston valve and piston examination mileage went up from 20–24,000 to 30–36,000 even to 40–45,000 in the case of 2-6-0 locomotives with Walschaerts valve gear and the three-cylinder 4-6-0 'Patriots'. There was now a total of 30 examination items, which covered the whole of the conventional steam locomotive fleet, numbering about 9,000 in 1932. Separate schedules applied to special types such as the Sentinel. One of the latter, No 7191, was allocated to Kettering to shunt in the large goods yard there and I was despatched more than once to fit a new firehole door to its vertical cross-tube boiler. My recollection is that the door was made from some alloy material which fractured rather easily and the door itself re-quired to have a good seating on the firebox shell plate. These 'extramural' activities were very welcome as they carried 1s per day expenses if one could manage to spin out the job over the meal hour.

Although the new examination schedule still required the by-pass valves fitted to large numbers of ex-MR and LMS designed locomotives to be examined at 5–6,000 miles, it was not long before the order was issued to sheds to remove these fittings and blank off the cylinders appropriately. Apparently Mr W. A. Stanier, the recently appointed CME, considered that the cost of maintenance of by-pass valves and of the traffic delays when they failed in service was not balanced by the free-running qualities bestowed upon the locomotives which carried them, due to reduction in cylinder back pressure.

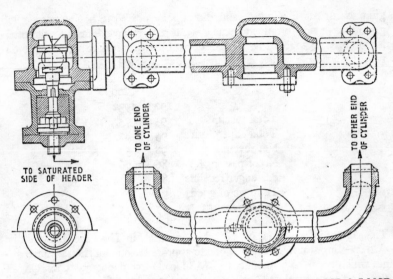

Fig 27. Anderson's cylinder by-pass valve as fitted to superheated MR & LMSR locomotives.

A glance at the arrangement of the valve and breeches pipe which connected the two ends of a cylinder (Fig 27) shows that the cross-sectional area either through the pipe or the valve was very much less than the cross-sectional area of the cylinder, so that some compression would still be set up when coasting. But that the valves should be removed as not worthwhile, was an opinion quite definitely not shared by Wellingborough enginemen. They contended that whereas a Fowler Class 4F 0-6-0 would coast with its load of empty wagons the 14 miles from Sundon to Bedford when by-pass valves were fitted, the application of steam was required most of the way after they were removed. I have often wondered whether any controlled tests were made to try and quantify in discrete terms the pros and cons of by-pass valves in all classes so fitted: or whether they and bogie brakes were removed by a new broom who had little experience of such fittings, looking for something to sweep clean, eagerly aided and abetted by elements in the drawing office who had not been brought up in the Midland tradition either. My view has been that it was a mistake to remove them from *all* classes, they were no trouble if conscientiously maintained.

The issue of the new examination schedule was accompanied by a directive from higher management to assess and make effective the resultant savings in manpower forthwith. Moulang remitted to me the job of making the calculations, on the basis that the average annual mileage of Wellingborough locomotives was then 25,000. With a twinkle in his eye he bade me not to forget the inevitable increase in running repairs which would result from the extension of the examination mileages. A few additional examinations applicable to the more modern engines had been inserted into the schedule, and I noted carefully the actual times incurred in carrying out these new items, together with the time involved in the removal of by-pass valves and fitting blank flanges to the cylinders.

The net result was a saving of 28 man hours per week—little more than half a fitter! I then proceeded to Bedford (at 1s per day expenses!) and performed the same exercise in respect of the 45 locomotives allocated there. The stud then comprised three Class 1P 2–4–0, five Class 2P 4–4–0, eleven Class 3P 4–4–0, five Class 1PT 0–4–4, three class 1FT 0–6–0, eight Class 2F 0–6–0, six Class 3F 0–6–0 and four Class 4F 0–6–0. Because there was a much higher proportion of passenger engines at Bedford than at Wellingborough, the average annual mileage per locomotive was higher; consequently the impact of the examination extensions was higher. Nevertheless by the time I had done all the adding and subtracting, the net saving was little more than 2000 man hours per annum, or again less than one fitter. I did not learn of the result for Kettering, which then had about 28 small locomotives, but I doubt very much whether the pundits at Derby succeeded in squeezing a single man out of Moulang's complement at the three sheds.

Indeed the work in the District appeared to be increasing, due to additional day to day repairs arising, particularly at Bedford which was a favourite point for a passenger train driver to give up a failing steed, as it was the first shed at any distance from St Pancras or Leicester where he would be likely to find a sizeable passenger locomotive as replacement. The extent to which this occurred was brought home to me when I was despatched post haste to Bedford following the first visit there of D. C. Urie, the newly appointed Superintendent of Motive Power and unknown to Midlandites. Apparently the visit got off to a bad start when Urie criticised the manner in which the ends of some small boiler tubes were being swaged by a boilersmith, adding: 'I am not a bloody fool, Moulang'. To this Moulang, who did not use expletives, replied: 'I am delighted to hear it, Mr Urie'.

Urie and his party, who stayed at Bedford overnight, were joining their inspection saloon at Bedford station the next morning when Harry Booth, the shedmaster, put in an appearance, ostensibly to see that the steam heating was in order. According to Booth's subsequent account, Mr Urie, seemingly much mollified by the overnight hospitality of a Bedford hostelry, asked Booth conversationally his opinion of the quality of current overhauls in the main works—which were, of course, governed by the CME. Booth, emboldened by a cordiality so sadly lacking during the tour of the shed the previous afternoon, promptly castigated main works personnel; their slack work, he averred, was responsible for increased work, not only on his own engines but also on those which expired on his doorstep.

This was like manna from heaven to Urie who, it was strongly rumoured, was disappointed because he had not been appointed Chief Mechanical Engineer. Reaching Derby, he promptly upbraided Colonel Rudgard, who was now the (Midland) Divisional Superintendent of Motive Power, for not telling him about this shortcoming on the part of the main works. In turn Rudgard, caught off guard by Urie's fulminations, summoned Moulang and Booth with equal celerity to Derby the next day for a justification of Booth's criticisms and to explain, if such justification was forthcoming, why he had not been informed. Rudgard demanded facts and terminated the meeting abruptly.

The next day, after suitable briefing by Moulang, I left for Bedford. For the next week I examined there dozens of casualty report forms, repair cards, boiler inspector's reports and any other documentary evidence which might reveal support for Booth's allegations of faulty shop work. Whilst there had been 35 cases of heated axleboxes at Bedford in the first eight months of 1932 compared with 34 in the whole of 1931, there was no indication that this was due to a deterioration in shop repair or inspection standards. A significant feature of the greater trend towards heated axles in 1932 was the contribution made by the tenders of 'Claughton' class locomotives allocated to Kentish Town and Leeds. Indeed, far more foreign engines failed at Bedford than did engines of Bedford's own allocation, which was a penalty suffered by more than one comparatively small main-line passenger depot. The only conclusive evidence I could find of bad workmanship in a main works of the CME in the previous 20 months on engines which failed at Bedford was in the dossiers of three locomotives —Johnson Class 1P 2–4–0 No 188, Fowler Class 4F 0–6–0 No 4529 and Claughton Class 5P 4–6–0 No 5974.

No 188 had received a general repair at Derby in April 1930 and had been stopped four times between then and February 1932 with the rh driving wheel key loose. On each occasion the offending pair of wheels had been sent to Derby main works for attention, but after a short period of service the key was loose again. A core plug worked loose and blew out of the by-pass breeches pipe on No 4529 and the outside web of the lh inside crank of No 5974 moved inwards, pinching the connecting rod big-end brasses, causing them to heat. Booth and I discussed fully my findings before reporting to Moulang. But with only three cases obviously debitable to the main works out of a total of some 180 investigated, it was clear that Booth had given Urie an incorrect picture, since even the increase in heated axleboxes in 1932 could not be ascribed to defective shop repairs.

Moulang delivered some homilies to Booth on the evils of generalising without facts, particularly when speaking to senior officers whose sympathies, affiliations and ambitions were unknown to lesser individuals such as Running Shed Foremen (the term 'shedmaster' did not become current on the former LMSR until after nationalisation). The whole business was a valuable lesson to me in mechanical investigation, industrial politics and the foibles of all levels of mankind. If I was ever asked a question by a superior in the ensuing 40 years to which I had not the answer, I promptly said so and set out to find it—quickly. To conclude this anecdote Table IV

Table IV

Locomotives which failed at Bedford 12 months ending December 31, 1932
(Heated axle boxes not inlcuded)

Engine No	Class	Owning Depot	Nature of casualty	Conclusion as to cause
4982	Garratt 2-6-0 + 0-6-2	Toton	Drop grate falling in ashpan	Carrier bars burnt away
4968	Garratt 2-6-0 + 0-6-2	Toton	Flexible oil pipe to outer coupled axlebox, trailing unit, broken	No obvious cause
4996	Garratt 2-6-0 + 0-6-2	Wellingborough	Bolt missing from lh by-pass cylinder flange, leading unit	No obvious cause
4984	Garratt 2-6-0 + 0-6-2	Toton	Lead plug fused in firebox	Mismanagement by driver
9572	7F 0-8-0	Toton	Lh coupling rod gradient pin nut, washer and split cotter missing	Cotter pin incorrectly fitted
9575	7F 0-8-0	Toton	Lh by-pass actuating steam supply pipe broken	Failure of previous brazing
5974	Claughton 5P 4-6-0	Kentish Town	Lh inside connecting rod big end hot	Crank web moved on axle
5955	Claughton 5P 4-6-0	Kentish Town	Small tubes leaking in firebox	Tubes insufficiently expanded
5978	Claughton 5P 4-6-0	Kentish Town	Lh outside connecting rod big end hot	Brasses too tight on crankpin
5964	Claughton 5P 4-6-0	Kentish Town	Unable to maintain vacuum	Rubber neck ring on engine vacuum brake cylinder piston rod broken
13146	4F/5P 2-6-0	Derby	Lh connecting rod big end hot	½in knock on crank pin
13172	4F/5P 2-6-0	Kentish Town	Lh crosshead top side metal fused	Intense cold caused oil to congeal (sic)
13174	4F/5P 2-6-0	Kentish Town	Rh connecting rod big end hot	Cause of heating destroyed
13173	4F/5P 2-6-0	Kentish Town	Wash out plug loose in firebox wrapper plate	Insufficiently tightened by boiler-washer
1053	4P 4-4-0	Nottingham	Difficulty in maintaining vacuum	Main train vacuum pipe broken under disc valve
1009	4P 4-4-0	Leeds	Small tubes leaking in firebox	One tube very loose 'in plate', insufficiently expanded

Table IV—*continued*

Engine No	Class	Owning Depot	Nature of casualty	Conclusion as to cause
927	4P 4-4-0	Nottingham	Rh connecting rod big end hot	Due to developed knock
1044	4P 4-4-0	Derby	Short of steam	No obvious defect
3949	4F 0-6-0	Toton	Lh injector failed, rh not reliable	Cones badly scaled in both injectors
4529	4F 0-6-0	Kentish Town	By-pass breeches pipe blowing	Core plug blown out
3931	4F 0-6-0	Cricklewood	Brick arch collapsed	Brick arch supporting bars burnt at front end
4414	4F 0-6-0	Nottingham	Short of steam	Small tubes insufficiently expanded, firebox end
4027	4F 0-6-0	Kentish Town	One tube leaking badly in tube plate	Insufficiently expanded
3934	4F 0-6-0	Cricklewood	Lh connecting rod big end hot	Excessive knock due to slack cotter
4419	4F 0-6-0	Derby	Tender steam brake pipe broken	Insufficiently secured
3910	4F 0-6-0	Bedford	Superheater flue tubes leaking in firebox	Ferrules badly burned
4548	4F 0-6-0	Nottingham	Engine drawbar hook broken	Defective material
4263	4F 0-6-0	Rowsley	Lh trailing tender brake hanger pin worked out	Split safety pin missing
4508	4F 0-6-0	Kentish Town	Lh connecting rod big end cotter missing	Cotter set pins slacked back
4293	4F 0-6-0	Leicester	Tubes leaking in firebox	Slack in plate
4332	4F 0-6-0	Wellingborough	Short of steam	Firehole door stuck open
764	3P 4-4-0	Bedford	Rh fore gear eccentric fork end broken through pin hole	Pin had seized due to shortage of lubrication
759	3P 4-4-0	Kentish Town	Lh trailing engine brake hanger disconnected	Defective brake hanger bracket
765	3P 4-4-0	Bedford	Lh connecting rod big end hot	Defective lubrication
755	3P 4-4-0	Bedford	Small tubes leaking in firebox	Tube ends very thin
762	3P 4-4-0	Bedford	Rh middle tender spring hanger broken	Defective material

Engine No	Class	Owning Depot	Nature of casualty	Conclusion as to cause
701	3P 4-4-0	Leicester	Rh trailing engine spring broken	Fracture in top plate developed
724	3P 4-4-0	Nottingham	Lh trailing crank pin hot	Cause of heating destroyed
719	3P 4-4-0	Bedford	Short of steam	No obvious cause
765	3P 4-4-0	Bedford	Vacuum train pipe nut loose	Insufficiently tightened
755	3P 4-4-0	Bedford	Lh trailing crank pin hot	Cause of heating destroyed
765	3P 4-4-0	Bedford	Small tubes leaking in firebox	Insufficiently expanded
765	3P 4-4-0	Bedford	Leakage in vacuum system	Vacuum pipe joint missing
763	3P 4-4-0	Bedford	Lh injector clack sticking	Clack dirty
763	3P 4-4-0	Bedford	Short of steam	Tube plate and tubes very dirty
719	3P 4-4-0	Bedford	Short of steam	Superheater element tube burst
760	3P 4-4-0	Bedford	Short of steam	Element tube burst
544	2P 4-4-0	Leicester	Short of steam	Mismanagement by driver
533	2P 4-4-0	Peterborough	Short of steam	Not in fit condition to work train
559	2P 4-4-0	Kentish Town	Short of steam	By-pass valve joints blowing on rh cylinder
3217	2F 0-6-0	Bedford	Short of steam	Mismanagement of fire
3112	2F 0-6-0	Bedford	Tubes leaking in firebox	Tube ends thin and short
3119	2F 0-6-0	Bedford	Tubes leaking in firebox	Tubes loose in plate
3112	2F 0-6-0	Bedford	Injectors failed	Mismanagement by driver
3112	2F 0-6-0	Bedford	Rh injector not working	Overflow pipe damaged, obstructing flow of water
265	1P 2-4-0	Bedford	Small vacuum ejector failed	Loose scale in internal steam supply pipe to ejector
257	1P 2-4-0	Bedford	Both injectors failed	Mismanagement by driver
1272	1P 0-4-4T	Bedford	Lh driving tyre fractured	Defective material

lists brief details of the failures, other than heated axle boxes, which occurred at Bedford in the 12 months ending December 31st, 1932.

Because so many variables affected steam locomotive operation on a big railway, such as number in a given class, pattern of allocation over a countryside network, variation in quality of feed water and a dozen other features, it is unwise to generalise too freely when drawing any conclusions from the above table. Nevertheless it contained some definite pointers. Only a handful of 'Claughtons' were allocated to the Midland Division, at Leeds and Kentish Town, yet four of them had failed at Bedford, each time from a different cause. Their stay on the Midland was comparatively short-lived and it is probably fair to say that former LNW enginemen found Midland locomotives more congenial and adaptable than former MR enginemen found ex-LNW engines. Apart from engines Nos 765 and 3112 there was little evidence of repetitive failures. Both inside and outside connecting rod big ends added their quota of trouble, but it is worth noting that despite the relatively large proportion of Wellingborough-based locomotives which passed Bedford depot daily, there was no instance of one coming off there with a heated big end. This I ascribe to the very thorough manner in which this component was maintained at the former shed.

Apart from the economies sought by reorganisation of maintenance schedules, there was a great drive to secure the benefits predicted through feed water treatment, which had already accounted for a substantial capital expenditure in full-scale softening plants and wayside treatment facilities. Those in authority who had been the loudest advocates of water treatment were urging that boiler cleaning involving removal of a number of small tubes at a given periodicity, usually six months, should now be performed only when the monthly examination of the firebox or of the water spaces at wash-out revealed the presence of scale immovable by any other means. Similarly, it was argued, there should be a noticeable reduction in coal consumption which would not need to be expressed in ton-mile figures, but which would be revealed in the per-mile figures provided other factors, eg train loadings, remained about the same. In fact, because there were so many other variables, it was difficult to detect any substantial change in coal consumption figures which could be ascribed to a particular influence. The coal consumption of Garratt locomotives continued at about 112lb per mile, whilst that of the Class 4F 0-6-0 engines continued to vary more with seasonal influences than with the amount of scale in the boiler, as shown by the figures for No 3962 for 1931:

Four weeks ending	*Coal per mile, lb*
25 January	89
22 February	81
22 March	87
19 April	83
17 May	68

Four weeks ending	Coal per mile, lb
14 June	66
12 July	65
9 August	77
6 September	55
4 October	62
1 November	83
29 November	70
27 December	92

Steel tubes were beginning to appear in newly shopped boilers. This introduction of another variable in the economics of boiler maintenance made it difficult to frame a clear statement on the effect of water treatment *per se*, but I spent many interesting hours trying to do so in respect of Wellingborough engines.

Another avenue of economy explored in the early 1930s was means to secure maximum life from wheel tyres. To this end a tyre flange limit gauge was issued in 1933, which purported to indicate the maximum degree of wear that could be tolerated on tyres having the thick 'A' profile before an engine need to be taken out of service for this cause alone. In October 1933 Rudgard discussed the new gauge at a meeting of District Locomotive Superintendents, who expressed alarm if it was the intention to use it as the only criterion of wear limits, since in their view flanges would become far too thin. Rudgard hastened to reassure them that the gauge must be regarded as an absolute limit gauge: it was not intended that tyres should be allowed to wear to the extent it would permit. He added curiously that the superintendent's eyes and fingers were the deciding factor: the gauge was only to be used as a guide! In fact, the gauge was quickly withdrawn.

I became a student member of the Institution of Mechanical Engineers In January 1932, and having exhausted the useful possibilities of Wellingborough Technical Institute, I embarked on a correspondence course to prepare for the further academic requirements of the Institution. This work together with continuing interest in the MIC movement and contributions to technical and other journals like the *LMS Magazine* kept me busy. Every issue of the *LMS Magazine* had one page devoted to the MIC movement, usually carrying a drawing and description of component parts of new locomotives which affected the work of the driver. The item was very popular amongst enginemen and made a significant contribution to their training at little cost to the Company. Each year MIC pages were reprinted to form a separate booklet; in the foreword to the 1936 edition, D. C. Urie mentioned that two previous issues amounting to 23,000 copies had already been exhausted and there were demands for more. Mr Urie added that the reception given to the reprints was abundant evidence of the keenness displayed by the staff concerned; he may himself have derived a special satisfaction from the undoubted success of the MIC movement as a whole, since his father, R. W. Urie had fully endorsed and continued on the LSWR the pioneering work of Dugald Drummond in the education of enginemen.

In August 1933 instructions were received that the locomotive costing scheme first introduced in January 1927 was to be expanded by sub-dividing the schedule of locomotive parts under main headings to enable running repair charges to be allocated in much greater detail. The original scheme required purely running repairs and examinations to be coded only as appertaining either to engine or tender; this was sufficient, however, to show up in broad outline the relative running costs of huge classes of locomotives and thus provide one index of performance amongst several others, consideration of which would lead to the decision to withdraw or retain a given class. Now it seemed that the emphasis was being directed to establishing the relative costs of running maintenance of the component fittings of different classes, since locomotive depots were now required to code repairs under detailed headings as shown below:

Boiler
(1) Superheater elements, flue tubes and ferrules
(2) Small tubes
(3) Firebox
(4) All other boiler repairs including those to steam pipes internal and external, brick arch, smokebox and chimney, lagging and hand rails, ashpan, dampers, firehole doors.

Engine
(1) Valves and pistons
(2) Connecting rod big end and little ends
(3) Injectors
(4) Other standard examinations (eg brake)
(5) Axleboxes and bearings
(6) Connecting and coupling rods
(7) Valve motion (other than at valve and piston examination)
(8) Bearing springs
(9) All other repairs including those to cylinders, heating apparatus, tyres reprofiling, and any fittings or operations not included in 1–8 above.

Tender
(1) Axleboxes
(2) Bearing springs
(3) All other items not included in 1 and 2 above.

In theory the tradesman was supposed to enter the appropriate code against the time entry on the repair card; this he had to complete for every locomotive on which he had worked during a turn of duty. In practice, the great majority did so, but a glance at the lists above will quickly show that there could easily be differences of interpretation of the codes. Inevitably the kind of question soon arising was, for instance: did an injector steam supply pipe between the boiler and injector come under 'boiler' or 'injectors'? The artisan confronted with such a weighty problem would leave it for Foreman Fitter Moore to decide when he signed the cards. Since any predilections he may have possessed were certainly not towards paper work, it fell to me to check the codes on all cards each day. Such a chore may sound as tedious as this anecdote which has only been included because it is descriptive of a method that can be recommended to anyone who wants to acquire a detailed knowledge of the shortcomings and relative costs of maintaining machinery of whatever kind.

I went to Kettering and Bedford in an endeavour to get the same interpretations accepted throughout the Wellingborough district. At the latter depot I heard from Harry Booth the first whisper of a radical new shed organisation to come. His brother, E. L. Booth, who was District Locomotive Superintendent at Carlisle, had supplied him with snippets of information about what was happening at Rugby where, it was rumoured, a large-scale experiment was being mounted in methods of organising repairs. Nobody doubted that this would be another economy measure and all waited in some trepidation to hear what would eventually break. On returning from one of these gospelling missions at Bedford I was riding on the footplate of the locomotive hauling the passenger train when we were stopped specially at Oakley to pick up a passenger. The gentleman was none other than Mr Goodchild, who was Outdoor Machinery Assistant to the Chief Mechanical Engineer at Derby and who had been visiting the pumping station which supplied Oakley troughs in company with the District Outdoor Machinery Inspector and Charlie Brooks, of whom we have already heard in connection with the coaling plant. The story was that Goodchild had demanded the removal of the cover of one of the barrels of the Worthington pumps, but it remained obdurately welded to its barrel after removal of the securing nuts. He then directed Brooks to subject the cover to internal mains pressure, which would be fairly substantial due to the pumping station being at the bottom of the embankment, in an effort to dislodge the cover. Brooks was nothing if not anxious to please at all times and promptly opened the valve on the delivery line before Goodchild, who was standing on the longitudinal centre line of the pump, could get out of the way. Either the cover or a jet of high pressure water—nobody was sure which—struck Goodchild amidships and he returned to Derby a sadder but wiser man.

Before concluding this chapter and thus leaving for the time being the subject of costs, it is interesting to note the relative performance of various classes of locomotives in certain aspects which are not so avidly devoured by the enthusiast as figures of coal and water consumption per ton mile, maximum speeds and horsepower developed and all the visual and audible locomotive characteristics still so hotly debated. Important as these issues

Table V

Costing of individual locomotives, Western Division, LMSR
Average Running Repair Costs, Miles run, Coal per mile and Weekdays Out-of-Service for Repairs and Eaxminations 12 months ended December 31, 1932

Operating class of engine	Wheel arrangement	Number allocated to Western Division	Cost of running repairs and examinations (engine only) £	Miles run	Coal consumed lb per per mile	Weekdays out-of-service for—		Remarks
						Heavy and light repairs	Shed repairs and examinations	
6P	4-6-0	60	427	63,047	48·75	35	50	'Royal Scot'
5X	4-6-0	10	386	56,712	46·94	31	63	Improved 'Claughton' Caprotti gear
5X	4-6-0	10	360	45,468	51·70	32	65	Improved 'Claughton' Walschaert gear
5	4-6-0	66	289	39,686	51·14	21	51	Ordinary 'Claughton'
5	4-6-0	15	203	25,250	56·62	19	87	Ex-L&Y four cyl
4	4-6-0	219	190	35,002	51·40	23	39	'Prince of Wales'
4	4-4-0	55	242	41,469	47·31	23	48	Standard Compound
3	4-6-0	1	50	12,963	73·61	33	8	'Experiment' four cyl No 5554 Prospero superheated
3	4-6-0	41	105	19,215	67·66	13	33	'Experiment' saturated
3	4-6-0	1	139	39,890	64·58	12	24	'Experiment' saturated (conversion) No 5472 Richard Moon
3	4-4-0	65	126	23,744	53·07	11	35	'Precursor' superheated
3	4-4-0	21	95	15,875	61·06	5	26	'Precursor saturated'
3	4-4-0	90	96	18,634	55·36	10	27	'George the Fifth'
3	4-4-0	1	52	16,147	36·48	—	8	No 5413 (ex-North Stafford No 171)
2	4-4-0	1	122	22,206	52·96	16	31	No 391 (ex-Midland saturated)
2	4-4-0	10	156	43,221	43·75	4	40	Standard superheated

7	0-8-0	14	125	27,392	65·59	8	43	Standard '9500' class
7	0-8-0	56	128	23,000	76·30	18	43	ex-LNW G2 superheated
6	0-8-0	340	124	20,319	72·92	14	40	ex-LNW G1 superheated
6	0-8-0	9	88	16,442	69·27	18	27	ex-LNW G1 superheated (conversion)
5	0-8-0	30	93	16,317	80·22	20	26	ex-LNW saturated
4	4-6-0	138	123	20,978	71·30	11	31	ex-LNW '19in' goods, saturated
4	2-6-0	83	191	36,603	58·84	17	40	Horwich designed 'Crab'
4	0-6-0	163	141	23,487	66·60	14	38	Fowler type
3	0-6-0	16	81	23,278	61·17	10	24	ex-Midland saturated
3	0-6-0	8	84	13,649	65·26	12	21	ex-Furness saturated
3	0-6-0	4	82	14,307	55·97	10	38	ex-L&Y superheated
2	0-6-0	117	71	14,896	46·69	10	25	ex-LNW 4ft 3in coal
2	0-6-0	154	74	15,030	59·76	7	23	ex-LNW 'Cauliflower'
2	0-6-0	28	76	19,778	55·79	8	28	ex-Midland
2	0-6-0	26	55	10,244	54·69	4	23	ex-L&Y
5	0-6-4T	8	168	27,234	59·42	47	27	ex-North Stafford superheated
4	4-4-4T	5	134	19,009	59·04	19	57	ex-Furness saturated
4	4-6-2T	47	193	24,502	54·48	26	65	ex-LNW 'Prince of Wales' tank superheated
4	2-6-4T	39	187	40,834	50·44	16	38	LMS standard
4	0-6-4T	8	224	31,196	59·28	30	36	ex-North Stafford superheated
3	4-4-2T	38	138	24,367	61·06	20	33	ex-LNW 'Precursor' tank saturated
3	4-4-2T	7	162	21,324	58·15	29	59	ex-North Stafford 'K' class superheated
3	2-6-2T	32	166	33,064	53·23	18	47	LMS standard
7	0-8-4T	30	154	16,544	65·05	12	68	ex-LNW superheated
6	0-8-2T	25	85	14,339	55·10	13	24	ex-LNW saturated
3	0-6-0T	243	93	20,782	48·90	13	28	LMS standard
3	0-6-0T	8	126	23,429	43·41	9	27	ex-Midland
1	0-6-0T	17	62	15,972	43·70	4	19	ex-Midland
0	0-4-0T	1	48	10,893	20·77	—	33	Sentinel No 7160

are, the kind of information equally, if not more, necessary in the management of a large fleet of locomotives may be sampled by reference to Table V. This shows in detail some of the lesser publicised indices of performance for the year 1932 for the more important groups of locomotives working on the Western division.

It will be noted that a number of former Midland and L&Y types had been drafted into former LNW territory. Their performance would certainly have suffered to some extent because of the spares situation and the fact that maintenance and footplate staffs would be relatively unfamiliar with them. Unfortunately I have not the corresponding data for the Midland and Central divisions, but readers whose interest lies in such matters should consult E. S. Cox's *Chronicles of Steam*, which contains a number of highly interesting tables of different indices of locomotive performance.

The inferences to be drawn from a study of Table V could only develop if one was in possession of further background information on the apparent inconsistencies. Why, for instance, should the coal consumption of the solitary four-cylinder 'Experiment' No 5554 *Prospero* have exceeded that of all other passenger locomotives; and how indeed had this locomotive, rebuilt in 1915 with Dendy-Marshall valve gear, managed to survive with all its non-standard components until 1932? Or what lay behind the apparently exemplary performance of the sole remaining North Stafford Class 3 4-4-0 No 5413 (originally NSR No 171), which used saturated steam but returned a creditable 36·48lb/mile as against its saturated sister, Class 2P Midland 4-4-0 No 391, which returned nearly 53lb/mile. The answer could only be found by ascertaining precisely how the locomotives were utilised during the year under review, because in 1931 No 5413 had returned 59/lb mile whereas the 24 Class 2P saturated Midland locomotives still extant on various parts of the LMS had averaged less than 51lb/mile. One could devote a whole chapter to speculation aroused by the figures in this Table; but the main, overriding implications relating to the performance year after year of the numerically larger classes were clearly discernible for higher management to see and act upon.

6 The Silver Lining

As the new year was heralded in 1934, I still could see no escape from a never-ending succession of valve and piston examinations, renewal of superheater element joints, refitting of axleboxes and all the heavy and dirty chores inseparable from the operation of a running shed. Because of the reduced demand on the main works for intermediate repairs due to reduced locomotive mileage, the pits in the shop at Wellingborough were closed; no longer were the more extensive repairs carried out there. Yet within a few weeks my personal horizon was extended to a degree I had never even imagined.

The rumours anent reorganisation of running sheds which had rumbled so persistently around Wellingborough district during the latter part of 1933 erupted quite suddenly into fact at the beginning of the following year. Consultation with staff at all levels as it is practised today was then unknown. Thus when I was summoned to Moulang's office on a morning in early January 1934 to make extensive calculations to ascertain the number of staff which would be required to deal with a greatly enhanced number of valve and piston and other major examinations, also boiler cleaning, on engines not allocated to Wellingborough, the artisan staff were still unaware of the details of the impending scheme.

Briefly, the intention was to concentrate at the biggest depot in a District all the major standard examinations, also repairs such as renewal of boiler tubes, attention to hot axles, collision damage, etc—indeed, any job which would necessitate a locomotive being out of service 24 hours or more. The depots thus denuded of work were to become merely garage depots, at which only boiler washing and the small examinations would be carried out and at which no engine would be stopped for more than 24 hours—in theory. Apparently Sir Harold Hartley, a vice-president of the LMS executive, had brought the concept back with him after visiting some North American railroads and was anxious for the new arrangements to be implemented as quickly as possible. Originally the scheme had envisaged an even more radical re-distribution of work, whereby the maintenance of particular classes of locomotives would be concentrated at major depots; these would specialise accordingly. For instance, on the Midland Division, it was proposed that Leeds would concentrate on its own Class 5X locomotives plus those allocated to Kentish Town and Carlisle. Nottingham was to be the maintenance centre for 2–6–0 'Crabs', whilst Derby would look after all the compound locomotives on the Division. Curiously, Burton-on-Trent was to have become a large concentration repair depot for freight locomotives allocated on the Derby-Bristol line, apart from a substantial portion of Saltley locomotives destined for Wellingborough's attention.

205 tank locomotives of various types at certain garage depots were not allocated to a specific repair concentration centre, because of the light mileage which would be involved in getting them there. These were to be concentrated at some larger garage depots still to be selected.

It was an ambitious scheme by any of the standards then prevailing. It is interesting to note that Saltley, which had a well-equipped outstation shop and was destined a few years later to have the biggest individual locomotive allocation of any depot on the LMSR, did not figure in the proposals as a concentration depot at all: whilst the depot at Burton-on-Trent, which had been created largely to meet the needs of the brewing industry, was to blossom into a concentration repair depot for some 235 freight locomotives, plus its own limited passenger locomotive allocation.

The intention to concentrate at Derby the heavy examination and repair work of all the 107 standard compounds then allocated to the Midland Division was based on the fact that their intermediate and general overhauls were carried out in Derby main works, where a comprehensive stores was also maintained. Expertise in dealing with the peculiar foibles of the compounds would thus, it was held, always be available.

The plan as outlined above did not materialise. This was probably due to intensive staff reaction at all levels; the lack of repair and machining facilities at some of the concentration depots selected, and the absence of a sufficiently large number of regular freight engine workings to enable locomotives allocated to garage depots to be worked to and from their concentration depots when due for examinations, etc, without incurring light mileage. The proposal to concentrate the repairs on standard compounds at Derby was also ill-conceived in my view, since there was no means at Derby running sheds of drilling by machine even a small hole. All components requiring remetalling and/or machining had to be transported into the main works, where the nominal agreement that they should have preference over material for new construction or for general and intermediate repairs seemed to be honoured always in spirit but not invariably in fact. The same hesitation was noticeable on the part of the main works supervisory staff (with a few brilliant exceptions) in the prompt despatch of their staff to lavish their expertise on the rectification of the more difficult jobs cropping up in the running shed. Such hesitancies were perfectly understandable. Again, whilst in no way deprecating the undoubted skill of the artisan in the main works who had probably performed the same, if difficult, job for many years, I have always held that the expertise in diagnosing and rectifying the more mysterious defects which afflicted steam locomotives in service needed to be of a rather different brand to that normally found in a main works.

As already indicated, a modified plan and indeed a much more practical and sensible one was about to be introduced on the Midland Division. When I returned to Moulang with my calculations for staff, he revealed that Wellingborough was to be the guinea pig depot. All engines allocated to Leicester, Bedford and Kettering were to have their major examinations and repairs carried out at Wellingborough. The scheme was to be known under the grandiose title of the Area Locomotive Supply, Repairs Concentration and Garage Scheme. The work at Wellingborough was to be organised on a three-shift system, thus reducing substantially the number of locomotives stopped for repairs at any one time, whilst no locomotive was supposed to be stopped at any of the three garage depots for more than 24 hours. The staff to cope with the increased work at Wellingborough was to be drawn from the district and other more distant garage depots, such as Peterborough and Walton where, in common with all garage depots, there was to be a substantial reduction in staff commensurate with their reduced maintenance commitments. The HQ staff elements were as usual out for their pound of flesh and there was to be a net reduction of staff on the Midland Division to make the scheme financially viable. Moulang then added the cryptic comment that 'there might be something in it for Hardy and you'. Edgar Hardy was a fitter 10 years my senior who had been Deputy Foreman Fitter since Renaut had retired and a good colleague and friend.

In less than a fortnight Hardy and I were summoned to Moulang's office on a Friday morning. We were informed that the new scheme was to be introduced the following Monday and that he and I were appointed leading hand fitters from that date at a rate of 5s per week more than that of a top rate fitter. Hardy was to start the night shift and I was to book on at 1.00pm to supervise the afternoon shift; this arrangement would alternate in succeeding weeks. The majority of artisan staff were to be divided into three shifts and additional staff were to be drafted in from garage depots as soon as possible. Hardy and I were to maintain voluminous records of man-hours incurred on every job, material issued down to the last split pin, engine non-availability and a mass of other data.

Appointment as leading fitter in sole charge of a shift whilst still graded only as an improver fitter was an innovation so foreign to the conservatism endemic in a running shed organisation of the period that it took a lot of comprehending. The prospect of shift work did not daunt me; in fact, I was elated at the thought of two hours regular overtime every week and payment for time and one-third for hours worked between 6.00pm and 6.00am.

This rosy vision of wealth amounting to an average of 82s per week (on a basic rate of 51s) was clouded by another, of disappointed colleagues and the justifiable anger which this promotion of the most junior fitter in the shed might well arouse. I need not have been apprehensive. To their great credit, everyone, each in his own way, helped me and that is something for which I shall be eternally grateful.

Launching of the Area Concentration scheme at Wellingborough with an expedition that would have been the envy of many present-day managers heralded on the Midland Division the introduction of the District motive power organisation throughout the LMSR. At grouping in 1923 there had been 33 principal locomotive depots on the MR (together with a few small sub-depots), each with its own superintendent. A few of them situated on remote tentacles of the Midland such as Brecon, Upper Bank and Carnforth had been absorbed into the Western Division; conversely the Midland over the years had assumed responsibility for a few former LNW and NS depots. The new organisation postulated the formation of Districts, each consisting on average for the Midland Division of between four and five depots, a lower figure than for the Central and Northern Divisions, where either there was a concentration of average-sized depots in a small area or a large number of small depots over a wide area. The depot at which heavy running maintenance was to be concentrated was usually the largest in the proposed Districts already and was also that chosen for the District administrative headquarters. The exception on the Midland Division was Kentish Town, which although nominally a garage depot continued to house the District Superintendent because of its importance to traffic working on the Midland main line and St Pancras in particular. Wellingborough was a reasonable focal point for its garage depots, because the same superintendent had governed Kettering and Bedford in recent years. The annexation of Leicester was achieved without fuss, although Moulang exercised a very loose rein over its former superintendent, G. A. Frost, until his retirement in 1935. The final grouping of depots into districts on the Midland Division was as under:

Shed No	Concentration Depots	Garage Depots	Remarks
13A	Plaistow		
13B		Devons Rd (ex-NLR)	
13C		Tilbury	
13D		Shoeburyness	
13E		Upminster	
14A	Cricklewood		
14B		Kentish Town	
14C		St Albans	
15A	Wellingborough		
15B		Kettering	
15C		Leicester	
15D		Bedford	
16A	Nottingham		Included Southwell and Lincoln

Shed No	Concentration Depots	Garage Depots	Remarks
16B		Peterborough	
16C		Kirkby-in-Ashfield	
16D		Mansfield	
17A	Derby		
17B		Burton-on-Trent	Included Overseal
17C		Coalville	
17D		Rowsley	
18A	Toton		
18B		Westhouses	
18C		Hasland	
18D		Staveley	Included Sheep-bridge
19A	Sheffield (Grimesthorpe)		
19B		Millhouses	
19C		Canklow	
19D		Heaton Mersey	Joint with LNER
19E		Belle Vue	
19F		York	
19G		Trafford Park	Joint with LNER; included Widnes (M) and Brunswick
20A	Leeds		
20B		Stourton	
20C		Carlton (Royston)	
20D		Normanton	
20E		Manningham	Included Ilkley
20F		Skipton	Included Keighley
20G		Hellifield	
21A	Saltley		
21B		Bournville	Included Redditch
21C		Bromsgrove	
21D		Stratford-on-Avon	Included Blisworth
22A	Bristol		
22B		Gloucester	Included Tewkesbury, Dursley and Thornbury

Shed No	*Concentration Depots*	*Garage Depots*	*Remarks*
22C		Bath	Included Radstock
22D		Templecombe	
22E		Highbridge	Included Wells

The first few weeks of operation of the new scheme at Wellingborough were hectic enough. The garage depots were not slow to realise that any defect which presented difficulty in diagnosis or rectification and was therefore likely to cause a locomotive to be stopped for more than 24 hours, could promptly and legally be dispatched to Wellingborough. Very quickly a morning conference with the District garage depots had to be instituted to regulate the influx of work to the concentration depot. Some of the staff who were supposed to have transferred from other depots either had not arrived or had left the service, although there were very few of the latter, since jobs were so scarce. The stores at Wellingborough had never stocked spares for passenger locomotives of classes other than those for the smaller types allocated there and a wholesale transfer of stocks from garages had to be organised to enable standard compounds and Class 2P and 3P locomotives to be dealt with promptly. Hardy and I tried to cope with the paper work, as well as continuing to do our share of fitting and seeing that others did the same. In this we were encouraged but not assisted by Foreman Fitter Moore, who had suddenly found himself landed with much more work but also much more assistance pro rata than ever he had enjoyed. He had not been upgraded to compensate for the greater volume of work passing through the depot, the specious but typical argument being advanced by the staff barons that until parallel reductions in supervisory expenses could be effected at those depots at which work had been reduced, no increase in pay could be granted to those whose responsibilities had increased.

Despite the lack of adequate preplanning work on many details of the scheme, its inherent soundness began to triumph over the initial confusion and frustrations by the time the next reorganisation descended upon us some three months later to cause yet more travail. This added complication, more imagined than real, rejoiced in the title 'Locomotive Maintenance and Mechanical Efficiency on Washout Basis', but quite quickly it became known universally as the 'X' scheme of repairs. It was applied at every depot at which boilerwashing was carried out; thus the garage depots were included.

Before the introduction of this scheme, boilers had been washed out either on a mileage or time basis and it was fortuitous if examinations or major repairs were carried out at the same time. Under the new arrangements every locomotive due for boilerwashing was thoroughly examined by an examining fitter and examining boilersmith. All repairs they found together with any standard examinations due were carried out at the same time. By synchronising the washing-out operation with the 'mechanical' functions, the authorities expected to increase availability of locomotives for traffic working, to improve their mechanical efficiency, to prevent the development of defects by thorough, detailed examination at predetermined periods and to reduce effectively repetition repairs.

Yet again a major scheme of repair reorganisation was introduced virtually overnight. At Wellingborough the burden was borne largely by Hardy and myself, since we were charged with testing in steam, examining and recording repairs required on every locomotive due for boiler washout, and then subsequently re-examining it to see that the repairs had been carried out properly, finally signing a certificate to this effect. We were also required to peruse every 'Repairs Required' card submitted by drivers and decide what specific repairs could be deferred until the next 'X' day, thus contributing to greater availability. If there was still any spare time left on a shift, the architects of the scheme had ensured that it would be fully occupied by devising numerous records, the maintenance of which was mandatory: of time engine on pit; time commenced to blow down steam; etc, etc *ad nauseam*. All this data came under critical examination by representatives of higher management during their daylight excursions from the hallowed precincts of Divisional headquarters at Derby into the outer world of reality.

For a never-to-be-forgotten month, during which yet a further refinement of the repair costing scheme was introduced, resulting in time on standard examinations, time on repairs arising, total time on 'X' repairs and running ('Y') repairs, all having to be shown separately, Hardy and I struggled to cope with an impossible task. We were afraid that if we complained we would be thought unequal to it. Then at about 12.30am one morning Moulang called in at the Foreman Fitter's office en route to a derailment and found me still there two hours after booking-off time, bringing records up to date. He enquired, and was told, the reason; and from then on an elderly fitter carried out the initial 'X' examination and either Hardy or I would check the repairs on completion.

Taken together, the Area Repair Concentration Scheme and the 'X' Scheme probably constituted the outstanding advance outside the main CME workshops in steam locomotive maintenance in the later days of its operation in this country. Indeed, when integrated with the schedule of standard examinations, these new schemes provided a maintenance philosophy which was ordered, simple and sound and withstood the test of time until the steam locomotive disappeared.

This revolution was made even more effective in promoting higher availability by the attention focussed on the peregrinations of a locomotive after it arrived on a depot, but before it was stabled on a pit in the shed. A committee of four, all trained in some aspect of motive power operation, was formed on each Division. They were charged with examining the progress of locomotives through selected depots as they underwent coaling, watering, cleaning of firebox and smokebox, cooling down of boiler and boilerwashing, examination, repair, tube sweeping, steam raising and preparation including oiling ready for further service. The method was for one committee member on each shift of eight hours to record on pre-prepared sheets how every locomotive was occupied from arrival on the depot until departure, including all waiting time. This exercise lasted for a total of 72 consecutive mid-weekday hours, after which the results were collated and transferred to summary sheets. Reference to these showed very clearly any bottlenecks occurring in locomotive operations, whether they were caused by physical limitations of the depot layout, staff or material shortages or simply bad management. The committee chairman took a regular day turn and liaised with the District officer and local supervisory staff, with whom the committee's final report would be discussed before submission to the Divisional management. The whole exercise was an excellent tool of management, which enabled the 'worst' depots to be pinpointed on a basis of facts and earmarked as requiring capital expenditure to bring them up to the best modern standards.

By the middle of 1934 the various new facets of repair procedures were beginning to function with a fair degree of efficiency. In order to get some uniformity of artisans' time charges for standard examinations, I embarked on a series of method studies, after first explaining fully to the participants the reason for them, which was simply an endeavour to be fair to every member of the staff. Everyone co-operated in these exercises with a much greater willingness than I had anticipated. Most of Wellingborough's traditional times proved to be about right; a few were 'tight' and a few over-generous. The studies anticipated to some extent the more sophisticated ones carried out in connection with productivity schemes in post-war years, although they were made without the use of a stop watch.

Within two or three months a reasonable pattern of working had emerged, which enabled pre-planning of work loads and eliminated mutual recriminations amongst staff who had originated from different sheds or who had practised different methods.

Anyone who is concerned with the maintenance of preserved locomotives still capable of working in steam may be interested in Table VI, showing times which an experienced fitter (and mate where appropriate) might be expected to take in the examination of specific components. Included as a matter of interest are some times issued by the Western Division authorities at Crewe in 1935, showing corresponding times reached by entirely independent investigations at WD depots. In the case of the latter, the times were issued with an instruction for District officers to comply with them and some of them must have met with a frosty reception. Reference to the table shows a remarkable variation in the times for piston and piston valve examination as between the two Divisions, amounting in some cases to 100 per cent. This was probably due to the relative extent to which refurbishing of the various components associated with pistons and valves was carried out. At most former Midland depots, the piston tail rod bushes, where fitted, would either be reversed or renewed at each piston examination; similarly piston valve spindle bushes in both front and back steam chest covers were remetalled and rebored at each piston valve examination. Likewise, slide valve engines had the brass bushes for the valve spindles in the steam chest cover renewed at each 10–12,000 miles examination and valve spindles were also put in the lathe for polishing and checking for truth. At some of the small depots where there were no remetalling or machining facilities, these refinements could not be observed; this, coupled with different methods of stripping and reassembling, may have been a major reason for the quite significant variation in times for jobs of all descriptions throughout such a vast railway system, with a corresponding variation in mechanical efficiency and maintenance costs.

As the year wore on I began to enjoy myself immensely. However humble the position of Leading Fitter, it was one in which decisions or otherwise about the fitness of things mechanical had to be made promptly and at every hour of the day. To hesitate or defer a decision until the Foreman Fitter's opinion was available was to invite loss of confidence in those whom one supervised. A running shed also engendered an atmosphere in which forthright, uncomplicated speech was not only necessary but appreciated. Equally a supervisor had to be prepared to receive with good humour the comments of an exasperated fitter for whom nothing had gone right that day, or the strictures of a driver who had reported a defect several times without it being properly rectified – probably because the engine was agreed for a main works overhaul and was not having money spent upon it. In dealing with Wellingborough drivers I found enormous benefit from having identified myself with their Mutual Improvement Class activities; but a driver lodging at the depot with a 'foreign' locomotive occasionally became difficult when I tried to persuade him that I had no more resources to devote to an ailing, aging locomotive than the depot to which he and it belonged.

One such driver was Parry of Saltley, who used to bring No 8829, an ex-LNW 19 in 4-6-0, to Wellingborough on a lodging turn. These locomotives were quite suitable for working fitted or even partially fitted trains, but their brake power was woefully inadequate for non-fitted mineral trains, as one brake cylinder on the engine had to serve both engine and tender. As slack developed between the engine and tender, with progressive wear of the intermediate drawgear, it became unwise to adjust the tender brake blocks close to the wheel tyres, otherwise the blocks were binding when the engine began to exert tractive effort. I told Parry that it was up to Saltley to put the intermediate drawgear right: if he was not satisfied with the brake power available, he must either get his load reduced or run at reduced speed. I do not know what he did, for the engine did not last long at Saltley; it was another instance of a class of LNW locomotive being unacceptable in an area where it was completely unknown.

Table VI

Typical times taken for certain standard examinations based on mileage (Wellingborough 1934-35)

Examination Item	Milage Basis 000s	Standard Compound Fitter hrs	Standard Compound Mate hrs	2P 4-4-0 Fitter hrs	2P 4-4-0 Mate hrs	7F 0-8-0 STD / 4F 0-6-0 STD Fitter hrs	7F 0-8-0 STD / 4F 0-6-0 STD Mate hrs	3F 0-6-0 Midland Fitter hrs	3F 0-6-0 Midland Mate hrs	3FT 0-6-0 Standard Fitter hrs	3FT 0-6-0 Standard Mate hrs
Inside connecting rod, big and little ends remove, examine, replace	10–12	2 (2½)	2 (2½)	3½ (4½)	3½ (4½)	3½ (4½)	3½ (4½)	3½	3½	3½ (4½)	3½ (4½)
Big end brasses, refit	10–12	1 (1)	1 (1)	1 (2)	1 (2)	1 (2)	1 (2)	1	1	1 (2)	1 (2)
Outside connecting rods, remove, examine, replace (bushed type)	10–12	3	3	—	—	—	—	—	—	—	—
Coupling rods, examine in position	10–12	½ (½)	½ (½)	½ (½)	½ (½)	1 (1½)	1 (½)	1	1	1 (1½)	1 (½)
Crank web, examine	10–12	½ (½)	½ (–)	½ (½)	½ (–)	½ (–)	½ (–)	½	½	½ (½)	½ (–)
Wheels and tyres, examine and gauge profiles	5–6	1 (½)	1 (–)	1 (½)	1 (–)	1 (½)	1 (–)	1	1	1 (½)	1 (–)
Bogie, examine in position	10–12	¼ (½)		¼ (½)							

Pistons, remove, examine, renew rings and gland packings, tail rod bush, remove crossheads for remetalling and replace	30–36	17 (24)	17 (24)	22 (11)	22 (11)	20 (11)	20 (11)	7	7	7 (10)	7 (10)
Piston valves, remove, examine, renew rings and packings or remetal bushes	30–36	5	5	12 (7)	12 (7)	12 (7)	12 (7)				
Slide valves, remove, examine, replace	10–12	8¼ (8)	8¼ (8)					5	5	5 (3)	5 (3)
Slide valves, fit new if required (per valve) (includes renewal of valve spindle packing)	10–12	2 (2)	2 (2)					½	½	½ (2)	½ (2)
Blast pipe, remove, clean and replace	30–36	6	6	5 (3)	5 (3)	6 (4)	6 (4)	4½	4½	3½ (2)	3½ (2)
Intermediate drawgear, uncouple engine from tender, examine and recouple	30–36	2½ (2)	2½ (2)	2½ (2)	2½ (2)	2½ (2)	2½ (2)	2½	2½		

NOTES.—(1) Figures shown in brackets show corresponding times issued on the Western Division.

(2) Times shown are for operations mentioned and do not include time for work arising when defects were found which could increase the total examination time.

(3) Two hours extra per locomotive was taken when Class 2P 4–4–0 locomotives were fitted with double exhaust piston valves.

Another incident was a sharp reminder of the different characteristics possessed by the passenger locomotives we had begun to maintain. A Class 3P 4–4–0 No 764 was piloting a 'Patriot' class 4–6–0 rebuilt from 'Claughton' No 5971 on the 7.20am Nottingham–London express, which left Wellingborough at 8.40am for St Pancras, calling only at Bedford; it was the most important and heavily patronised train of the day from Wellingborough and when piloted would reach 75/80mph towards the foot of Sharnbrook bank. Approaching the latter point the rh connecting rod of No 764 fractured completely through the little end, wrenching the other end of the rod from the strap (Fig 28); the rod itself

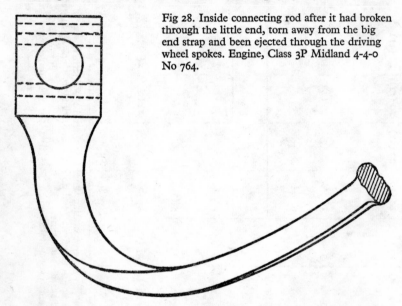

Fig 28. Inside connecting rod after it had broken through the little end, torn away from the big end strap and been ejected through the driving wheel spokes. Engine, Class 3P Midland 4-4-0 No 764.

was ejected *through* the spokes of the rh driving wheel into the four foot of the down fast line. It was necessary to dispatch the breakdown vans to clear the up fast line as No 764 could not be moved until the valve gear, completely wrecked by the flailing connecting rod, could be cleared away. Fortunately oxy-acetylene burning tackle was by this time available to release the damaged motion; only a few years previously such a chore would have to be performed with a hacksaw, large hammers and cold chisel setts! No 764 was towed back to Wellingborough and had to be pushed off No 2 shed turntable on to a pit as a 'dead' engine was opposite. I was on duty and summoned all available hands to push it off the table. There was no resistance from her stationary pistons and valves and their associated motion parts, so that when the heavy balance weights in her 6ft 9in coupled wheels passed over the top centre the engine began to accelerate rapidly. Despite the frantic efforts of the man on the tender handbrake, the trailing pair of tender wheels (leading in the direction of travel) climbed nimbly over the rail stops at the end of the pit and the tender buffers struck the shed wall. I blessed the generous proportions favoured by the architects of earlier years, for that wall never budged and the engine was quickly pulled back on to the pit.

About this time, too, I escaped censure for failing to notice that a crosshead arm was working loose on Class 7F 0-8-0 No 9541 by drawing attention to suggestions I had submitted previously to improve the design of crosshead and gudgeon pin. The radical weaknesses of the 'Austin Sevens' were becoming only too apparent as they aggregated mileage from new engine or heavy shop repairs; connecting rod little end bush wear was very heavy, it was impossible to keep gudgeon pin nuts tight for more than a few days, and longitudinal fractures developed in the gudgeon pins themselves. During 1934 no fewer than six of this class at Wellingborough, Nos 9501/05/11/25/61/79, suffered broken lh driving coupling rod crankpins, whilst No 9502 distinguished itself by breaking its lh piston head. These defects, coupled with the heavy incidence of heated engine axleboxes already described and a host of minor defects such as leaking injector steam and delivery pipes, made the class a heavy drain on shed maintenance resources. It redeemed itself only by good steaming qualities and efficient use of the steam when in service.

Standard compound locomotives which were little known at Wellingborough prior to the repair concentration scheme, but which now came from Leicester for their major maintenance, posed problems for the artisan staff. What, for instance, was acceptable wear in the high pressure piston valve liner? What cylinder and steam chest fractures could be tolerated? What degree of carbonisation of valves and pistons was normal? These and other pointers to the mechanical health of the locomotive needed assessment. For some reason, I kept my rough notes relating to the valve and piston examination of No 1043 as follow:

Carbonisation
Thickness on high pressure piston head $\frac{1}{8}$in.
Thickness on high pressure cylinder front cover $\frac{1}{8}$in in patches.
Thickness in high pressure liner ports $\frac{1}{16}$in.
Thickness on rh low pressure piston Nil.
Thickness on lh low pressure piston $\frac{3}{16}$in.

Condition of pistons
Good, all rings renewed, tail rod bushes reversed, grooves worn out.

Condition of cylinders
Good, fracture in lh low pressure exhaust port bar, will continue to run safely.
Hp piston valve liner, good, 10in Full.
Lp port faces, corded in centre, well lubricated.

Condition of valves
Hp piston valve, rings renewed (narrow type).
Lp valves $\frac{11}{16}$ in thick, replaced, corded in centre of face.

Piston rod packings
White metal good, MacNamee slack, renewed.

Valve spindle packings
2, MacNamee garter springs renewed.

Blast pipe
Clean.

The internal condition of this engine as revealed by the above particulars could be regarded as 'good' for this class after 30–36,000 miles running. The curious feature to be noted is the cleanliness of the rh low pressure piston head, which had no deposit on it; that suggests a paucity of lubrication somewhere, although there was no evidence of local excessive wear.

Standard compounds could give audible warning if things were going wrong internally. Badly worn high pressure piston rings would pass so much steam to the low pressure receiver that the exhaust beats would sound noticeably louder when full compounding at low speeds. The proximity of my home to the main line had made me extremely sensitive to variations in the audible characteristics of all types of passing locomotives. Thus my ears were affronted when one Sunday morning a Nottingham compound, No 1098, after starting an up passenger train from Wellingborough station, produced two beats close together followed by a long pause and then another two beats close together. Normal emission was, of course, four equally spaced beats per revolution as the low pressure cylinder cranks were at 90 deg to one another, the angle of 270 deg being bisected by the high pressure crank. I could not believe my ears. I rang Nottingham to inform them of this enormity, fully expecting to be told that the engine was stopped for repairs somewhere in the London area. Instead a somewhat superior voice said that No 1098 was fitted with a crank axle with the three cranks nominally at 120 deg, hence the irregular sequence of exhaust beats. Whatever the purpose or result of this experiment, the arrangement was neither perpetuated nor extended.

Comparatively few of the Horwich-designed 2–6–0 locomotives had yet penetrated to the south end of the Midland main line, although introduced in 1926. On occasions such as the Grand National at Aintree or Blackpool Illuminations, Cup-Ties, etc, two or three of these locomotives would be sent to Wellingborough to work excursion trains thence to the North-West. In the early hours of a very busy Saturday No 2747 was sent light engine from Nottingham to work an excursion from Wellingborough via Derby and Manchester to a point on the Central Division. The incoming driver reported the lh bottom main steam pipe joint blowing in the smokebox. Butterworth, a dour Lancastrian who was the running shift foreman on duty, immediately informed me, as there was only about two hours turn-round time during which the engine had to undergo disposal and prepara-tion operations. Wellingborough had no really suitable engines for heavy passenger work and the Class 4F 0-6-0 locomotives used before the advent of the 'Crabs' were not suitable for the 2-6-0 timings. I tested the extent of the blow in the smokebox by holding a lighted rag on the end of a brass rod against the joint with the regulator open. It was an appreciable blow and I told Butterworth that I would pass the engine fit for the Wellingborough–Derby section, but would not guarantee its behaviour on the grades between Derby and Peak Forest. I got a fitter's mate to cut some large sods of earth from the bank behind No 2 shed and pack them round the offending steam pipe joint, although I doubt whether it did the slightest good.

In the days of good maintenance, when to put an engine into service with a known defect of this kind was to court the severest displeasure, my action was little less than intrepid. It got Butterworth off the horns of his immediate dilemma, but it brought down the wrath of Rudgard on to the head of Moulang at 9.00am the same morning. The locomotive had man-aged to get its train to Derby on time and the latter depot, also very busy on summer Saturdays, had with difficulty turned out a replacement, which promptly lost 30 minutes between Derby and Millers Dale. H. V. Buckle, the District Locomotive Superintendent at Derby, related this dismal story to Rudgard, who in turn lost no time in acquainting Moulang with all the pungency of which he was capable, which was considerable. By this time Butterworth and I were at home out of harm's way, but on the following Monday Moulang delivered a homily on the consequences of buck-passing without, however, indicating a satisfactory alternative course of action which we could have followed.

Two months later another unfortunate episode in passenger train operation occurred when the Springboks were playing at Leicester. A special was run from Bedford, picking up at Wellingborough, Kettering and Market Harborough, and timed to arrive at Leicester about an hour before the match. My personal *béte noire*, Class 4F 0-6-0 No 4035, was sent specially to Bedford to work the train, but when I saw it on the Saturday afternoon passing my home about 1.30pm having difficulty making enough steam to keep the brakes off, it was evident that all was not well. It reached Leicester at half-time, causing a most serious breach of public confidence for those days, and by 5.00pm Moulang was fetched specially from his home to his office at Wellingborough and exhorted by Rudgard to find out what had happened—quickly. Moulang sent for me and at 6.00pm I was on my way to Leicester to examine the offending steed. I tested the engine in steam, but could find nothing obviously wrong. It transpired when the enginemen were interviewed that misman-agement of the fire had been the major cause of the fiasco. The driver had been only recently passed for driving duties and the firemen was a cleaner only recently passed for firing duties. Whilst such combinations, caused by the method in use at some sheds in covering spare jobs, often produced some first-class work, this pair did not; the over-anxiousness of both led to gross over-firing, a process heartily disliked by a Fowler 4F. I relate these anecdotes to try and portray the gravity with which heavy delays were viewed in those days of forty years ago and the prompt action demanded by higher management to get the facts quickly and avoid a repetition.

There were, of course, more momentous events in the locomotive world on the LMSR in this year of grace 1934 than I have recorded in detail here, simply because they had little impact on a motive power District organisation such as that at Wellingborough, which existed principally to provide power for mineral, secondary passenger and branch line trains. The new Stanier Class 5MT and 5XP 4-6-0 locomotives began to make spasmodic appearances on express passenger trains powered by Kentish Town and Trafford Park, but it was some months before we country bumpkins at Wellingborough got a chance to get a close look at either.

Stories were current that they were not too free steaming, but in other respects they seem to have established themselves quickly in the esteem of the top link men of the Midland Division. It was later in 1934 that the Stanier three-cylinder tank locomotives sometimes came on to Wellingborough depot en route to Plaistow, the first five having been allocated to Watford because the track on the Tilbury section was not ready for them. The taper-boilered 2-6-0 freight locomotives made only rare appearances at the south end of the Midland main line and the two Pacifics operating on the West Coast main line might as well have been performing in North Carolina for all the interest shown in them by the majority of Wellingborough staff.

Such was the parochial attitude engendered by preoccupation with the struggle to keep one's own engines in good condition. A quick look at other people's had to be taken during the annual holiday (taken *without* pay for artisan staff), and it was during such a busman's holiday that I saw my first 'Royal Scot' locomotive and also the LNER Beyer-Garratt locomotive. In the latter instance I was staying with the stationmaster at Normanton during an August bank holiday weekend and on the Sunday afternoon hired a bicycle and pedalled the 24 miles to Mexborough shed to see No 2395, as it was then. My visit was prearranged and I was met by a deputy running foreman who conducted me to the engine in a dark and gloomy shed. The dismal impression created by the shed was dispelled to some extent by a visit to the stores, where I found that the method of dispensing lubricating oil was far in advance of anything I had yet seen.

The silver lining continued to shine. One Saturday afternoon in mid-January 1935, I was absorbed in trying to divine why Johnson Class 2F 0-6-0 No 2968 had moved forward towards the turntable when the reversing lever was in back gear. The crank axle had been stripped for examination of some flaws in the eccentric keyways and when the fitter reassembled

1 (*Above*) Tangyes tandem compound
steam engines geared to two-throw
sewage pumps. Installed circa 1895 at
Wellingborough, Northants.
/*Wellingborough UDC*

2 (*Below*) Another view of Tangyes
pumps. Part of the cylinder indicator
gear can be seen immediately above
the crosshead. /*Wellingborough UDC*

3 (*Top*) Midland Railway, Johnson 'Single' No 662. /*F. Moore*

4 (*Above*) Kirtley Class I 2-4-0

No 21 photographed at Derby circa 1925 after the LMS crest had been added to the cab sides. /*W. C. Good*

5 (*Top*) Kirtley Class 1 0-6-0 No 2778, Midland Railway. /*Ian Allan Library*

6 (*Above*) LNWR Class 'E' four-cylinder compound 2-8-0 locomotive No 1886, sister engine to No 1888 which for many years worked coal trains from Nuneaton to Wellingborough. /*British Rail*

7 (*Top*) LNWR 'Precedent' class No 2191 *Snowdon* worked for many years on the Northampton-Peterborough line./*IAL*

8 (*Above*) Thos Butlin & Co's 0-4-0 locomotive No 1 built by Hudswell Clarke in 1894. /*Author*

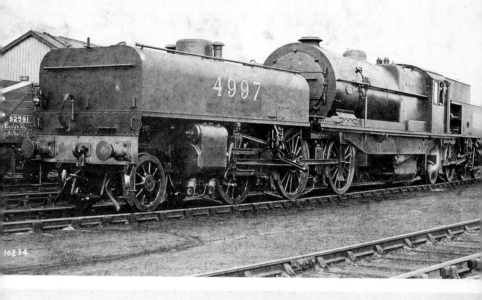

9 (*Top*) LMS Beyer-Garratt
locomotive No 4997 made its debut in
1927. /*IAL*

10 (*Above*) Ljungström condensing
turbine locomotive built as a private
venture by Beyer-Peacock in 1926. /*BR*

11 (*Top left*) Fowler Class 7F 0-8-0 locomotive No 9500, first of a class which proved to be a mixed blessing. /IAL

12 (*Bottom left*) The author's *bête noir*, Fowler Class 4F 0-6-0 No 4035 in LMS days, shown here as No 44035 hauling a coal train near Wickwar in post nationalisation days. /G. F. Heiron

13 (*Top*) Johnson Class 3F 0-6-0

No 3580 in LMS days shown here as No 43580 after nationalisation working a train of empty wagons down the Erewash Valley at Bennerley Junction. /J. F. Oxley

14 (*Above*) LMS Beyer-Garratt locomotive No 4986. The vertical column of the feed water tanks' contents gauge is clearly seen behind the right hand cab door at the side of the rotary bunker.

15 (*Above*) The Baltimore and Ohio 4-4-4-4 locomotive. Chapelon was mystified because only four exhaust beats were audible from two, uncoupled, two-cylinder simple engines.

16 (*Right*) 'Precedent' class 2-4-0 locomotive No 5031 *Hardwicke* in all the pristine glory of its LNWR days. The LMS renumbered it 5031.
/*J. Edgington*

17 (*Top*) The train which ran away
to Olney. (*Above*) Some of it fell in
the River Ouse.

18 (*Top*) Wellingborough's 15 ton capacity breakdown crane cleared up the mess at Olney—it was the only one available at that time.

19 (*Above*) Johnson Class 1F 0-6-0T No 1854, one of a class which worked Midland passenger services from Swansea to Hereford in 1913. /*E. D. Bruton*

20 (*Above*) Rear unit of LMS Beyer-Garratt locomotive with bunker removed. The cylinders and motion of the bunker engine can be clearly seen behind the worm shaft. The pivot centre of the unit is in middle foreground. /*LMS*

21 (*Left*) Lt-Colonel Harold Rudgard. /*Hay Wrightson*

22 (*Top right*) 'Claughton' No 6001 which the author often fired when working at Bedford in 1932. Note 'MM' tender from a withdrawn Robinson 2-8-0 former WD locomotive. /*F. R. Hebron*

23 (*Centre right*) Another Midland Division 'Claughton' with different external lines. /*T. G. Hepburn*

24 (*Bottom right*) 'Claughton' No 5973 having its bogie lowered on Bedford wheel drop. /*BR*

25 (*Top*) An easier engine to fire
when returning to Wellingborough in
the afternoon was rebuilt Johnson
Class 2P 4-4-0 No 553 here shown
standing outside Bedford shed. /*IAL*

26 (*Above*) Class 1P 0-4-4T No 1230
formerly S&DR No 52 which
provided many lessons in locomotive
engineering. /*W. S. Garth*

27 (*Top*) Johnson Class 1P 0-4-4T
No 1374 fitted with condensing
apparatus for working in Moorgate
tunnels and a sister engine to No
1373 mentioned in Table III. /*IAL*

28 (*Above*) No 1373 as rebuilt in later
years with Belpaire firebox and Ross
pop valves.

29 (*Top*) The original Deeley compound Class 4P 4-4-0 No 1005 as fitted for oil burning in 1926. /*IAL*

30 (*Above*) The ill-fated LMS high pressure locomotive No 6399 *Fury*. /*BR*

31 (*Top*) Sentinel locomotive No 47191 (formerly 7191). /*L. Elsey*

32 (*Above*) Anderson's cylinder by-pass valves were fitted to many classes of superheated MR&LMSR locomotives. In this picture of rebuilt Johnson Class 3P 4-4-0 No 768 the casing over the breeches pipe and steam pipe to the actuating cylinder can be clearly seen below the front end of the footframing. /*F. Moore*

33 (*Below*) LNWR 'Experiment' class 4-6-0 No 1361 *Prospero* rebuilt as a four-cylinder engine with Dendy-Marshall valve gear in 1915. /*BR*

34 (*Bottom*) *Prospero*, now renumbered 5554, at Coventry in the LMS days of 1929. /*A. Flowers*

35 (*Top right*) LMS Class 3P 4-4-0 locomotive No 598, formerly NSR No 171, which lasted until 1933. /*IAL*

36 (*Centre right*) Persona non grata at Wellingborough; ex-LNW '19in Goods' 4-6-0 No 8829 was a frequent but unwelcome visitor in 1933. /*IAL*

37 (*Bottom right*) This '19in Goods', No 8849, was fitted with bogie brake gear; it is shown here without brake blocks. /*S. J. Rhodes*

38 (*Top*) Horwich designed Class 5F 2-6-0 locomotive No 2774, a favourite class for working excursion trains in the 1930s. /*C. C. B. Herbert*

39 (*Above*) One of the early arrivals of a famous class, Stanier Class 5MT 4-6-0 No 5006. Engines of this class powered the 4.25am St Pancras–Manchester newspaper train in 1935. /*via John Edgington*

40 (*Top right*) Johnson 2-4-0 No 20266 at speed near Kimbolton on a Cambridge–Kettering train. /*H. C. Casserley*

41 (*Centre right*) A rebuilt 'Claughton' class locomotive No 5946 with large boiler and Caprotti valve gear. These engines were taken off Liverpool–London expresses in 1934 mainly because of smokebox leakages. /*P. Ransome-Wallis*

42 (*Bottom right*) Part of the Locomotive Operations Analysis Committee at Stourton in 1935. Left to right: Frank Barber, shedmaster, Charlie Brown, member, C. Hollis, chief clerk, Author, chairman.

43 (*Top*) Stanier Class 8F 2-8-0
locomotive No 8003. Five of this
class were allocated to Westhouses
when almost new in 1936 and used
mainly for banking trains from the
Blackwell branch to Tibshelf
sidings. /*Real Photos*

44 (*Above*) An ex-LNW
'Cauliflower' (see crest over driving
wheel splasher). It was an engine of
this class which tested the elasticity of
the shed wall at Westhouses. /*BR*

45 (*Top*) The interior of Westhouses
MP depot taken in 1967; the engine in
left foreground has obviously been
derailed. [*J. R. Hillier*

46 (*Above*) The ex-NLR crane engine
which tripped the stores van between
Bow Works and Devons Road MP
depot every day. [*BR*

47 (*Below*) The other class of NL engine at Devons Road in 1937, 0-6-0T No 58860, shown here at Middleton Top on the Cromford and High Peak line where it finished its days. |*John Edgington*

48 (*Bottom*) An LMS Broad Street–Richmond dc electric train of 1937. |*IAL*

49 (*Top right*) An ex-LNW class 6F 0-8-0 known as 'G1' No 9190. |*IAL*

50 (*Centre right*) A 'G1' rebuilt as a 'G2a' No 9329 and reclassified as 7F. Principal difference was in the boiler pressure, 160lb/sq in in the 'G1' and 175lb/sq in in the G2a. |*IAL*

51 (*Bottom right*) 'Jubilee' Class 5x 4-6-0 locomotive No 45614 *Leeward Islands*. |*G. W. Morrison*

52 (*Top left*) General view of Plaistow MP depot; the lifting shop is the high building on the right. /IAL

53 (*Centre left*) A Derby-built, LTS design, Class 3P 4-4-2T No 2112. /IAL

54 (*Bottom left*) Stanier Class 4P 2-6-4T of three-cylinder design, No 2525; all 37 of this class were originally allocated to the LTS section. /IAL

55 (*Below*) The double bogie electric locomotives of the former District Railway which hauled the Ealing–Southend through train as far as Barking. /London Transport

56 (*Bottom*) Class 3P 4-4-2T No 2111 approaching Leigh-on-Sea with the through Ealing–Southend train. /John Edgington

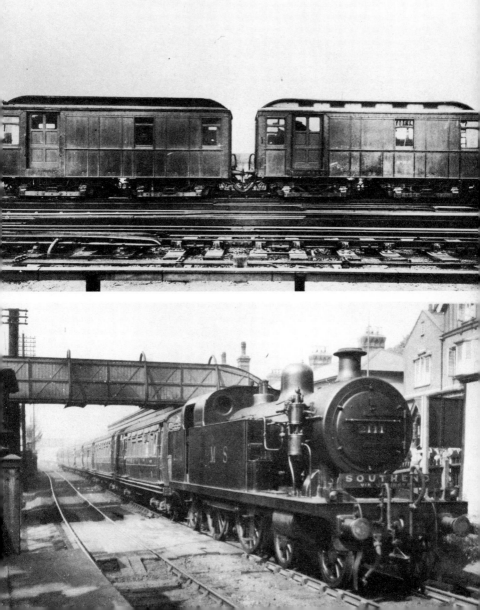

57 (*Top left*) The engine which fell in the bomb crater at Warley, Class 4P 2-6-4T No 2513 near Westcliff with a typical commuter train. *IAL*

58 (*Centre left*) Double heading was rare on the LTS section but here Nos 2506 and 2521 are seen together on a train near Southend. /*IAL*

59 (*Bottom left*) Stanier Class 3P 2-6-2T No 105 working Broad Street–Potters Bar service experimentally. /*Eric Treacy*

60 (*Below*) Anti-glare sheets were effective but made the cabs extremely hot; here is shown the arrangement on a Jubilee Class 5xP. /*John Edgington*

61 (*Bottom*) Plaistow 20 ton capacity Cowans Sheldon breakdown crane. /*BR*

62 (*Above*) The Plaistow breakdown train in 1938. /*D. Cardew*

63 (*Left*) Is it high enough? The author bends to look at 0-6-2T No 2224. /*D. Cardew*

64 (*Bottom left*) The Plaistow gang deals with a derailed District line coach of London Transport at Barking. 'Tim' Wood rests hand on footboard, John Killingback, the district controller, occupies foreground. /*D. Cardew*

65-68 (*Right*) The scenes of devastation at Plaistow after an air raid, September 7th, 1940. /*BR*

69 The author spends a happy day at Bressingham with one of his former charges—the restored 4-4-2 Tilbury tank engine, *Thundersley*./*J. Edgington*

the eccentric sheaves he fitted them the wrong way round on the axle. As the fore and back gear sheaves for each separate engine of the locomotive were manufactured as a unit component, split only to enable it to embrace the axle, the mistake was perpetuated in both fore and back gears automatically. The fitter assembled the rh side first and then followed a similar pattern in the assembly of the lh side; thus the reversal was complete. I was checking first to see that the wheels had not been put in the wrong way round (i e left hand to right hand and vice versa), when summoned to Moulang's office.

Wondering what else had gone wrong, I found that gentleman in expansive mood. Apparently there had been a discussion at Derby that morning at which it transpired that at some concentration repair depots the weight of the extra work was causing the existing artisan supervisory staff to become vocal. Foreman fitters in general had been chosen for their ability as mechanics rather than for administrative qualities and the increase in the volume of their work, and in the associated costing procedures, was proving too great a burden for some of them. Hence a decision had been made to create a new grade of workshop supervisors to assist in every facet of shed maintenance work thus providing much needed help for some foreman fitters. Equally important, it offered a more realistic training ground for young men entering the motive power department after apprenticeships in the main workshops than did the more common system whereby young supernumeraries were employed at the larger depots as part of their training.

Moulang said that he was recommending Hardy and myself for the two positions at Wellingborough, which would involve exactly the same work as we were already doing but which would carry salaried status. His recommendations were favourably received. On January 22nd, 1935, Hardy and I each received a missive, signed by Moulang, reading as under:

'*Reorganisation of Motive Power Depots*
I have pleasure to inform you that it has been decided to appoint you as Workshop Supervisor at a rate of £190 per annum as from February 1st, 1935.

A medical examination will be arranged with a view to considering your entry into the Superannuation Fund.

Although you are being appointed Workshop Supervisor, you will be a working foreman and must attend in overalls and assist with the fitting work as at present.'

This was the first of a series of Irishman's rises which extended over the next 20 years. Apart from salaried staff status, which carried two weeks *paid* annual leave and a somewhat condescending, nebulous promise of admission to the Superannuation Fund (which was in fact delayed for four months), the new grade was financially less attractive. £190 per annum was the lowest adult salary then current and its recipient in Class 5, like the midshipman in the navy, tended to be regarded as the lowest form of animal life in the department. I had received more than £4 per week for 12 months as a leading fitter and the new rate was only £3 14s per week with no enhanced payment for shift work. The all-powerful staff pundits had scored again by securing the same amount of work for less pay by calling the youthful aspirant's financial reward salary instead of wages, whilst still insisting on a modicum of manual chores. But even so I had sense enough to know that it was a necessary step in the ladder, however humble, and I was sincerely grateful to Moulang for his efforts on my behalf.

In the event I did not suffer much financial loss and my silver lining still shone. On the day on which Hardy and I were to have assumed our new aura of respectability, I was packed off to Kettering to take charge of the shed tucked away behind the station, as the newly appointed shed-master (Class 2!), a man named Cox, who originated from the S&D, was unable to take up his duties immediately through sickness.

This unexpected assignment presented a real challenge—not in the supervision of maintenance, which was easy since Kettering was now only a garage depot of about 28 locomotives, but in the fact of having foot-plate staff to supervise directly for the first time. The management team under the District Superintendent consisted of a Running Shed Foreman (shedmaster) on a regular day turn with a lower graded Running Shift Foreman on the afternoon and night shifts respectively, all of whom were supported by a chief clerk with two assistants.

I plunged into the unplumbed depths at 7.00am on the Monday morning. I was greatly relieved to find that Moulang had arranged for one of the Running Shift Foremen, Charlie Cooper, to accompany me for the first few days until I got some idea of how to roster footplate men, deal with the traffic control and special train notices and the myriad of other facets of the purely running side of a locomotive depot as distinct from its main-tenance functions. Cooper was formerly a driver, a man of small stature but great heart, and he showed no resentment at losing the chance of a day turn because of my incursion.

I had to work hard to establish the principle, not always readily apparent at many old Midland depots, that the shedmaster and not the chief clerk had overall charge of the shed. The drivers proved co-operative; they knew my history, since Wellingborough was only seven miles distant and no doubt the bush telegraph had been busy.

During this spell at Kettering the first 'On Time' day throughout the whole of the LMSR was introduced by C. R. Byrom, the Chief Operating Manager. Every driver had to be seen by the shedmaster of every depot on the railway and exhorted to do everything possible to keep time on a certain day in March. Many and varied reactions resulted from my efforts to impress every Kettering driver with the gravity of the occasion, but in the event they did extremely well. Less fortunate was the driver of mid-morning Manchester express which suffered 18 mins late start from St Pancras due to loss of train pipe vacuum. The driver was the redoubtable Howard of Kentish Town, who recouped most of the lost time to Derby and was congratulated personally by Rudgard on arrival. A week or two afterwards it was rumoured that Howard had passed a signal at danger somewhere and had suffered a day's suspension from duty in consequence. Whether or not this was true, it is a fact that laurels gained on one occasion cannot be used to cancel out serious sins of omission of railway operating grades on a subsequent occasion, although this maxim does not always appear to have applied to the hierarchy unless dishonesty was involved.

The assignment at Kettering brought me into my first real contact with the Stanier Class 5MT 4-6-0. I had to reach Kettering before 7.00am, which entailed travelling on the 6.11am newspaper train from Wellingborough (4.25am from St Pancras). The engine now worked through to Manchester and was invariably a 'Black Five' manned by Kentish Town and Trafford Park men on alternate days. I approached every driver on arrival at Wellingborough, told him who I was and where I was going and was never refused a ride, although I pointed out to them that the local pass which I held referred only to Garratt locomotives. Many of the drivers invited me to 'have a go' over the seven-mile run, for which I believe ten minutes were allowed. The load to Leicester was only about 130 tons and one could keep time easily by using $\frac{1}{2}$–$\frac{3}{4}$ regulator and 20 per cent cut-off, shutting off at Kettering Sewage Works and commencing to brake at Kettering South signal box. I used to return to Wellingborough on an afternoon local train, which had started from Wellingborough in mid-morning and, called at every station en route, arrived back at Wellingborough about 3.30pm without reversal by using the curve from Syston South Junction to Syston East Junction and returning via Melton Mowbray, Manton and Corby. The engine was always a Kirtley 2-4-0 manned by Wellingborough men and again I enjoyed the privileges of the footplate.

Supervision of Kettering included keeping an eye on the few LMS enginemen at Cambridge, who had their own booking on and off point within the precincts of the LNER locomotive depot there. A visit once a fortnight was sufficient to see that weekly notices were being signed for and the cabin kept clean and to interview any men as necessary, although this was an infrequent occurrence; but the visit was not to be missed, for it afforded an opportunity to become acquainted with another type of branch working.

The single Kettering-Cambridge line was largely to Huntingdon North, where LNE metals were joined, and was worked partly on a token system and partly by staff and ticket. The gradients were considerable and the schedule of 85 minutes for the 47$\frac{3}{4}$ miles with ten stops called for an average speed of over 33mph, the last 14$\frac{3}{4}$ miles from St Ives to Cambridge over LNE double track requiring an average of 44.2mph. The motive power was invariably a Kirtley Class 1P 2–4–0 of the later builds with 6ft 9in wheels, and if ever firing was required to be 'little and often' it was on such a duty as this, for with an overall speed restriction of 45mph on the Midland portion of the route, uphill running had to be fast. The combination of small coal and a small grate demanded skilled firing despite the light loads conveyed; equally smart work was required at the stops and I have records of station times which would not have shamed London Transport's underground performances.

As Kettering was the centre from which the maintenance of all outdoor machinery for the Wellingborough district was arranged, I became acquainted with a variety of equipment, such as capstans and cranes in goods yards, turntables and a motley collection of pumping machinery and water treatment plant all of which in total represented a substantial capital investment. All of this machinery was interesting and its maintenance afforded a wide scope of training in mechanical, electrical and hydraulic principles and practice.

When I returned to Wellingborough after 11 weeks of this *locum* tenancy, I had the temerity to apply for some extra financial reward for the higher grade work. The official reply was to the effect that I should regard myself as fortunate as having had the opportunity to gain experience in another field, but that payment of 3s per day lunch expenses would be considered.

I had hardly settled down again at Wellingborough when the news broke of Moulang's impending retirement; he was to be succeeded by Ivor E. Mercer from Bolton, who was to take complete charge of Leicester also now that Frost was about to retire therefrom. My guide, mentor and friend for so long was leaving and I have to put on record without the slightest disrespect to valued friends and colleagues of later years that this homely Irishman, with his endearing sense of fun and sometimes infuriating idiosyncrasies, has remained high in my humble estimation of what a good engineer should be. Would that I had possessed his inventive turn of mind and ability, like Agatha Christie, to look at problems from angles other than the obvious. He was, perhaps, too easy-going to be a good administrator but few took advantage of his warm-hearted approach to the task of management.

Mercer spent a few weeks touring the district with Moulang and with what proved to be characteristic vigour began to familiarise himself with his new area, even to the extent of riding and firing on most of the locomotive types used by Wellingborough men over the various routes for which they signed. He had no respect for normal hours until he moved house, and would frequently drop into the Foreman Fitter's office in the late evening, begrimed and physically weary; but he was quite capable of sustaining a discussion for the next two or three hours on a wide variety of mechanical and administrative subjects provided he was fortified by copious draughts of the coffee which Hardy and I used to brew to facilitate the business of handing over shifts.

Hardly had Moulang vacated the chair than Mercer informed me that he had decided to bring me on to a regular day shift to assist him in certain aspects in the running of the district. At that time he had no assistant graded as such and now that the responsibility for Leicester was borne fully by the District Superintendent, the latter was becoming increasingly aware of the burdens laid upon him. Mercer remitted to me matters concerning the individual costing of locomotives, indices of depot performance and *ad hoc* mechanical investigations into whatever happened to be going wrong at the time. The clerical efforts and supervisory scrutiny required to collate the details for the compilation of the 'Comparative Statement of Motive Power Depot Performance' (Fig 29) was the scourge of many chief clerks and also supervisors, who had to explain why the current year's results were not as good as last year's.

A weakness of the document was that it had no provision for *forward* looking. Explanations given to account for apparently less satisfactory figures tended to become stereotyped and of little use to higher management who, notwithstanding, continued to press for them. I spent some time in the District trying to find explanations for some of the more pronounced variations between depots and often stumbled on some archaic local instruction governing a practice, the origin of which was lost in the mists of antiquity.

During a week at Wellingborough, in which I was developing proposals for reducing the cost of drying and handling sand for locomotive use, I first encountered C. Ross Campbell, who was Rudgard's assistant at Derby for mechanical matters. He had an essentially practical outlook and his visits were very welcome.

On this occasion he asked about the operation of the Area Repair Concentration Scheme and the 'X' scheme, which gave an opportunity to draw attention to the associated voluminous paper work still mandatory. Campbell asked for all current records, examined them and wrote in the front cover of at least half of them 'Cancelled C.R.C.' together with the date. I do not recall anyone who worked for Harold Rudgard acting in this direct way when one of his own instructions was involved.

Certainly Ross Campbell made an impression. Since he also appeared to be approachable, I broached the matter of the niggardly salaries still paid to the workshop supervisors. He agreed that they were not such as to induce young, suitable artisans to become foremen and promised to add Wellingborough's complaint to the swelling chorus of discontent arising all over the LMS from this feature, although I did not know of this at the time. In the event the salary of workshop supervisors was raised to £205 pa and Hardy and I had ours back-dated three months to the date of our initial appointment. Campbell's popularity and the respect he commanded was assured on the Midland Division, although the decision to raise salaries would not, of course, be his, but he was undoubtedly one of those who brought pressure to bear on those who guarded the purse strings with

....DEPOT.

Sub-Depots Included....................................

L M S   COMPARATIVE STATEMENT OF MOTIVE POWER DEPOT

	Week ending	Corresponding week last year	Week ending	Corresponding week last year	Week ending	Corresponding week last year	Week ending

1. WAGES PAID:
(a) Suptdce., Inspectors, &c.
(b) Drivers and Firemen (including Passed Cleaners Firing)
(c) Electric Motormen
(d) Chargemen Cleaners and Cleaners (inc. Firemen cleaning)
(e) I. Boilerwashers and W.O. Plant Attendants
 II. Steamraisers
 III. Emptying Ashpits and Loading Ashes
 IV. Other Shed and Yard Staff (Conciliation)
(f) I. Coalmen
 II. Stacking
 III. Lifting from stock
(g) Water pumping E'men and water softening plant attendants
 Messroom attendants (Shed)
 Lodging House Stewards, Matrons and Attendants
(h) O.M.S. Conciliation Staff (other than 'g')
(i) I. Artisans and Shop Staff
 II. O.M.S. do.
 TOTAL (To agree with Abstract E.R.O. 23290)

2. WAGES COST PER:—
1000 Engine Miles { (b) Drivers and Firemen (c) E'tric Motormen (e) IV. Conciliation grades in (e) IV.
Engine Cleaned (d) Chargeman Cl'ner and Cleaners (inc. Firemen cleaning)
Washout (e) I. W.O. Plant attendants and Boilerwashers
Engine turned off Shed (e) II. Steamraisers
Wagon of Ashes Despatched (e) III. Emptying Ashpits & loading Ashes
Ton of Coal Issued (f) I. Coalmen

3. ENGINE MILES (To Agree with E.R.O. 23536)
 Coaching
 Freight (inc. Dept'l)
 TOTAL
3a. Total Electric Miles
4. Loco Dept'l Shunting miles inc. in (3)
5. ENGINE HOURS. (To Agree with E.R.O. 23404) (Traffic and Loco Duties)
6. Engine Miles per Engine Hour.
7. Drivers' Man Hours (actual plus guar. day and week)
8. Percentage of Engine Hours (5) to Man Hours (7)
9a. Total engine miles (Steam) by engines allocated to Depot
 (b) Coal consumed by engines allocated to Depot (cwts.)
 (c) lbs. per engine mile
10a. Oil Lubricating (pints)
 (b) Pints per 100 Engine Miles
11. Total Electricity consumed (Units) (a) Power
 (b) Lighting
12. Total Gas Consumed (c.f.)
13. Loco Water (Galls.)
14. No. of engines cleaned (equivalent)
15. No. of Boilers Washed out
16. No. of times water changed in Boilers

TO..

Fig 29. Comparative statement of motive power depot performance, LMSR.

PERFORMANCE. Four Weeks ended...19

Corresponding week last year			Four weeks this year				Corresponding period last year				Increase (or decreases in RED) in payments for									
											ORDINARY			SUNDAY DUTY			OVERTIME		
£	s.	d.	Average equated No. of Staff.	£	s.	d.	Average equated No. of Staff.	£	s.	d.	£	s.	d.	£	s.	d.	£	s.	d.

REMARKS

a miserliness reminiscent of the darker days of the Industrial Revolution.

In July, Mercer said that if I had perpetrated any misdeeds whilst acting shedmaster at Kettering earlier in the year, the fact had not come to light, therefore he intended to ask Rudgard if he would agree to me acting in a similar capacity at Bedford as Booth, the shedmaster, had requested extended leave. The next I heard of this proposal was a summons at 9.00pm on a Saturday evening, delivered by the signalman at Little Bowden Junction, Market Harborough, where I was staying for the weekend, to proceed *at once* to Bedford and take charge of the depot. I arrived there at midnight, found accommodation at a small hotel near the station and descended on the depot at 1.00am on Sunday morning expecting to find some dire situation demanding my immediate attention.

The Running Shift Foreman did not appear surprised to see me, but assured me that all was well and asked if he was to call me for breakdowns and the like, to which I replied in the affirmative. I then repaired to my bed feeling somewhat deflated that my powers of succour were not immediately required. I was awakened after an hour by the night porter who had conducted the night shift boilersmith to my room. No 764's superheater tubes, he said, were leaking badly and all the ferrules wanted changing; should he get on with it or send the engine to Wellingborough? The running foreman wanted to know urgently as he was short of Class 3P engines for Monday morning, etc, etc. Despite the mental mists induced by the sleep of exhaustion known only to youth, I realised immediately the political implications of this question.

It was a sore point with garage depots that loss of overtime and Sunday duty had resulted from sending work to Wellingborough to comply with the rule that no engine must be stopped for more than 24 hours at a garage depot. I told the scout crisply to get on with the job if he thought he could complete it within the Sunday shifts. As I expected, the job was finished well within the time required. For the next month my slumber was undisturbed and there was a gratifying reduction in the somewhat inordinately long time that Bedford staff had hitherto taken to change ferrules in superheater flue tubes.

An interesting little investigation arose from a wish expressed by Mercer that whilst at Bedford I should make a special effort to find the cause of heated leading coupled axleboxes on the Johnson Class 1P 0-4-4T engines, of which four were then allocated there, Nos 1239/60/72 and 1302. In the previous three months these locomotives had suffered seven hot leading axleboxes between them. For a first stab I examined all the main worsted trimmings in the oil wells formed in the top of the solid brass axleboxes; for this purpose it was necessary to jack up the engine to give sufficient clearance between main frame and axlebox to enable access to be gained to the oil wells. As a consequence of this inaccessibility all four trimmings per axlebox were found in dirty condition on every locomotive, thus decreasing their capillarity; No 1239 had only three trimmings in the lh leading box, thus further restricting the supply of oil. Four new trimmings per axlebox were fitted, having four strands in plug 2½in long and four tails 8in long in three locomotives, thus halving the number of tails originally found; but the holes from the oilwell to the bearing surface on No 1239 were plugged, reliance being placed solely on the auxiliary underpad feed. It worked the 3.27pm Bedford-Hitchin without heating on the next day and the day following I rode with it on the two-coach (54 tons) motor train over the 'Mounts' between Bedford and Northampton as this was a fairly severe duty even with that load. The lh leading axlebox promptly ran warm again, but fortunately the white metal was not fused. After refitting the bearing, the engine was again put on the Northampton duty and this time behaved satisfactorily.

My recommendation to Mercer was to the effect that the leading coupled axlebox oilwell trimmings should be examined and renewed if required at every 'X' day, and that all axlebox underkeeps of the class should be modified to receive pads to rub on the journal if not already fitted. Mercer accepted these recommendations. Although I never saw the result of their implementation I am still satisfied that it is good advice for people concerned with the preservation in steam of old locomotives. The most common cause of heated axle bearings on all ex-Midland engines was, of course, inadequate bearing design for the loads imposed, but at the time of which I am writing the hot axlebox situation was not understood at running depots as well as it was in later years after E. S. Cox's labours in this field.

The creators of the 'Punctuality Day' had realised that it was useless to foster a competitive spirit amongst enginemen and other traffic grades without supporting it by a similar scheme designed to promote a healthy rivalry amongst Motive Power Districts in the matter of mechanical casualties. To this end the exciting year of 1935 saw the introduction of a Motive Power League. It was organised for the whole of the LMS which, as regards motive power functions, now comprised 29 Districts. The District which obtained the highest number of miles per casualty of locomotives allocated during each four-weekly period was awarded 29 points, that with the next highest 28 points and so on. The minutes of meetings of District Locomotive Superintendents held during the initial period of the scheme reflected the great emphasis directed towards the reduction of mechanical casualties. The total number of these for 1935 showed a drop of 19.5 per cent compared with 1934, or an improvement expressed in miles run per casualty of 25.7 per cent. These figures are as likely to have been influenced at least as much by a very keen personal interest displayed by District officers in the compilation of the results as by improvement in the quality of inspection and maintenance.

The 25 per cent improvement in mechanical reliability reached over a period of twelve months was an extraordinary achievement by any engineering standards. The rapid rate of replacement of old locomotives by fewer, but more powerful, new ones, resulting in an increased annual mileage per locomotive, must also have made a substantial contribution to the spectacular result. Some districts on the Western Division must have felt that they had an impossible task. When an objective of 50,000 miles per casualty was being set by the Divisional hierarchy at Crewe, performance at some WD depots was so poor that the situation must have seemed hopeless, as the figures for a typical four weekly period in the early part of 1935 show:

Depot	Miles per mechanical casualty
Willesden	8,104
Rugby	9,962
Nuneaton	11,783
Bushbury	12,418
Bangor	7,438
Widnes	12,842
Stockport	9,249
Preston	11,583
Barrow	10,244
Workington	9,505

District Superintendents were being exhorted to put into store the maximum possible number of 'Georges' and 'Precursors' and a glance at Table VII shows why; as long ago as October 1934, 'Claughtons' fitted with Caprotti valve gear had been taken off important expresses because they were responsible for 35 per cent of Edge Hill's failures in traffic. In fact, one of them had disgraced itself 15 times in five months with smokebox leakage on Liverpool-London trains. Nevertheless over the whole of the Western Division the average miles per mechanical casualty during the four weeks ending March 23rd, 1935 was 37,527, compared with 26,810 for the corresponding period in 1934. Things were getting better.

Just before the termination of this further *locum* tenancy at Bedford, Mercer informed me that instead of returning to Wellingborough, I was to become chairman pro tem of the Midland Division Locomotive Operations Analysis Committee, the functions of which have already been briefly described. This committee had been at work for some 12–18 months and had visited Wellingborough under the chairmanship of S. T. Clayton, who ultimately became the Motive Power Superintendent of the LM Region some years after nationalisation. By the time I came to occupy the chair, the conservators of the cash box had been busy again and the team had been reduced to three; the chairman had to take his turn in recording locomotive movements, etc, on the day shift, his two colleagues being relegated to the night and afternoon shifts during the 72 hours during which observation was kept. The grading of the committee members had also been drastically pruned; I was to remain Class 4, but my two colleagues, Charlie Brown and Bob Sowry, were not even on the salaried staff. Brown was a fireman at Grimesthorpe, Sheffield, whilst Sowry occupied some sort of supernumary post at Burton, the nature of which

Table VII

Analysis of certain engine casualties—January 1st to June 1st, 1935 (LMSR—Western Region)

Concentration Area	Prince of Wales 4-6-0						George V 4-4-0				4-6-2 Supr Tank			
	Allocation	Heated Bearings Coupled Wheels			Big Ends	Vacuum Brake Failures	Allocation	Heated Bearings Bogie Boxes	Big Ends	Vacuum Brake Failures	Allocation	Heated Bearings Coupled Wheels		
		(A)	(B)	(C)								(A)	(B)	(C)
Willesden	—	—	—	—	1	1	—	—	1	—	—	—	—	—
Rugby	25	3	2	1	7	2	28	14	14	9	2	—	1	—
Bescot	11	1	1	—	2	1	5	2	3	1	7	—	—	1
Shrewsbury	6	—	—	1	2	1	—	—	—	—	—	—	1	—
Crewe	31	8	2	—	3	3	22	1	25	2	3	—	—	2
Fresh off Wks	—	1	—	—	—	—	—	—	—	—	—	—	—	—
Chester	12	—	1	—	1	3	15	—	7	1	5	—	—	—
Llandudno Jct	4	2	1	—	—	—	16	3	2	1	4	—	1	1
Edge Hill	5	2	—	—	2	1	9	—	—	—	7	—	—	—
Longsight	5	1	6	—	2	—	1	—	—	—	4	—	—	—
Springs Bch	21	6	—	—	2	5	10	1	—	1	12	—	1	1
Carnforth	4	1	1	—	2	3	—	—	—	—	3	1	1	1
Carlisle	3	—	—	—	—	1	1	—	—	—	—	—	—	—
TOTAL	127	26	14	2	24	21	107	21	52	15	47	1	4	6

(A)—1st coupled; (B)—2nd coupled; (C)—3rd Coupled

was never very clear. During a briefing session at Derby, Rudgard's other principal assistant, J. E. ('Tim') Wood, made it clear to all of us that assignment to the work of the committee was an indication that we were destined for higher things if we behaved ourselves. He comforted my helpmates by informing them that they would enjoy the lodging expenses applicable to the lowest salaried grades, which included me. I never ceased to wonder during a lifetime of railway service how the term 'enjoy' continued to be used with enduring frequency whenever a superior wanted to give the impression that he was conferring on some lesser mortal a benefit to which common justice entitled him anyway. In this case the munificence consisted of 7s 6d per day and night; admittedly good lodgings could be found almost everywhere for 28s from Monday evening to Saturday morning, but the margin of income over outgoings was not such as to encourage moral turpitude amongst committee members during their off duty hours.

The first depot given to us to examine was Toton and an improver, Richard Tildesley, was assigned to us for this first commitment, as he had had a spell as a committee member and was familiar with the paper work, which was somewhat daunting at first sight. Toton was one of the bigger depots on the Midland, having an allocation of about 150 freight locomotives but no passenger engines; the nearest town was Long Eaton, where Tildesley was already lodging with an elderly widow, Mrs Fells, who possessed a large house and a large heart, for she hoarded all four of us for three weeks for a very modest sum.

After sitting up half the night to find a 'lost' half-hour on the summary sheets, we presented the report on Toton to Wood at Derby on the third Saturday after commencing the study. It was a statistical portrait of operations at Toton which did not displease Wood. He was afflicted with a severe speech impediment which did not embarrass him in the least; indeed, when one came to know him well, this stammer seemed to add to an already attractive personality.

The next exercise of the committee was staged at Millhouses, Sheffield, followed by another one at Stourton, Leeds. Both depots then had an allocation of about 50 locomotives; Millhouses engines were almost entirely passenger types whilst freight locomotives only were in evidence at Stourton. Study of the two depots in an organised way provided a classic example of the contrast between a purely passenger and a purely freight depot.

At the passenger depot every locomotive arrived off its train at almost the same (booked) time every day. Staffing throughout the 24 hours in every grade was thus simplified and the spare cover required was only a small proportion of the total staff complement. On the other hand, few locomotives arrived at a freight depot at the time shown on the working diagrams and in winter time the lateness could amount to several hours. This irregularity resulted in a number of peaks and troughs in graphs of the various kinds of activity involved in the servicing of locomotives; it also reduced the productivity of a given number of staff whilst increasing unit costs. The committee was unable to make any substantial proposals to improve performance at either depot without incurring heavy capital expenditure for coaling and ashlifting plants; it is doubtful if these would have shown sufficient return on the investment.

It is worth noting that Ronnie Pinchbeck, the shedmaster at Millhouses, had so organised affairs that during the 72-hour observation period, the total time shown under 'waiting repairs' was only 18hr 7min, and that time was incurred only because an engine which arrived at Sheffield station with a heated axlebox was released to Millhouses instead of Grimesthorpe, the parent depot where this type of repair was concentrated. The only criticism made in the report referred to the number of locomotives taking coal when leaving the shed merely to 'top up' the tender, which practice involved locomotives in conflicting movements, thus causing 'waiting ashpit' delays. It was a practice to be deplored but one to which drivers were very prone at passenger depots. Pinchbeck's death at an early age deprived the railway, in my view, of a man who would inevitably have made his mark in motive power circles.

Our next and my last analysis committee assignment was to my own depot of Wellingborough. By this time I had enjoyed the opportunity of studying quite intensively the working, including maintenance activities, of several depots, some of them larger and some smaller than the one in which I had grown up. Thus I had no anxiety about the outcome of our investigations there. I was able to present a satisfactory report which required no 'whitewashing' and I was pleased for Mercer who had been very kind to me. I had the impression then, strengthened in later years, that he had not been Rudgard's nominee as Moulang's successor and in consequence could not afford to give the Colonel any reasonable cause for complaint.

On presenting the report on Wellingborough to Wood at Derby and enquiring where we were to go next, he informed me that Mr Kinsman wished to see me. O. E. Kinsman was Rudgard's principal assistant. He specialised in general matters affecting the running of the Midland Division and staff matters in particular, as compared with his immediate subordinates Campbell and Wood, who each had well-defined areas of responsibilities for locomotive maintenance and utilisation respectively.

Kinsman asked me if I was interested in becoming a running shift foreman at Westhouses, a small depot in the Erewash Valley which only provided power for coal traffic originating from collieries in the Notts and Derby coalfields. He said that the post was Class 3, which would mean that I would have an immediate rise of £25 (per annum!). Although I was taken completely by surprise I answered in the affirmative. Within a week I was summoned to Rudgard's presence. He told me that I had got the job, that I was very lucky and should not forget to take my overalls with me as I might occasionally have to undertake some running repairs. This latter warning proved to be the understatement of the year.

7 A Course in Management

I arrived at Westhouses on a foggy Monday in late October travelling on a local Nottingham–Chesterfield train which, by virtue of its stop at every intermediate station, coupled with the numerous and lengthy permanent way slacks which then abounded on the Erewash Valley line due to colliery subsidences, made the weary traveller even wearier through lengthy contemplation of the dismal landscape dominated by colliery spoil tips and their spidery overhead connections. Even occasional green countryside was spoilt by the coal-blackened stream which meandered sluggishly through it.

By the time the train reached Alfreton, the station immediately to the south of Westhouses, I had formed a poor (and erroneous) opinion of Derbyshire's claim to contribute to the beauty of the English scene. By now, too, I was unimpressed with the fact that I was about to start work on the most congested portion of the Midland main line, that between Cudworth and Toton. At Alfreton, however, my mental horizon brightened considerably when a very plump man with a thatch of greying hair entered the compartment and, almost before he had sat down, enquired if I was the new shift foreman for Westhouses. I suppose my obviously new bowler hat and blue suit proclaimed the typical locomotive foreman of the period whom he was expecting to appear that day, for he proved to be the chief clerk at the depot, Harry Chandler. In view of my previous strictures about certain chief clerks, I must put on record quickly that Chandler was the complete antithesis of the type I had previously considered as typical of the breed.

During the $1\frac{1}{4}$-mile ride to Westhouses, he made me feel that I was welcome. During the remainder of our association I learned from him a great deal about the conditions of service of footplate grades and how to apply them. He was a local Labour councillor and respected by the men at Westhouses as much for his forthright explanations when they had imagined grievances about staff entitlements as for his moderate political leanings.

On arrival at Westhouses we walked to the depot by its only means of access, a footpath which passed under the main lines and again under the lines connecting Blackwell South Junction with Blackwell East Junction. The depot itself was situated at the commencement proper of the Blackwell branch, which served Blackwell 'A' Winning, 'B' Winning and New Hucknall collieries. It was a six-road straight shed, all roads converging on to a junction with the outgoing road, beyond which was the turntable. The offices, stores and fitters' shop were situated at the south side of the shed and looked out over green fields with Sherwood Forest in the far distance. There was a set of shear legs of standard design and lavatories of the most primitive kind. Coaling was effected by manual tipping from a stage and all ashes had to be loaded with hand shovels. Due to colliery subsidence the rear wall of the shed was propped with huge timber beams, a fact for which I was soon to be thankful.

Arrived at the depot, Chandler introduced me to the Shedmaster (then known as Running Shed Foreman), a tall, thin, red-headed man about 30 years old named I. M. Howard. He made me welcome enough and showed me round the depot in about ten minutes flat, by which time my opposite number on the shifts had arrived, one George Dobson. The latter was a short, stocky man of 35, with great energy, little knowledge of locomotives and even less of motive power depots, which deficiency he proclaimed freely within the first few minutes of our initial meeting. He had been a chargehand hydraulic fitter at Somers Town goods depot and had come to Rudgard's notice when the motive power function included supervision of outdoor machinery. He was a man of considerable person-ality and proved a first-rate colleague, determined to master the motive power scene, which was virtually unknown to him before being appointed to Westhouses a few months earlier. Rudgard's contention was that anyone with intelligence, enthusiasm and an engineering training could acclimatise himself to the motive power environment without necessarily having served his apprenticeship on locomotives. Although this was an an arguable theory, the hapless subject of experiment in its application was hardly likely to receive the maximum guidance or encouragement by banishment to a depot like Westhouses for duties which included only a small mechanical content.

The Westhouses allocation of about 28 locomotives in 1935 consisted of Johnson Class 3F, Fowler Class 4F and a few ex-MR shunting tank engines. Later, in 1936, a few of the new Stanier Class 8F 2–8–0s appeared, but no engines had standard examinations or boilerwashing carried out on them at Westhouses at that time. Instead, the Class 3F and later Classes 7F and 8F were maintained at Staveley, whilst the Class 4F and tank engines were dealt with at Hasland. Toton was the repair concentration depot for the district. Thus any criticisms of the quality of work done at Hasland and Staveley on Westhouses engines was contained within the family enclave and could be dealt with by the District Officer at Toton, Mr Slade.

The object of denuding Westhouses of boilerwashing and maintenance work was to minimise costs there. This was achieved by withdrawing boilerwashers and boilersmiths and reducing the number of fitters to one poor soul who was condemned to a regular night shift, being assisted by a tuber named Penrice who I am sure never realised the contribution he made to the running of the LMSR. He would enter a firebox to examine a leak or expand a tube without the boiler being cooled down and then mention the circumstances casually to the foreman on duty.

I soon realised why Rudgard had told me to take my overalls with me to Westhouses. The man who had arranged for the maintenance of the depot's locomotives to be done elsewhere was A. W. F. Rogerson, who had once been in charge of Westhouses, Hasland and Staveley, before they were incorporated in the Toton district. He had then moved on to sunnier climes, succeeding E. E. A. Talbot as District Locomotive Superintendent at Kentish Town. Rogerson was no mean enthusiast. He would not permit such a trifling circumstance as the absence of fitting staff for 16 hours a day at a shed of 28 locomotives to ruin the practical aspects of his financially attractive plans if he could avoid it by the simple expedient of ensuring that the salaried foremen were mechanically trained and would fill the breach when necessary. It was clever reasoning, which ultimately failed in its purpose when the volume of coal traffic increased in 1936-7 and the engine allocation and repair staff had to be increased.

Before taking charge, I spent a fortnight sampling the afternoon and night shifts with Dobson and also in travelling over most of the routes over which Westhouses men worked. These included the Blackwell, Pilsley and Teversall branches and the main line to Birmingham, Peterborough, Wigston, Rowsley via Ambergate and Gowholes via Chesterfield and the Sheffield–Manchester line. About a quarter of the jobs were lodging turns, none of which, however, qualified for mileage bonus payments. My role on the railway was again cast amongst men who worked pretty hard without getting any fringe benefits—unless one rates overtime as such. This was fairly common on the main-line turns during the winter months. The Erewash Valley is prone to bouts of fog which can last for days on end; the movement of traffic deteriorated and the backlog could only be eased by working throughout the weekend at enhanced rates of pay. Not that the salaried staff were permitted to participate in this pre- and post-Christmas treat; extra Sunday turns were covered invariably by deputy foremen, who were drawn from a specially selected, voluntary panel of drivers and passed firemen.

That practice was changed after I had been called out twice without notice on a Sunday to sort out a particularly difficult rostering situation which a certain deputy had felt unable to resolve—largely, I suspected, because the small village of Westhouses contained so many railwaymen that he could not help upsetting some of his immediate neighbours if he booked them to certain turns. Thereafter Dobson and I alternated on Sunday turns at times of great activity, which usually extended over the months of December, January and February. I would not like it to be inferred that drivers and passed firemen did not in general make good Deputy Foremen. The great majority who acted in this capacity did well. Many ultimately became salaried supervisors such as Foremen, Locomotive Inspectors and Regulators—in fact, key figures in the motive power organisation. It was just that at some small depots, a deputy could in certain circumstances find it difficult to be completely impartial in the allocation of work and continue to enjoy harmonious relations with his off-duty neighbours.

Before assuming the awesome responsibility for a shift I also visited the District Control Office at Tibshelf Sidings, presided over by the District Controller, W. H. Bullimore. I had already of necessity overheard a number of telephone conversations with members of his staff whilst Dobson was acquainting me with local contacts, and had felt a vague disquiet that the latter appeared always to be on the defensive when talking to the Control. Ever since I entered the service of the railway eight years before I had been aware of an undercurrent, a kind of 'them and us' attitude between the 'Loco' and the 'Control'. Now I was to hobnob with Traffic Control staff for some part of every hour of every shift, I thought I might as well beard these strange creatures in their den so as to know to whom I should be talking in the future.

The Traffic Control system almost universal on the LMS in 1935 appears to have had its genesis on the Midland in January 1909. From that date the movement of all goods and mineral trains between Cudworth and Toton came under the scrutiny of District Controllers at Cudworth, Masborough, Staveley, Westhouses and Toton, from whom signalmen were liable to receive orders affecting their own work and also instructions to transmit to other members of the staff respecting theirs. In succeeding years, Cecil Paget in his role of General Superintendent of the MR, had developed this initial concept until it covered the whole of the Midland system. By sheer weight of personality, he seems to have invested the early denizens of Control offices with a mysterious aura of superiority over those more ordinary mortals whose job it was to drive locomotives, to ride brake-vans, signal trains, and by extrapolation provide locomotives at the times required. There is no doubt that in many areas there was bad feeling between enginemen and members of Control office staff, many of whom lacked experience in outdoor movement operations, but felt qualified on occasions to conduct telephone conversations with drivers and signalmen in somewhat peremptory or supercilious tones from the safe confines of their Control office. The immediate reaction of a less articulate enginemen or guard would be to reply in rich, pungent dialect, which did not help very much and often terminated the conversation abruptly.

I believe this behaviour was quite traditional on the Midland. It probably was elsewhere and may well have been one of the principal reasons why a major change was made in 1935 in the structure of Divisional management. That year saw the appointment of a Divisional Superintendent of Operation at the three Divisional headquarters at Crewe, Derby and Manchester; to him both District Locomotive Superintendents *and* District Controllers were responsible. The Divisional Superintendent of Operation had two principal aides, one for operating and one for motive power matters. The Midland Division was fortunate in having Rudgard in the latter position, his personality and authority was such that little impact of the new organisation was felt by junior supervisors like myself. Nevertheless it was necessary constantly to remind the gentlemen in the control offices that there were *two* legs to the divisional body. In fact S. E. Parkhouse, the Divisional Superintendent of Operation at Crewe found it appropriate in March 1936 to deliver a homily at a joint meeting of District Locomotive Superintendents and District Controllers on the evils of trying to saddle one another with the responsibility for adverse operating results, so the real issue was frequently obscured. Mr Parkhouse found it necessary to reiterate his plea for greater co-operation at a meeting of mostly the same Western Division officers held at Crewe in December 1937; whilst he was satisfied that the closest co-operation did exist between the District Controllers and the District Locomotive Superintendents themselves, he felt that the same spirit was not shared by their respective staffs at lower levels. I might add that the twain are not yet fully integrated at the time of writing.

At the conclusion of my fortnight's 'teach-in', I armed myself with rubber, pencil and overalls and commenced work at 4.00pm. The first job on every shift was to ascertain the number, owning depot and position of every locomotive inside the shed signal. This process was made easy by the former Midland practice of providing all locomotives with a cast depot number plate attached to the lower part of the smokebox door. Since the formation of the new Districts, the letter which now followed the numeral indicated to which shed in a particular district an engine belonged, an essential piece of information on a railway still operating over 7,700 locomotives. On this itinerary I also checked the state of the coal stage and ashpits and the availability of dry sand, of which there was a heavy user at Westhouses during the winter months.

Arrived back in the office, the next job was to confirm by reference to the roster book that every driving, firing and guard's duty had been covered as far as possible for the next 24 hours. This was a job which could not be delegated to anyone else, since Foreman Howard on the day shift was the only one blessed with a foreman's assistant, a recognised wages grade, in which many performed a range of duties far beyond a strict interpretation of the agreed job content.

The filling of vacant positions by spare men was a simple business at most small sheds on the Midland Division. Firemen passed as competent to undertake driving duties and cleaners passed for firing duties were divided into two roughly equal groups; one was rostered on duty turns starting between midnight and midday, the other between midday and midnight. If there was a vacant driving turn within this am and pm division, the senior am passed fireman with 12 hours rest since the previous turn of duty and the requisite route knowledge would be rostered to the driving vacancy; the resulting firing vacancy would be filled by the senior am passed cleaner available, again subject to his having had at least twelve hours rest.

Described thus briefly, the system sounds delightfully simple; but there were traps for the unwary. The filling of one vacancy involved much rubbing out of names and a lengthy interruption in the middle of that could cause a name to be wrongly inscribed. One had to remember that if a man was moved to work a lodging turn, his regular booked job had to be covered for *two* days. On one occasion, Dobson on the afternoon shift had to move a registered driver, Edwin Wright, from his regular local turn to a Birmingham lodging turn, but forgot to rub out his name from the local turn on the next day when Wright would be returning *from* Birmingham. I was on the night shift when at about 2.00am a diminutive call boy rang me from Westhouses and Blackwell signalbox to say that he had been to call Driver Wright for his regular turn, but his wife said he was not at home; he was supposed to have gone to Birmingham and if he was not there, she demanded to know where he was! As Edwin Wright had had a somewhat wild reputation in his younger days, I hurried to establish where from his signing-on card. I told the boy to tell the enraged lady that her consort should be returning to the fold about 10.00am, and that we were very sorry to have disturbed her slumbers. Wright was an easy-going giant of a man who never mentioned the incident, although Dobson apologised to him later.

In 1935-6 there was still an intense quest for economy. The allocation of a driving or firing turn to the wrong man incurred the severe displeasure of the headquarters staff office, who had perforce to give the man who should rightfully have had the turn credit and sometimes payment for higher grade duty which he had not performed. Credit for higher grade turns was the important thing, since pay increments were partly based on the aggregate number of turns performed in the higher grade; therefore this aggregate was quite naturally and properly watched closely by each man concerned. The strong community spirit which pervaded the small village of Westhouses, where the male members of most families were employed either on the railway or at the mines, was balanced by an equally strong determination on the part of individuals to see that nothing was done which would affect their seniority position one iota then or in the future. This keen but healthy rivalry even invaded families; I can recall one man who was adept at reading the roster book upside down by peering through the hatch window of the foremen's office to ascertain what his two brothers were doing.

This passion for justice made it very easy for the supervisors to manage the depot. It had nothing to do with trade unions—in fact at that time many men were still disenchanted with them and did not belong. But all foremen respected the solidarity of a group of responsible men living in a fairly isolated area and there were virtually no labour troubles. The issue of a disciplinary charge form was a rare event; nearly all of them related to incidents outside the depot and were issued at the direction of the Divisional office at Derby, where the facts relating to such events were collated.

An aspect of rostering which worried me during that first winter was the operation—or rather non-observation—of the twelve-hour rest clause. I had heard so much of the sanctity of this provision in the National Agreement that I was flabbergasted on the first occasion I exhausted the supply of men with twelve hours rest who could be upgraded, when the chief clerk assured me that it was alright to bring them on after a minimum of nine hours rest provided that: (a) I had explored all avenues of supply at neighbouring sheds within the district; and (b) individual men were prepared to come without demur. It was within the 'law' for a man to take up his own booked turn after less than twelve hours rest if he so desired, also at the resumption of work after lodging away, but this local custom was a new one on me. No attempt was made to persuade a man to come under 12 hours for a spare turn, although all but three passed firemen and two passed cleaners elected to do so.

The reason for this situation was not far to seek. The volume of traffic declined sharply in the summer months with the advent of colliery holidays and there was no higher grade duty for passed firemen, although passed cleaners often elected to go to Newton Heath, Preston, Accrington and Blackpool for firing duties over busy weekends, such as were caused by Blackpool Illuminations, etc.

The engine arrangements board was as far as possible marked up for several hours ahead, to enable the steamraiser to have engines with a proper head of steam when required. Once the men's rosters were completed, and after perusing the 'Repairs required' cards, the next job was to assign locomotives to specific duties for the next 16 hours or so, so that trains of given weights were powered with the correct class of engine with the appropriate route availability. Great care was taken to see that engines were put on turns to enable them to terminate easily at Hasland or Staveley, if they were due for boiler washout. During very bad weather it was not uncommon for the shed to be completely denuded of locomotives from about 2.0pm to 10.00pm. The men booking on for the few turns which started during that shift simply sat in their messroom waiting for a locomotive to arrive on the shed; when one did appear there was an orderly scramble to clean the fire, empty the smokebox, fill the tender tank and sand boxes, oil the motion parts, coal it and get it off the shed again. When the supply of power was adequate and trains were running with reasonable punctuality, it was a grave sin to incur a late start from the shed from any cause.

Certain members of the District Controller's staff appeared to be under the impression that there was an unfailing supply of locomotives sitting at

the shed waiting to be marked up in the place of locomotives which had
not arrived due to late running. It was often possible to reallocate Westhouses locomotives to local turns, but there was a limit to the 'hotching up'
process. One senior shift controller in particular was frequently cynical
when any of the foremen told him that there was no more suitable
power to use; he would enquire sarcastically whether we had asked the
surrounding depots for assistance, knowing full well that none was
available.

After a month of such pointless and supercilious comments, I decided
that something must be done about him. On a particularly trying shift
when I had not paused to eat for about five hours, I decided (to use
Marshal Foch's words to General Joffre in 1914) that the situation was
excellent for attack, since my centre was giving way and my right was in
retreat. I assembled all the diagrammed workings relating to Westhouses
engines and made a list of the times at which locomotives were booked to
arrive at the depot from traffic. I compared this list with the actual
arrival times during the previous 24 hours and found that, apart from
certain shunting and banking engine turns, not a single main line engine
had been released within two hours of the time shown on the workings;
most of them were detained much longer. I then called up my controller
friend and lectured him on the crass stupidity of expecting the 'Loco' to
turn out locomotives to time if they did not come on the shed to time.
There was a pregnant silence and then a muttered 'Blimey' as the 'phone
clicked into silence. For my remaining two years at Westhouses, relations
were cordial. I doubt whether at the majority of depots communications
between the two functions, 'Control' and 'Loco', were at such a low level
as they had been at Westhouses.

Disruption of services due to bad weather not only caused power
shortages but also resulted in locomotive types or classes alien to Westhouses arriving on the shed. One afternoon I came on duty at 4.00pm
and the only locomotive on the shed was an ex-LNW 'Cauliflower' 0-6-0
standing forlornly at the inner end of a pit road. All foreign unbalanced
locomotives (ie locomotives without a return working) were reported by
wire to a Power Controller at the Divisional Control office at Derby, who
would arrange return to the home depot by the best means. I cannot
recall where this engine was allocated, but I received a wire from the
Divisional Power Controller to put in on the 7.55pm Westhouses—Toton
coal train, normally booked to a Stanier Class 8F 2-8-0.

The driver was Percy Ball, a man of imposing proportions, but one who
disliked too much deviation from normal working arrangements. When he
saw what was marked up for his train, he informed me that he knew
nothing about 'Cauliflowers' and accused me of rough justice in saving
this locomotive specially for him. I pointed out that the train would stand
if he did not take this locomotive and offered to show him the controls and
the more obscure oiling points. I still marvel at my temerity, for apart

from seeing them dashing along the Northampton–Peterborough line in my youth, 'Cauliflowers' were as unknown a quantity to me as to Ball. I mounted the footplate, released the handbrake and wound the reversing lever in a clockwise direction preparatory to setting the engine for oiling.

The boiler was full and the safety valves were simmering as I opened the regulator; whereupon the engine promptly moved *backwards*, propelling the tender over the rail stops at the end of the pit until its movement was arrested by the shed wall, which was already propped up outside, as mentioned earlier. The wall deflected slightly, but resumed its position when I reversed the engine and opened the regulator smartly: whereupon the tender bumped back over the stops back on to the rails. I had forgotten that the reversing screw of several types of ex-LNW locomotives turned in the opposite direction to the more natural movement for fore and back gear respectively on the great majority of British locomotives. F. W. Webb was remembered without enthusiasm on that evening, but Ball eventually rumbled off with his unusual steed after I had quickly examined the tender for any sign of disturbance of bearings or spring gear.

I saw no reason to report my lapse from grace, since I had not yet been passed by a locomotive inspector as competent to move an engine in steam within the yard limits; but as the result of another incident a few weeks later, this omission was soon rectified. On a very frosty and very busy night I had asked the driver and fireman known as the 'shed set' if they would take their meal earlier than usual as a rush of engines tardily released from traffic was expected to arrive on the depot later in the shift. The 16-year-old fireman had been borrowed from Hasland and was enjoying his very first firing turn; he finished his meal quickly and came to enquire if there was anything else which required doing urgently. I instructed him to accompany me to the ashpit, whence I intended to move Fowler Class 4F 0-6-0, No 3978, into the shed as it required brake blocks renewing and was due out in about an hour.

Arrived at the bottom points in the yard, we both descended from the locomotive. I told the boy how to work the newly-installed one-way spring points, stressing the necessity for him to hold them until the whole of the engine had passed over them. He was a very willing but small boy, obviously anxious to please on his first firing turn; but he was wearing a brand-new pair of hobnailed boots, one of which slipped on the glistening wooden cover over the point mechanism just as the leading coupled wheels of the engine were about to run on to the switch rail. The boy was thrown off balance, released his grasp of the points lever, and the leading wheels of No 3978 settled down on to Mother England gently but firmly, as if with a sigh of regret. I felt the bump and applied the brake, thus preventing the driving wheels from following suit. The poor lad was almost in tears as I sent him off for the steamraiser, the fitter and some wooden scotches; I needed a full head of steam if I was to get the leading wheels back, since the layout at the point of derailment made it impossible either to push or pull the locomotive. The fitter and I placed the wooden scotches so as to lead the wheels back to the rail and protect the chairs; I then reversed the engine, opened the regulator wide and to my intense relief it was rerailed without damage to itself and with only the corners chipped off two slide chairs. On this occasion I reported the facts in the log book, since another department, the permanent way, was involved and I did not want a fuss made of a minor incident caused by the inexperience of a very willing boy. I mentioned in the report that I was not authorised to move engines in steam within yard limits and in less than two weeks Locomotive Inspector Tom Mellor came up from Nottingham to perform the sacred examination rites, after that an entry was made on my service record to the effect that I was now entitled to handle the regulator within shed yard limits. I never abused this privilege by moving an engine in circumstances in which the use of a set of men was justified, but I was often able to further the smooth working of the shed by relieving a driver for a few minutes whilst he ate his well deserved 'snap'. The men knew that I loved to drive an engine and if there was any complaint, I never heard of it.

One piece of feedback information from locomotive depots to the Divisional diagramming and timing offices which is worth mention was the 'Breakdown of Booked Workings' daily return. By now the itineraries of locomotives were no longer governed by the route knowledge and mandatory rest periods of the men who worked them; intensive efforts were made to increase the hours a locomotive spent in traffic, usually increasing daily mileage at the same time. For instance, a locomotive which hauled a freight train from Peterborough to Westhouses was required to work from Westhouses to Wigston and back before returning to Peterborough. The object of the return was to focus attention on booked workings which frequently broke down due to inadequate terminal margins or consistent late running. After filling in many forms which constantly recorded breakdown of certain workings, but which failed to move the Divisional diagramming office at Derby, I submitted alterations of some workings under the Staff Suggestions scheme. In due course I received an expression of thanks, and an intimation that the breakdowns occurred because of some tight pathing margins which were being modified; that action would put things right. It did nothing of the sort. And so, after getting Dobson to collaborate on his shift, we implemented my proposals, which continued to operate up to the time and maybe after I left Westhouses without anybody being the wiser and with great benefit to the working.

The Mutual Improvement Class at Westhouses was a very healthy one, held in the Railway Institute on Sunday afternoons and usually attended by 50 to 60 footplate staff or about half the total strength. In 1936 coal production was increasing and a number of extra staff were engaged and extra turns allocated to the depot, thus creating more driving and firing positions necessary to cope with coal traffic which increased by 12 per cent during the next twelve months. The young fireman at Westhouses was at a disadvantage because he rarely saw an engine dismantled; all such work was performed at Hasland, Staveley or Toton.

I quickly found that a great deal of practical demonstration was necessary before the youngest class members could comprehend the drawings and charts exhibited at the lectures. Accordingly, I took a number of passed cleaners and firemen to the shed each Sunday morning at times when there was no weekend working and dismantled portions of locomotives so that they could see what a slide valve, a piston valve, a connecting rod big end or an injector cone looked like. The succeeding session in the Institute in the afternoon was thus made much more comprehensible.

A factor which helped to sustain the exceptional interest in Mutual Improvement Classes at that time was the introduction by the LMSR in 1936 of a biennial examination of all drivers and firemen passed for driving in their knowledge of rules and regulations. There had been some serious incidents on the line in the early 1930s due to non-observance of what were really elementary, commonsense operating rules. Higher management considered that the examination would be a safeguard against the continued employment in a responsible position of a driver with known deficiencies in his knowledge of this part of his job. No resentment was openly expressed about the examination at Westhouses. I believe the majority of the men concerned there welcomed the opportunity to demonstrate that they had not ceased to take interest once they had passed the initial driving examination.

I always entertained some doubts as to the value of a formal periodical rules examination, since some men who knew the rule book and the general appendix to the working timetable backwards were not necessarily those who performed best in an emergency. Drivers should encounter an Inspector at least once a year and the latter can quickly establish whether a man is dangerously ignorant of any aspect of his work. On the other hand, the former drivers who now became Rules Inspectors specially appointed to carry out the new edict on the LMS did much valuable work in bringing to light some working difficulties, since many drivers became much more articulate when talking to one of their own ilk than to a shedmaster, who had not the same background experience. The examination was discontinued after nationalisation due to union pressure.

I was thankful for the outlet which the MIC movement provided for my youthful energies, for once the snares and pitfalls of the roster book had been mastered in the first three months there was little else to absorb my interest due to the absence of any maintenance activities other than purely minor running repairs.

However, Ross Campbell sent me a note from Derby saying that the Colonel (Rudgard) would like some figures relating to the life of a number of consumable items fitted to Class 3F ex-Midland 0-6-0 locomotives, the standard Class 4F 0-6-0's and Class 7F 0-8-0s. Collection of this data over the next few months provided an interesting exercise with the results shown below:

Firehole deflector plates ('smoke' plate) (Fig 30)
Average mileage, 1,100 (the mileage varied according to class of coal used).
A deflector plate fitted to an engine which had burnt a lot of coal such as
Pilsley, which tended to form a non-porous clinker, had only about 60 per
cent of the life of one fitted to an engine burning a non-clinkering coal;
the difference was due to the greater amount of air admitted through the
ashpan dampers when a clinkering coal was in use, which in turn caused
more rapid burning of the inner end of the deflector plate.

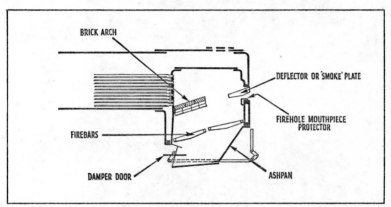

Fig 30. 'Consumable' items in the firebox.

Firehole mouthpiece protector (Fig 30)
Average mileage 2,500 (the life of these also was influenced by the type of
coal in use).
Engine brake blocks
Average mileage 3,000; this was the performance on engines engaged
mainly on loose-coupled mineral and empty wagon trains and was a little
better than the performance on engines employed solely on shunting duties.
Firebox brick arch
The life of a brick arch appeared to be a function of time rather than of
mileage and varied from five to eleven weeks according to class of engine
and work performed. The effective life of the arch was frequently curtailed
by the necessity to remove it to permit repairs to tubes and ferrules.
White metal gland packing (Fig 31)
Average mileage (a) valve spindle 10–12,000. (b) piston rod 30–36,000.
The mileage achieved by piston rod white metal packing on superheater
engines was dependent upon the maintenance in good condition of the inner
McNamee brass ring segments, also on a close watch on lubrication of piston
glands and development of initial clearances of crosshead slide blocks in
slidebars.
  I did a few sums also on oil consumption on an average basis and found
that 5½ pints of machinery oil, as distinct from cylinder oil, was being used

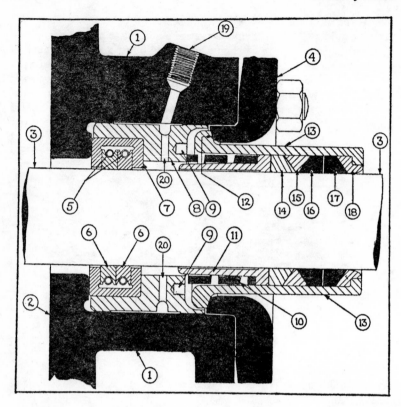

1, Stuffing Box Casting, integral with 2, Cylinder Cover;
3, Piston Road; 4, Gland Cover; 5, Garter Springs to hold
McNamee Rings up to Piston Road; 6, McNamee Packing
Rings, special Bronze Alloy; 7, McNamee Packing Box;
8, Gland Neck Bush; 9, Holes tapped $\frac{3}{8}''$ Whit: to take
Extractor for Withdrawing Bush; 10, Gland Spring;
11, Follower; 12, Spherical Joint between Gland Cover and
Sleeve; 13, Brass Sleeve; 14, Inner Packing Ring, Gun-
metal; 15, Packing Ring, Gun-metal; 16, Packing Ring,
White metal (Copper Alloy in std. Compound H.P. Gland);
17, Packing Ring, White metal (Copper Alloy in std.
Compound H.P. Gland); 18, Outer Packing Ring, Gun-
metal; 19, Oil Feed to Gland from Cylinder Mechanical
Lubricator; 20, Oil Ducts in Neck Bush.

Fig 31. A typical piston gland arrangement for a superheated locomotive.

per 100 engine miles. I discovered years later that an almost identical figure was the Line average for the LMS in 1938. It was virtually impossible to compare the consumption on different types of locomotives in different areas on a realistic basis because of the variety of methods used to feed oil to the bearing surfaces, the design of those surfaces and the different practices followed by drivers in different areas. Some men were not content unless an engine was swimming in oil; like Oliver Twist they were always asking for more—more, that is, than the strictly controlled ration determined and issued for each locomotive duty. They rarely got permission to draw additional oil unless it was for an engine which had been standing for several days.

The new Class 8F (originally classified 7F) 2-8-0 locomotives, five of which were allocated to Westhouses a few months after emerging new from Crewe Works, proved to be another stimulus to sustain interest in things mechanical. As is invariably the case with a new locomotive design, there were many minor teething troubles. I submitted several suggestions for improvement of details, illustrated by Dobson's wonderful freehand sketches for the production of which he had a remarkable gift. Ideas related to the armouring of the flexible oil pipes to the trailing coupled axleboxes to withstand the heat of the firebox; the provision of an expansion bend in the steam control pipe to the continuous blowdown valve; rearrangement of the middle ashpan damper to facilitate ashpan cleaning; provision of separate gauge frame drain taps; modification to the steam cylinders which operated the dry sanding gear; and to the layout of connections to the sand gun fitted to the boiler backplate for cleaning the tubes whilst running. Many innovations on the 2–8–0 previously unknown to Westhouses men were appreciated by them, including the bushed type connecting rod big end fitted with a fluted restrictor instead of a worsted trimming (Fig 32) and a host of grease nipples on the brake rigging and intermediate drawgear which reduced the number of oiling points requiring the use of the traditional oil feeder.

One frequent subject of comment was the 2–8–0's apparently inferior braking performance compared with that of the standard Class 7F 0–8–0's. This is not surprising as the brake percentage (ie the ratio of the sum of the forces on the brake blocks divided by the static weight on the rail and expressed as a percentage) of the latter was 78.5 compared with only 65.8 on the new 2–8–0. Yet as so often happens, drivers quickly adjust themselves to a new set of circumstances. The complaints quickly died as they became accustomed to what was still a good brake on the 2–8–0.

The continuous blowdown valve mentioned above was also a new innovation. It was fitted to the boiler backplate for the purpose of drawing off a portion of the water in the boiler whenever the engine regulator was open. At that time, despite the efforts of the water softening chemists, some soluble compounds often remained in suspension in the feed water after treatment and caused excessive priming when a locomotive was

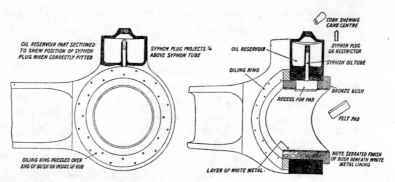

Fig 32. The type of bushed outside connecting rod big end with which Stanier locomotives were fitted.

worked hard. The blowdown valve was controlled by steam under pressure led through a small bore pipe from the rh cylinder; the water drawn off amounted to 2–3 gpm and was led through a coil in the tender tank where some heat was recovered before the water was discharged on to the ballast. Enginemen disliked the arrangement because they considered (rightly) that they were having to shovel more coal, although the heat losses were doubtless more than counterbalanced by the cleaner water side heating surfaces which resulted from feed water treatment. The civil engineers in due course came to dislike the apparatus also and produced impressive figures of the additional costs incurred in permanent way maintenance due to the discharge of boiler water on to the ballast.

With the advantage of hindsight, the necessity to fit the contraption at all now appears to have arisen because *all* the possible effects of water treatment were not considered initially; or if they were, someone in the hierarchy objected to capital expenditure being earmarked to counter the harmful side effects. Not that we were overmuch concerned at the MIC with the financial results of water treatment; when stalwarts like Johnny Duroe, Albert Lee, Bill Younger, Sam Harris and 'Ferd' Whitaker got going about the new fittings, of which usually no one knew anything until a locomotive so equipped made its first appearance on the shed, their preoccupation was with problems such as whether an additional water stop would be required on a given working. Countless highly competent engineers have launched and still do launch their products and systems on to long-suffering users without a thought that any steps taken to acquaint the latter with the purpose of the equipment and invite their wholehearted co-operation in making it work, would pay handsome dividends.

In early 1937 Rudgard visited the depot as a reconnoitering exercise immediately in advance of an even more awe-inpsiring state visit headed by no less than a Vice-President of the Executive, Mr E. J. H. (later Sir Ernest) Lemon. At the time we received the special train notices indicating that the officers inspection saloon would be used on each occasion, the shedmaster, Howard, was a sick man and intended to take some leave. He asked me if I minded taking charge as Dobson, although senior, did not yet feel competent to undertake the day shift. I said I did not and put into effect the lessons which I had learned so hardly at Wellingborough, Kettering and Bedford. The ashes were almost as high as the street-type gas lamps on the ashpit and there was an accumulation of spilt fuel under the coal stage sufficient to have bunkered a moderate-sized frigate, or so it seemed. The ornate fire-irons in the hearth of Howard's private sanctum were red with rust because he did not bother to have a fire lit to dispel the damp. The graphs of coal consumption and long hour cases and all the other paraphernalia of management required updating; and to complete the picture, heavy snowfalls were imminent and staff sickness was high.

I had the weekend to prepare for the visitors as Rudgard was due on Monday morning, to be followed by the top brass on Tuesday afternoon. I persuaded the Control office to bring on two or three extra relief sets on Sunday in view of the weather forecasts and brought in specially every available member of the shed staff who could wield a shovel. Every man co-operated loyally; top-rate drivers were busy with emery paper on the fireside fittings in the offices, lesser mortals were picking coal off the ground or loading ashes into wagons and the repair staff—all two of them—were clearing up the fitters' shop. As dusk fell on that Sunday afternoon I reflected that it was many a long day since Westhouses had looked so clean —and that it would be a long time before it did so again.

Rudgard arrived to time on Monday morning and expressed himself as well pleased with what he saw. His only comment arose from the heat still radiating from the sand-drying oven which he felt with his hand in passing. Its use was taboo due to the prodigious quantity of coal which it consumed to dry a given amount of sand. In theory, sand for locomotive purposes was supposed to be supplied ready dried in bags in a sheeted wagon. Too often it was not dry when received, or an indent had not been honoured. Westhouses was an area where serious trouble arose if there was not a good supply of dry sand in the winter months, so recourse was made to the old-fashioned but effective brick drying furnace. I assured the Colonel that it would cool completely during the next 24 hours and he passed on with a twinkle in his eye. It was impossible to fool him on any question of shed management and provided one did not try, he did not waste time in pointless recriminations.

When Lemon and his cortège arrived the next afternoon, it seemed like an anti-climax; the great man was courteous and his questions to the point. More important, he appeared to be satisfied with the answers.

Two months later I got a welcome break from the boredom of a job which had by now little else to offer than the opportunity to make a living without too much effort, mental or physical, which is not good for a young man of 26 years. 'Tim' Wood, who had by now succeeded H. Rihll as

District Locomotive Superintendent at Plaistow, had requested the Divisional Superintendent of Operation at Derby to send someone pro tem to take charge of the former NLR locomotive depot at Devons Road in Bromley-by-Bow.

Devons Road had previously been a sub-depot of Willesden, but came under Plaistow's jurisdiction with the introduction of the 1935 District organisation. In terms of its total staff, which numbered 524 in 1937, Devons Road was appreciably bigger than the parent depot of Plaistow. For this reason the Assistant District Locomotive Superintendent was located at the former place and acted as a kind of super-shedmaster, normally only working at Plaistow when acting *vice* the superintendent. The current assistant was named Jeffries, who had reported sick and who was not expected to resume work at Devons Road. In fact, he never did, but was sent instead to Saltley in a similar capacity where he reigned only a few months before resigning from the service. His predecessor at Devons Road, Morris, had suffered an unfortunate end allegedly due to worry and overwork. The District Superintendent who immediately preceded Wood at Plaistow also found difficulties at Devons Road, as he himself related to me many years later.

I was not aware of all these personal tribulations as I wended my way to Devons Road on a Monday morning in May, but I must confess that my spirits were somewhat dampened when I surveyed the private office. It seemed a sort of Vallombrosa of gloom despite or because of, the rich mahogany furniture with which it was furnished. The surrounding atmosphere was redolent of the dog biscuits turned out in their millions in the factory on the opposite side of the main line from Dalston Junction to Poplar. The flavour of this ambrosia was supplemented by the pungent, almost visible odours which arose at times from the still but not limpid waters of the Lee Cut, which formed the southern boundary of the shed precincts. I found Laurie Taylor, then an improver, holding the fort and although we were previously unacquainted, I have not forgotten the pleasant manner in which he effected introductions, showed me the premises and got me fixed up in his digs off Highgate Road. In the afternoon we went to see Wood at Plaistow, who said he had asked for an established foreman to take charge of the depot until Jeffries' successor arrived, because he wanted somebody who would get the men about their work without issuing a lot of disciplinary forms.

During the ensuing month of my locum tenancy I needed whatever native wit I possessed coupled with every artifice I had learned during the previous ten years to counter the wiles of a small section of the largely cockney staff. Most of them were as attentive to their work as their counterparts further north, but there was a minority who needed constant reminders of their obligations and they got them. I suspected that there had been some harsh interpretation of agreements and in our early dealings a driver named Mathieson, who was secretary of the Local Departmental

Committee, was inclined to be very rigid; but I found him to be an honest negotiator whom I quickly came to respect. Another driver named Bolam, who sported a pair of the most immaculate waxed moustaches, was chairman of the committee and its very effective mouthpiece. After a few encounters, I began to enjoy myself; these were people with whom one could work just as in my beloved district of Wellingborough and later Westhouses. I had the support of some excellent Running Foremen, all of whom had been drivers, although not at Devons Road; the senior of them was named Oxlade, who went to great lengths to dispense fairness through the roster sheets, the compilation of which I never fully understood at this depot.

In its North London days the shed had been a very large one of 26 roads, which must have enabled the 99 locomotives that the company possessed in 1922 to be housed simultaneously under cover. Now, half the roof had been removed and three pits covered over, so that there were ten pit roofed-over roads available to house the allocation of 71 tank locomotives. About 60 of them were standard Class 3FT 0–6–0 engines and the remainder ex-NL 0–6–0 tanks, together with the little NL crane engine No 27217 (Plate 46). The depot had been modernised with coaling and ashlifting plants, but had no worthwhile machine tools, as it was argued that Bow Works was only half a mile away and would be happy to oblige. To do them justice, they normally did; but the arrangement suffered from the same disadvantages already described in connection with Derby.

The maintenance of the locomotives, which went to the area repair concentration depot at Plaistow for major examinations and boiler cleaning, presented no serious difficulties, although some of them were worked very hard on the Broad Street—Great Northern line passenger and freight trains over the considerable gradients of the North London section. A proportion of the Class 3FT engines were reserved as far as possible for passenger working, because they had been specially fitted with screw-operated reversing gear; this obviated the need to close the regulator in order to notch up and thus avoided the surge noticeable in a close-coupled train when the lever reverser was in use.

Two minor but irritating difficulties seemed to persist on the standard engines. One related to the amount of moisture which always seemed to permeate the sand in the sand boxes despite alternative designs of filler necks which had been tried. The majority of the allocation had left the depot by 10.00am and along every pit road were little piles of sand where it had been emptied from the boxes. This trouble was not, of course, peculiar to this class of locomotive, but it was more in evidence than on any other class I have known.

The other source of trouble was maintenance of the light, brass whistle operating chain, which was not equal to its task and possessed attractive alternative applications.

In addition to the 150 sets of steam enginemen on duty daily, there were

16 electric drivers (or motormen as they were then called) who manned
the dc electric trains between Broad Street, Richmond and Watford. They
signed on at Broad Street, which I visited weekly to check their signatures
for operating notices and by talking to them learnt a little of the special
conditions surrounding this form of traction.

If I appear in earlier chapters to have been somewhat less than apprecia-
tive of the assistance rendered to me by the clerical and staff elements in
the great LMSR family, I would like to conclude this one by relating an
incident which occurred during this month. Foreman Oxlade sent to me
a man who was reporting for duty after a prolonged absence, an unusual
procedure which I noted with some wariness. When the man asked if he
could start work, I enquired why he had been absent. He replied that he
had just left prison. It appeared that he had thrown a jar of beetroot at
his wife; she found herself in hospital and as a result my problem found
himself in gaol. I had never been called upon to make such a delicate
decision, so I called up Wood, who gave me a number to ring in the staff
office at Euston House. This I did and describing the circumstances,
quickly received permission to start the man.

In January 1938, Mr Kinsman interviewed me at Derby and asked me
if I was interested in the job of Foreman Fitter at Plaistow, the occupant of
which post, Fred Millett, was retiring. 'O.E.K.' as Kinsman was universally known, was now Assistant Divisional Superintendent of Operation at
Derby and dealt with motive power matters for Rudgard, who had been
promoted Divisional Superintendent of Operation in 1937. I replied in the
affirmative and so in mid-February 1938, I said farewell to a job which
was never of absorbing technical interest, but one in which I had learned
a great deal about human relationships and their importance in the
industrial scene.

8 The World Outside

Most of the news concerning the great railway world outside which reached Westhouses locomotive depot had to be garnered the hard way; because locomotive boilers were not washed out there and no maintenance was performed other than purely running repairs, there were no visiting boiler inspectors, or other CME's representatives to bring the latest news, gossip or rumour as they did to most depots. We had to rely, either by personal purchase or regular visits to the public library, on the railway and engineering press to know what was going on. The house journal, the *LMS Magazine*, was excellent in itself and useful in some respects, but its information was often presented in the form of an exhortation to even greater efforts and ever-increasing economies, so that one felt that it was biased and just another 'plug' for the company which indeed it often was.

Our general picture of activities, outside our depot, of this allegedly largest corporation in the world was thus somewhat sketchy. But nevertheless there were some highlights in the years 1935-8, which had a lasting influence on post-war locomotive events. One of these was the attention focussed on budgetary control of engine repair costs of which not much had been heard at depot level before the end of 1935. By this time, however, a statement was available, compiled on a depot basis, showing the cost of wages per engine in service, split up into the component costs of major examinations and repairs arising therefrom, 'X' repairs carried out on the occasion of boilerwashing and 'Y', or purely running repairs, respectively. The District Locomotive Superintendents now had an analysis of at least the largest element of repair costs, controlled by themselves, which was that of artisan staff wages incurred at running sheds. Greatest emphasis was probably on the reduction to vanishing point of 'Y' repairs, which interfered with diagrammed workings and militated against punctual departures of engines from the shed into traffic.

Global figures in broader scale of locomotive running expenses were also available. For 1937 they totalled £13·19m for the LMS, of which £7.55m or 57.2 per cent was spent in wages (drivers, firemen, cleaners and shed staff) and £4·88m or 37·1 per cent in fuel; those two items absorbed no less than 94·3 per cent of the total. Concurrently with the increased demand for coal which became apparent in 1936, its price began to rise. By the beginning of 1938 it was obvious that to contain overall fuel costs within the 1935 level it would be necessary to save a further 4lb per engine

mile. Some examples were distributed to District officers showing how
checks in running militated against the achievement of this tall order,
thus:

A dead stop from 60mph with a 425 tons train cost 188lb of coal to
regain this speed.
A slack from 70mph to 20mph with a 425 tons train cost 234lb of coal to
regain 70mph.
A bad signal check with a 70 wagon coal train running on the level cost
280lb of coal.

It was stated that the above figures had been established as the result of
tests, the nature of which is not known to me; but it was claimed that they
could be used to support submissions for capital expenditure for improved
signalling and other equipment. Whatever their accuracy, they did
bring home to all the cost of unpunctuality, with its immediate and
adverse effects on those huge items of expenditure, wages and fuel.

It is an interesting exercise to ponder the effect on the finances of the
LMS if it had adopted the GWR system of reflecting very precisely in the
working timetables the mechanics of the train and steam rates obtainable
in practical operation. One feels that there would not have been so many
timings over uphill sections of the LMS which for their observance required locomotives to be always in first-class condition, coal to be of the
best quality, enginemen to be always of the top grade and attendance of
running inspectors a frequent occurrence. Even when all these desiderata
were obtained, firing rates were still very heavy on such sections and a
great deal of unburnt fuel was ejected.

Not that coal was the only consumer item to come under intense
scrutiny in 1936. At what appears to have been an abrasive meeting of
Headquarters and Divisional Motive Power and Operating officers in late
1936, chaired by D. C. Urie, Superintendent of Motive Power, the latter
found it necessary to enquire of Rudgard why the Midland Division had
not followed the general trend of the Line in restricting the increase in
locomotive maintenance costs to something like the budget figure; instead
the Midland had exceeded it by 2.4 per cent. Urie pointed out, for instance,
that although there had been a decrease of 2,731 in the number of small
tubes changed on the Midland Division in the first 36 weeks of the year,
equal to a decrease in material cost of £1,013, the wages costs had
increased; he would have expected that the cost of wages and materials
would rise or fall proportionately. It is difficult to imagine why Urie made
this comment unless his knowledge of running shed practice was very
limited. A good Foreman Fitter who would repair a pair of big end brasses
by the exercise of skilful methods instead of withdrawing a new pair from
the stores could well incur a greater labour cost thereby; but he would
show a significant net saving in total cost of the repair by avoiding the
expense of new brasses. Alternatively, as Rudgard pointed out in reply,

the answer could be that a greater proportion of secondhand tubes were being fitted, at consequently decreased material cost. Warming to his theme, Rudgard reminded his inquisitor that the wages cost per locomotive on the Midland Division was low in comparison with that on the Western anyway, obviously implying that it was unfair to select one index of performance without looking at the whole picture, which was nevertheless a practice often adopted by a senior officer who wished to make someone less senior but more capable look silly. Although the composition of the stud of 2,501 locomotives on the Western Division was very different to that of the allocation of 2,403 on the Midland Division, the latter made a good showing on costs, as shown in Tables VIII and IX below.

Table VIII
LMSR Running Shed Repair Costs (Wages only)
36 weeks ended September 5th, 1936

Total for 36 weeks (£) (£)

Western Division	..	..	..	159,963 equal to 63·9 per engine
Midland Division	..	..	..	110,556 equal to 46·0 per engine
Central Division	..	..	..	63,458 equal to 55·7 per engine
Northern Division	..	..	57,748 equal to 43·1 per engine

Cost of 'Y' repairs only

Western Division	..	..	..	34,728 equal to 13·8 per engine
Midland Division	..	..	..	18,617 equal to 7·7 per engine
Central Division	..	..	..	14,194 equal to 12·4 per engine
Northern Division	..	..	..	21,906 equal to 16·3 per engine

Judged by the above figures, the Midland made a good showing on any account, but in particular its low cost of 'Y' repairs, ie hour-to-hour repairs carried out between successive 'X' or boiler washout days, indicated that the repair concentration and 'X' schemes were working well.

Table IX is interesting in that it reflects a decreased user of small tubes, which was to be expected following the introduction of water treatment on a large scale. On the other hand, the increase in the number of piston heads renewed, many of them on the new Stanier locomotives, is indicative of the excessive wear thought to have been caused by priming following the introduction of treated water and before the introduction of more effective methods of lubrication (Fig 33). The phenomenal increased user of brake blocks in Scotland was attributed to the mixture of iron used when the blocks were cast at St Rollox, and also to the fact that the blocks were much smaller on the Stanier engines compared with the pre-grouping locomotives which they had displaced, so that unit block pressures on the wheels were much higher.

Urie must have been in a particularly belligerent mood on this occasion when he drew the attention of J. G. Barr, one of the Northern Division representatives, to the fact that he had 15 jobs booked for an allocation of

Table IX
Number of Tubes, Springs, Brake Blocks, Piston Heads and Piston Rings Changed at LMS Motive Power Depots during the 36 Weeks ended 5/9/36 Compared with 1935

PISTON HEADS		PISTON RINGS				BRAKE BLOCKS				Total Increase or decrease (£)
Increase or decrease	Increase or decrease at £1.13.11¾ per piston head (£)	First 36 weeks 1935	First 36 weeks 1936	Increase or decrease	Increase or decrease at 1/6 per piston ring (£)	First 36 weeks 1935	First 36 weeks 1936	Increase or decrease	Increase or decrease at 2/2¼ per brake block (£)	
261	443	4,058	5,370	1,312	98	79,958	90,492	10,534	1,163	1,064
19	32	3,898	3,405	493	37	95,523	88,769	6,754	745	4,450
30	51	1,438	1,771	333	25	28,237	27,758	479	55	1,937
82	139	2,894	4,003	1,109	83	41,283	147,943	106,660	11,777	12,539
392	665	12,288	14,549	2,261	169	245,001	354,962	109,961	12,140	7,216

17 Class 5X 'Jubilee' locomotives, whilst at the same time there were only two booked jobs for nine 'Royal Scot' engines. Mr Barr replied that he was covering Class 5X jobs with 'Royal Scot' engines because the former had been a great disappointment and from experience were only equal to a Class 4 (presumably he was referring to a standard compound). The Scottish 'Jubilees' were at that time fitted with superheaters having only 14

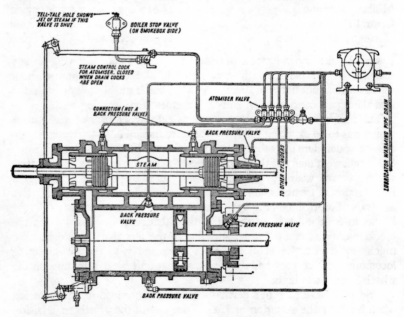

Fig 33. Atomised cylinder lubrication system, Stanier locomotives.

Division	TUBES				SPRINGS				PISTON HEADS	
	First 36 weeks 1935	First 36 weeks 1936	Increase or decrease	Increase or decrease at 7/5 per tube (£)	First 36 weeks 1935	First 36 weeks 1936	Increase or decrease	Increase or decrease at £3.3.0 per spring (£)	First 36 weeks 1935	First 36 weeks 1936
Western	39,174	40,328	1,154	428	6,327	5,988	339	1,068	218	479
Midland	65,553	62,822	2,731	1,013	5,810	4,957	853	2,687	99	118
Central	11,202	8,324	2,878	1,067	3,316	3,033	283	891	45	75
Northern	1,044	1,108	64	24	2,217	2,381	164	516	19	101
LINE	116,973	112,582	4,391	1,628	17,670	16,359	1,311	4,130	381	773

elements; this coupled with other dubious features of boiler design militated against production of enough steam of the right quality to feed three 17 in cylinders.

The situation was not improved by the absence of locomotive coal grading systems in Scotland. Barr was requested by Urie to come into line as quickly as possible with the English divisions in this respect and to grade coal delivered to individual depots according to the work performed by the locomotives allocated. Eventually, as is now well known, boilers with 24-element superheaters in conjunction with a larger number of small tubes of smaller diameter and a reduced diameter of blast pipe orifice were fitted, but the engines remained for the rest of their lives more sensitive to baleful influences than the two-cylinder Stanier 4-6-0s.

At the meeting under review, Urie suggested that as many of the new Classes 5 and 5X locomotives as possible should be stored during the 1936-37 winter under cover at the main workshops, so that they would be available for Christmas and Easter traffic and would only require a preliminary run before being put into service. He added that Mr Stanier had agreed to find as much suitable accommodation as possible. One wonders if the latter supported this remarkable proposal in order to gain breathing space to find a remedy for the ills with which his early batches of locomotives were afflicted, and which he acknowledged with such great courage and honesty, rectifying them with expedition although without the help of the sophisticated testing plant available in later years. I cannot find that any Stanier engines were, in fact, stored during that winter, even though Urie made a special plea for the 'Jubilees' on the Central Division to be put aside and the ex-L&Y Class 5 4-6-0 superheated engines to be used instead. Such a move would almost certainly have been unpopular with footplate and artisan staffs and would have evoked much adverse comment in the railway and technical press.

An interesting sidelight on the effect of commercial passenger policies on the power position was also discussed. It was revealed that the substantial programme of accelerated passenger trains introduced over the previous five years and the running of excursion trains at times which interfered with the movement of freight had had an adverse reaction on coal traffic, in particular on the Western Division. Urie said he had suggested to the Chief Mechanical Engineer that the power classification of the ex-LNW G1 0-8-0 locomotives, of which there were then 444, could be raised from 6F to 7F, ie the same as the G2 engines, by increasing the boiler pressure. Ten had been thus modified for trial purposes. Eventually a total of 254 were altered, becoming the G2a variety. This simple modification, which involved little change in general dimensions and arrangement of details, increased the potential of the locomotives for the movement of coal in the maximum possible trainloads, a traffic on which so much of the relative prosperity of the railway depended.

Another achievement of 1935-36 was the substantial reduction in mechanical casualties. The miles run per casualty for the Line in a period in October 1936 were 51,400, an increase of 8,400 over the corresponding period in 1935. There were dramatic decreases in 1936 in the numbers of heated axles, and connecting rod big and little ends; small wonder that nobody evinced any enthusiasm for storing Stanier engines which gave such better performances in those respects than the locomotives which they were displacing.

An extremely interesting meeting held in April 1936, was again chaired by Urie, but attended on this occasion by Stanier, Chambers (now his locomotive and personal assistant) and Coleman, Chief Draughtsman, together with every District Locomotive Superintendent on the LMS. This meeting was devoted to the performance and shed maintenance of both types of Stanier 4-6-0 locomotives, Classes 5X and 5MT, and all types of 2-6-2T and 2-6-4T locomotives. Two of the District Superintendents had prepared papers for discussion, Blakesley of Crewe dealing with the tender engines whilst Clews of Rugby dealt with the tank locomotives. As might be imagined, a wide variety of experiences and views were expounded, but on some items concerning the new Stanier locomotives opinion was unanimous or nearly so: these items were:

(1) Reversion to steam sanding should be made quickly; 'trickle' or dry sanding operated by steam actuating cylinders was a failure.

(2) Boiler washout plugs were badly sited and there were insufficient of them.

(3) Wear of regulator valves situated in the smokebox was high despite the sight feed lubricator provided; regulators in the dome were preferred.

(4) Excessive knock in trailing coupled axleboxes of Class 5MT 4-6-0 engines was mentioned but F. C. Moore of Newton Heath said he

had found that when the considerable clearance on the thrust block at the back of the reversing screw had been eliminated, the axlebox reports disappeared!

(5) Class 5X engines did not steam freely; one or two present had experience of the new 24-element superheaters and there had been some improvement. Follows of Sheffield said that the load for new 2–6–2T Stanier locomotives had been fixed at 270 tons on the Dore and Chinley line, but because steaming was inadequate, they would only take 170 tons. He was supported in this by Tandy of Saltley.

(6) Piston head wear on Classes 5MT and 5X engines was high; 26,000 miles was quoted as maximum for Class 5MT, although Wood of Plaistow said he had no trouble on Class 4 2–6–4 three-cylinder tank engines on the Tilbury section.

Most of the comments on the parallel boiler tank locomotives related to the carbonisation of piston valves, which had increased considerably since removal of cylinder by-pass valves; often now valves could only be removed from the liners when hot. In one case quoted a main steam pipe had had to be removed to enable the piston valve rings to be broken before the valves could be withdrawn.

It must have been an unwieldy meeting with no less than 45 people present, but at its conclusion Mr Stanier expressed his pleasure at being present. He was only sorry that the company's policy during the previous three years, in constructing large numbers of new locomotives so quickly, had not afforded sufficient time for the thorough testing of prototypes. He said he hoped to attend further meetings with the District Superintendents, who were the people with the experience and knowledge of the difficulties encountered; meanwhile he would make every effort to effect improvements. Mr Chambers said he was impressed by the fact that many of the troubles had been overcome at running sheds.

The necessity for boilers to be washed out at the mileages laid down for the various classes of locomotives provided the principal theme for another meeting of senior motive power officers, chaired by Urie and held in Glasgow in June 1937. The mileage permitted to be run between successive washouts by Classes 5MT, 5X and 6P (Royal Scot) locomotives was 1,600–1,800 miles, except in Scotland where higher mileages had been allowed because of the generally good water available. Instructions were now given, however, that Scotland must come into line with the English Divisions; the latter were in turn adjured to order things so that locomotives did not exceed the laid down mileages between boiler washout—which operation coincided, of course, with firebox examinations. This plea was repeated at innumerable meetings throughout the Line and many ingenious but impracticable schemes were designed to achieve the desired end. But in the last analysis it was most often the strength of character of the Mechanical and Running Foremen and the degree of co-operation between them which determined the relative healthiness of a depot's washing out arrangements.

This brief record of meetings picks out just a few of the enormous range of items needing attention to sustain and improve railway operation, a drama in which the locomotive is the principal actor. Despite an acute industrial depression, railway managements of the early and mid-1930s took the view that pursuit of improved operating methods, including higher speeds, should be continued relentlessly.

On the LMSR, these efforts were highlighted in the various runs made on the Western Division, some projected through to Glasgow, employing the new Stanier Princess locomotives. In one of the earlier runs made in 1935 by No 6200 with a load of 453 tons tare on the 5.25pm Liverpool–Euston, the 152·7 miles from a standing start at Crewe to the booked stop at Willesden Junction occupied only 129min 33sec. Three days later the same engine hauled a train of twenty vehicles equal to 461 tons tare from Crewe to Glasgow and back in order to assess the capacity of the locomotive for sustained effort with heavy loads over severe gradients; in this respect it succeeded as well as the later 'Coronation' class. On the first run the Camden crew consisted of Driver H. P. Smith and T. B. Pile, the latter being the youngest of three brothers who were firemen and drivers at that depot for many years. Test runs of this nature, where the load-hauling and general performance of a locomotive and its crew was being evaluated, always interested me more than those in which speed was the primary aim, important though that was in the field of passenger operation.

The next year, 1936, saw the introduction of an accelerated 'Midday Scot' train, followed closely by the exploits of Driver Tom Clarke and No 6201 *Princess Elizabeth* in running a train of 225 tons tare non-stop over the 401·4 miles from Euston to Glasgow in 353min 42sec, returning with 255 tons tare in 344min 20sec. At the conclusion of the down run, in a very human and thoughtful gesture, members of the train crew were entertained to an informal dinner chaired by Vice-President Lemon, and the toast of "Tom Clarke and his mates" (a relief fireman was carried) was drunk with musical honours. Since all the principal officers who had been concerned with the run were present or represented, the sense of achievement was shared by all. That has always seemed to me a very good way of promoting good industrial relations, although it is not mentioned in text books on the subject and has rarely been practiced by the talented amateurs of later years, who never knew the camaraderie engendered by the steam locomotive.

Another feature of those pre-war years was the wisdom shown by management in honouring all those humbler members of the staff who had contributed to a worthwhile achievement, not only those whose work inevitably gained the limelight. Thus, when a presentation was made to the train crew a week after the non-stop runs described above, the recipients were not limited to the driver, fireman and guard; they included Locomotive Inspector Sam Miller of Willesden, who had been responsible for the preparation of the locomotive.

The practical results of these exciting trials was the introduction in July 1937 of the 6½ hour service in each direction between London and Glasgow. That event had been immediately preceded by the record-breaking trial of June 29th, when No 6220 *Coronation* reached 114mph approaching Crewe.

Whilst these events on the Western Division provided the glamour, trials on the Midland main lines during the earlier months of 1937 were less spectacular, but equally deserving of notice culminating as they did in the substantial accelerations in September of that year. Class 5X 4-6-0 No 5614 *Leeward Islands* ran dynamometer trials between St Pancras, Nottingham, Sheffield and Leeds, whilst Class 5MT 4-6-0s Nos 5264 and 5278 did likewise between St Pancras and Manchester via Derby and Peak Forest. The Midland did not, and still does not, lend itself to high average speeds, because of the numerous permanent speed restrictions; but Kentish Town and Trafford Park men, egged on by Locomotive Inspector Harry Foulkes, knew how to take advantage of every opportunity to reach high maximum speeds which an intimate knowledge of an undulating road allied with strong nerves made possible. To coax a 'Black Five' with 258 trailing tons over the 61½ miles from Derby to Manchester Central in 68min 10sec may not appear exceptional; but anyone who knew that twisting, scenic line with its almost unbroken ascent from Duffield to Peak Forest, followed by a section with a line limit of 80mph into Manchester, could recognise the quality of engine-manship required to achieve such a result or to reach maximum speeds on the return journey of 86·6mph at East Langton and Sharnbrook and 91mph at Hendon.

9 Peace and War

I viewed the transfer to Plaistow with a great deal more enthusiasm than I had been able to summon when I left Wellingborough for Westhouses. I was already acquainted with the district and the people in it. Above all I was getting back to locomotive maintenance. Although the LTS section was, I suppose, a relative backwater in the great scheme of things on the LMSR, it was a very healthy backwater, which was purged twice daily of any sluggish action by the great tides of humanity which swept into and out of the metropolis over its metals. In fact the LTS section was popularly supposed—and I believe correctly—to enjoy the highest receipts from passengers per route-mile of any portion of the LMSR, generated by what was often a four-minute interval service at peak periods.

Small wonder that when I presented myself to Wood, the District Locomotive Superintendent, on a grey day in February 1938, he harangued me at length on the scale of delays which could build up from an injector clack which would not seat, a heated bearing or that more insidious shortcoming, an engine which would not steam or whose crew could not make it steam (the latter was a fairly infrequent occurrence). He described the working at the two platforms apportioned to LMS trains at Fenchurch Street and ended with an exhortation to watch the boilers, but not to upset 'George' and give him every assistance in keeping them well maintained. 'George' proved to be George Sutton, the Leading Boilersmith, of whom more anon; suffice now to say that he bore great responsibilities with true Cockney fortitude and was respected by all and feared by many.

Although Wood was prone to exaggerate the difficulties of maintaining trouble-free working on his beloved 'Tilbury', most people excused him because it was his first District command and because the working did, in fact, make considerable demands upon the staff of all grades. A failure in traffic almost invariably meant cancellation of the train, because it took too long to produce another locomotive. Although the passengers were turned out to await the next train, the latter was never far behind, though gross overcrowding resulted. The whole emphasis of effort on the 'Tilbury' was directed towards punctual passenger working; freight was relatively unimportant and moved mostly after the evening peak and into the night. A derailment which occurred during the day and did not directly affect the working on the main lines was usually left for attention until after peak hours; the breakdown crane was not permitted to travel fast enough to avoid upsetting the norms of John Killingback, the District Controller at Fenchurch Street.

The running shed at Plaistow contained eight pit roads and on the south side of it was a well-appointed lifting and machine shop with an overhead 45-ton capacity electric crane and some fairly modern machine tools. Coaling and ashlifting were manual operations and locomotive feed water was obtained from a borehole pump in the shed yard, supplemented by a supply from the MWB. At the back of the shed was the East London cemetery over the wall of which, I suspect, was irreverently consigned a great deal of bric-a-brac not fit for the enquiring eyes of a visiting notability, an over-zealous ferret of an inspector from the Divisional headquarters at Derby, or a CME representative from the same place. Derby seemed a long way off and the only time that its existence really erupted into one's consciousness was when Rudgard found it necessary to speak to Wood on the telephone or made one of his infrequent visits. Then everybody sat up and listened—hard.

The stud of locomotives for the maintenance of which I was completely responsible to Wood included the 37 Class 4P 2-6-4T three-cylinder Stanier locomotives built specially for the Tilbury Section, 44 Class 3P 4-4-2T locomotives of LTS design and varying vintage, 14 Class 3F 0-6-2T locomotives also built for the LTSR and three Class 1P 0-4-4T engines from the Johnson era; these latter were fitted for push-pull working over the Romford-Upminster-Grays branches and were numbered 1261/9 and 1360 respectively. In addition, I dealt at Plaistow with the major examinations and heavy repairs of the Devons Road allocation of 71 engines, already described.

Although the LTS section engines were nominally allocated to Plaistow, Shoeburyness, Tilbury and Upminster and carried the appropriate code number on the smokebox door, they were in fact all washed out and completely maintained, apart from purely running repairs, at Plaistow, where their records were also kept. This is not to denigrate the very excellent first-aid jobs carried out at the sub-depots, particularly Shoeburyness, to meet traffic requirements and avoid late starts.

Supervision of rerailing, etc, activities involving the use of the breakdown train was another responsibility for which I received a 5 per cent aggregation allowance on my basic salary with a further 5 per cent if I was called out more than 13 times in off-duty hours in a year. These terms were reasonable for the breakdown supervisor in a district of medium activity and few derailments, but at busy depots the hapless breakdown foreman often worked very long hours for scant reward although morally tied to his telephone for 24 hours a day, seven days a week. Such, however, was the romance of being 'on call' that I never heard any man in those days complain of the interruptions to normal social life which breakdown work imposed.

The supervisory organisation headed by Wood at Plaistow consisted of three Running (drivers') Foremen, Cook, Holland and Hampshire, George Sutton as Leading Boilersmith, myself as Foreman Fitter, a Shift Foreman Fitter and a Chargehand Fitter, together with a chargehand cleaner named Harry Hart. Of all these, the man who could probably influence events at the depot to a greater degree than any other was George Sutton. Although Urie had promised him salaried staff status on a visit during which George had made some particularly pungent comments about the rewards—or lack of them—for responsibility for maintaining boilers which used the worst water on the LMS, he was at that time still graded as a chargehand. Nevertheless he came to work in a bowler hat resembling the dome of a Tilbury tank, white collar and a waiter-type dickey. He supervised no less than eight boilersmiths, twelve sets of tubers and eight boilerwashers, probably the highest ratio of boiler maintenance staff to engines of moderate size to be found in the country. Although Sutton was nominally responsible through me to Wood for the condition of boilers, I only ever found it necessary to maintain a discreet watching brief over his activities to ensure that he did not spend money on the boiler of an engine which I knew would soon have to go to the CME shops for other reasons. We quickly established a working relationship which never faltered and which gave the required results. The work of drivers outside the depot was overlooked by Inspectors Jack Read and Jim Ryder, both of whom had been reared as drivers on the former LTSR.

Jimmy Platt presided over the clerical staff—that is, except for Grace Chipperfield, who acknowledged no peers but who, because of her lifelong service commencing in the Plaistow Works of the 'Tilbury' coupled with an uncanny knowledge of the detailed history of its locomotives, occupied a unique position in the motive power department for one of her sex. She acted as secretary to Wood and guide, mentor and counsellor to everybody else besides. In my early days at Plaistow I was known to utter strange oaths about women who interfered in my locomotive business matters. Within weeks I was often thankful for that quiet insistence and 'interference' from somebody who was saturated in the lore of 'Tilbury' locomotives. When 'Chips' as she was universally known, was forced to retire through ill-health at the early age of 45, the company lost a most valued and loyal servant.

The dominant feature of all maintenance and engine working activities on the LTS section was the internal condition of the boilers, besides which anything else paled into relative insignificance apart from matters of safety. Although there was a water treatment plant at Shoeburyness it was possible only to remove a portion of the scale-forming elements before introduction into the boiler. Kenneth H. Leech, an able raconteur and an articled pupil of Robert H. Whitelegg, Locomotive Superintendent in the last days of the LTS as a separate concern, has recorded that in the years 1910–1914, locomotive feed water at Shoeburyness contained over 2lb of solid matter per 1,000 gallons; elsewhere water was used in the raw condition and the result was an ever-increasing accumulation of dirt in the boilers, despite washing out at four to five day intervals in the case of the Stanier 2–6–4Ts, whilst the 4–4–2T engines came in for this attention about once per week when 'loose' dirt was removed by rodding between the tubes and along the barrel whilst high pressure jets of water were directed therein. Although brass rods were used in an attempt to dislodge the dirt, the Stanier engines were washed out so frequently that the rods wore grooves in the radius of the joint faces of the mudholes around the firebox foundation ring; it was sometimes difficult to make a satisfactory joint with the graphited asbestos joint washer then in use.

Every four months each of the 37 three-cylinder 2–6–4T engines was stopped at Plaistow to have about one-third of its small boiler tubes removed to facilitiate the removal of dirt from the barrel, unless this had already been effected at a classified repair in a CME works, either at Bow or at Derby. The dirt thus removed after four months running was allowed to drain of water and was then weighed. In the first six months of 1938 the average weight of dried dirt removed at such intervals was 27 cwt. In addition, of course, there was the weight of loose scale removed at every occasion of boiler washing.

The 4–4–2T engines made corresponding amounts of 'fixed' dirt, approximately pro rata to the lesser amount of feed water evaporated. They had tubes removed at about six-monthly intervals, despite the fact that they were fitted with manually-operated blow-down cocks on the firebox throat plate; these cocks were opened daily with the object of reducing the concentration of solids in the boiler, but the operation was of marginal value in dealing with the overall dirt problem.

Some of the 2–6–4Ts had originally been fitted with manual blow-down cocks on one side of the firebox, operated by a spindle which projected through the main frame. On an occasion in late 1937, the engine working a peak-hour evening train from Fenchurch Street—believed to be No 2513, but I cannot confirm beyond all doubt—was running through Plaistow station at speed when a roll of particularly high amplitude of the engine's superstructure on its bearing springs permitted the trailing section of coupling rod to strike the blow-down spindle. The cock was thus knocked off and the boiler emptied itself, squirting a high velocity jet of water throughout the length of Plaistow down fast platform at just above platform level. Fortunately there were only a few passengers on the platform at the time and no serious injuries resulted. Despite the efforts of Driver Garnham, the father of my shop clerk, to remove the fire quickly when the engine came to a stand west of Upton Park, the firebox was badly damaged and never fully recovered from its overheating during the three years I had dealings with the locomotive. The remaining Stanier 2–6–4T engines fitted with blow-down cocks had them removed, which made the railway more acceptable to people who lived in the vicinity of Tilbury section depots, owing to the reduced emission of the tremendous noise which accompanied the blowing down operation.

Meanwhile the dirt remained. Early in 1938, two of the 2-6-4T engines had a quantity of a proprietary liquid compound which rejoiced in the name of 'Everclean' added to the water in their tanks every day. The results at first appeared to be very promising and much of what had been hard scale came down as sludge; but the effects on the copper plates and stays was such that they quickly showed signs of rapid wastage and use of the product had to be discontinued after a few months. I never knew its composition, or whether the railway chemist did, but its effect was too devastating to make its use practicable.

About this time Urie issued instructions that the clearance between crossheads and slidebars was to be limited to 1/16in on passenger and 3/32in on freight locomotives. This was a very stringent requirement, with which few Foreman Fitters made any real attempt to comply. I have always considered that the person who conceived the instruction, whether Urie himself or one of his assistants, never paused to consider the cost of carrying it out. The only time I succeeded in observing the instruction, then or later, was in connection with the Stanier three-cylinder 2-6-4T locomotives, for the development of knock of the outside crossheads in the slidebars had usually reached about 1/16in by the time that the second batch of boiler tubes was due for removal at eight months from a classified repair in the CME workshops. As the boiler cleaning usually occupied at least one week, this gave an excellent opportunity and ample time to remove, remetal, machine and replace all three crossheads, the clearance of the middle one on its single bar being such by this time to warrant its rectification also. I could not have done the work at a valve and piston examination without adversely affecting engine availability. There was one really valuable dividend arising from this costly repair—the elimination of reports relating to blowing piston glands. This may have been Urie's objective; if so he achieved it on those 37 locomotives.

Urie made only one visit during my stint at Plaistow. He was a man of small stature sporting a wing collar which gave him a mildly clerical appearance, belying the considerable power which he wielded on the LMSR. He came into the shop where a crosshead was being planed, its two newly metalled fellows lying beside the shaping machine awaiting their turn. He enquired if I was having any trouble in meeting the new instruction. I informed him as related above and mentioned the cost in white metal; he grunted and passed on and I never saw him again.

The Stanier tank engines were complete masters of the work allotted to them and caused no maintenance difficulties apart from those described in connection with boilers. The other item which had to be watched carefully was the wear in the root of the flanges of the wheels of the leading truck and trailing bogie. This wear developed rapidly after about 25,000 miles running. Usually the bogie and truck tyres required reprofiling at about 32,000 miles, not because there was any element of safety involved, but because to have permitted further wear in the root of the flanges would have necessitated the ultimate removal of an excessive amount of metal from the treads in order to restore the profiles. Thus the overall life of the tyres would have been reduced, since the permitted thickness at last turning of tyres for these locomotives was 1¾in compared with 3in when new. The class averaged 55–65,000 miles between classified repairs in the CME works and if an engine was outurned with tyres at, say, 1 15/16in thick, it required careful judgment by the Foreman Fitter at the running shed to decide when to reprofile the tyres of carrying wheels, so as to avoid having to propose the engine specially for works attention because of tyre condition (Fig 34).

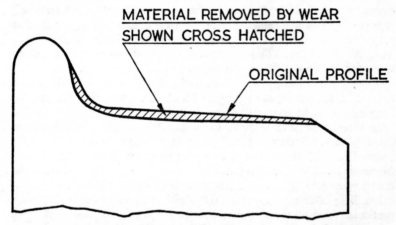

MATERIAL REMOVED BY WEAR
SHOWN CROSS HATCHED

ORIGINAL PROFILE

Fig 34. Stanier 3-cylinder 2-6-4T, worn tyre of leading truck after 31,000 miles. Wear was not serious at this stage, but because tyre was approaching last turning thickness, reprofiling was carried out at above mileage, thus prolonging life of tyre.

I had no wheel lathe at Plaistow, but the staff at the former NLR works at Bow under works manager Colonel Denning, Assistant Works Manager Adams and Senior Foreman Tom Beasley always co-operated nobly provided I gave them adequate notice of requirements. I had a first-rate team in the lifting shop at Plaistow, consisting of Fitters Dickens and Robinson and their mates working alternate am and pm shifts. The drill was for the pair on early turn to lift the engine, remove the bogie wheels, strip the axleboxes and load them into a Bow Works road vehicle, by which they were quickly conveyed to Bow. The job at that works of unloading, reprofiling, reloading to road vehicle and returning the wheels to Plaistow would occupy 2½–3 hours. On receipt at Plaistow, the wheels were unloaded, their axleboxes reassembled on the journals and the wheels replaced under the engine. Then followed removal of the pair of wheels from the leading truck for a similar cycle of events applied.

I believe an all-time record was established in the autumn of 1938. I had angered Wood by insisting that engine No 2505 must have its tyres turned during a week when the power position was more critical than usual. He agreed grudgingly and only, I believe, because he thought an element of safety was involved, which was far from the case. Wood was an excellent administrator, but not a notable engineer and it was a great temptation to practise mild deceptions on him at times when his knowledge did not enable him to appreciate all the mechanical aspects of a situation. Whenever I sinned in this fashion, I worked doubly hard not to let him down (and to justify my actions!). In the event No 2505 came on to Plaistow shed at 10.30am off an up train from Southend, had the fire cleaned but not withdrawn, had all the bogie and truck wheels removed, reprofiled at Bow and replaced in time for the engine to leave the shed at 5.13pm to take up a train from Ilford Carriage Sidings to Fenchurch Street the same day. This effort, really inspired by Wood, was due to team work which was thoroughly enjoyed by all the participants.

Coupled wheel flanges never wore to the same extent and would invariably run the full shopping mileage. Tread wear was greater than on the carrying wheels, but not critical.

In view of earlier comments made about exhaust steam injectors as fitted to Beyer-Garratt locomotives, it is interesting to note the reply which I assisted in concocting to a query received from the Divisional Superintendent at Derby in March 1938. He had asked whether the exhaust injectors fitted to the Stanier 2–6–4Ts were considered to be of value. The locomotive inspectors thought they were; I thought they had a particular value on these engines because some exhaust steam was being returned *free of scale* to the boiler. But I felt bound to point out that the fitter hours spent on purely running repairs on the exhaust injector was nearly seven times greater throughout the class than those spent on the live steam injector.

The reliability performance of the three-cylinder Stanier engines was very good. The fact that they were stopped for boiler cleaning at relatively frequent intervals enabled many other stitches in time to be made on the same occasion and failures in traffic were few. I believe it was No 2531 which disgraced itself on one occasion by stopping the job on the down line between Pitsea and Benfleet during the evening peak hour traffic. When negotiating the lh curve at Pitsea, where the direct line from Barking to Shoeburyness is joined by that from Tilbury, the bolt through the lh leading crankpin which held the crankpin washer in place fractured and released the washer. The leading section of the coupling rod was now able to 'whip' on the crankpin and strike the inside of the crosshead, producing a knock which attracted the driver's attention; because the connecting and coupling rod bushes were in good condition, without excessive end play, the coupling rod did not come off the crankpin, which was a mercy for all concerned. The fracture in the offending bolt had initiated at the root of a thread, but examination within 24 hours of the other 63 bolts in service (five engines were in the CME works at the time) did not reveal any more defects.

Many of my personal records relating to Tilbury section locomotives perished in the war, which as yet was only a shadow on the horizon to ordinary people and not something which they really thought would come to pass. But I can recall that the Stanier tank engines bristled with experimental fittings. Although again I cannot be certain of the individual locomotive, I believe it was No 2516 which was fitted with Trofinoff steam distribution valves (Fig 35), which were known in this country as

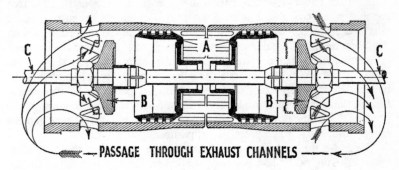

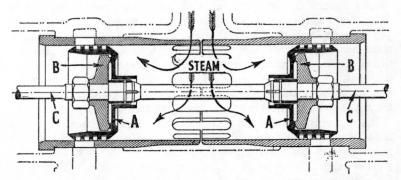

Fig 35. Trofinoff piston valves. (*Above*) Steam on. Piston valve heads 'A' are forced by steam on to discs 'B' and operate as ordinary piston valves on spindle 'C'. (*Top*) Steam off. Piston valve heads 'A' are left in middle of steam chest and there is thus a by-pass connecting opposite ends of cylinder.

T.A.B. valves after the patents had been acquired by the T.A.B. Engineering Co. The first locomotive to be fitted in this country was a Class 'G' 0-6-4T, No 94 of the Metropolitan Railway, on which the innovation was apparently successful for other Metropolitan locomotives were fitted later. The object of the fitting was to provide a by-pass of generous cross-section to connect opposite ends of the cylinder when coasting. Reference to Fig 35 shows that the piston valve heads which carried the usual narrow rings to make them steamtight were not, as usual, positively attached to the valve spindle, but were free to slide thereon when no steam was in the steamchest. When the regulator was open, steam was admitted between the 'loose' heads, which were then forced up to and held on to their respective stop discs and operated as conventional piston valves. When the regulator was closed and there was no pressure to keep them apart, they became marooned in the middle of the steam chest and thus provided a by-passing passage whose cross-sectional area was that of the steam ports and exhaust channels.

The Plaistow engine thus fitted quickly acquired a reputation for free running when coasting, but at about 15,000 miles, an irregular exhaust beat was reported. Examination of the valves showed a portion broken from one head. After this had been renewed, the same trouble recurred on another head, but this time the broken portion was ejected from the chimney and struck the driver's cab spectacle glass. It appeared that the inertia forces set up when steam was admitted between the two heads, forcing them on to their stop discs, was sufficient to cause fracture of the head. The engine reverted to the standard piston valve arrangement shortly afterwards and a promising experiment was ended.

The 4–4–2T locomotives of Tilbury lineage were all of the later vintages. Although they had been superseded on the heaviest duties by the Stanier engines, they were still required to cover day-to-day shortages in the required daily complement of the latter. To keep time with a train of 365 tons or more from Southend to Fenchurch Street one had to 'thrash' them over considerable portions of the route. The technique used was that of wide open regulator and steam reversing gear about $1\frac{3}{4}$ notches from mid-gear, which is about the shortest cut-off at which the gear would hold up. I do not know what percentage cut-off this position represented, but the knowledge would have been purely academic anyway.

It was the first time I had encountered full regulator working with a slide valve engine and the high steam chest pressure resulting from this practice was probably the principal reason for the high rate of wear of the gunmetal slide valves. Whereas the mileage for examination of slide valves for other classes so fitted on the LMS was 10–12,000, the Tilbury 4–4–2s would not run to this figure. In order to avoid failures which could occur if the valves wore thin, resulting in the laps fracturing or the valve falling out of the valve spindle buckle, it was Plaistow practice at 5–6,000 miles to remove the bushed housing in which the valve spindle extension was carried and insert a lighted taper in the steam chest. It was thus possible to see approximately how much the valve lap faces had worn and how slack it was in the buckle. The foreman would then decide whether to let the assembly run in existing condition a further 5–6,000 miles, or whether to remove the steam chest covers and either fit new valves or insert a liner between the back of the valve and the valve spindle buckle so as to lessen the likelihood of the valve falling out of the buckle as wear continued. Once, an attempt was made during a classified repair in Bow works to spray the faces of one of the valves of No 2153 with a proprietary non-ferrous alloy with the object of reducing wear, the opposite side being left standard for comparison. The engine did a trial trip running light from Plaistow to Barking and return, by which time it was sounding like a bronchitic buffalo running for its life. The experimental valve was removed when it was found that its intended protection had nearly all peeled off; worse still, it had badly grooved the cylinder port faces in the process, necessitating the return of the engine to Bow to get them refaced. The experiment was not repeated.

I have often wondered how these locomotives would have performed with piston valves, which latterly were more usually associated with superheated steam. Moulang once gave me some figures relating to coal and water consumption tests conducted in 1910 in the Leeds-Sheffield-Nottingham area with MR Class 2P saturated 4-4-0 locomotives on trains of about 145 tons. Three engines, Nos 403/6/25, were fitted with slide valves, whilst four, Nos 485/9, 503/8, were fitted with piston valves. The results were as shown in Table X.

From the table it will be seen that there was no significant difference between the coal consumption per ton-mile of the piston valve and slide valve engines respectively, but the former showed up slightly better than

Table X
Midland Railway, coal consumption tests
Piston valve versus slide valve engines of Class 2P 4-4-0 May–July 1910
COAL—Hickleton Main

Engine No	No of trips	Coal used cwt	Weight of train, tons		Miles	Ton Miles	Lb coal per	
			Net	Gross			Mile	Ton-Mile
PistonValve 485	6	292·5	145	244	991·5	241,920	33·0	0·136
PistonValve 489	4	176·1	140	239	661·0	157·485	29·8	0·125
PistonValve 503	5	237·75	145	244	826·25	201,920	32·2	0·132
PistonValve 508	4	208·5	145	244	661·0	161,364	35·3	0·145
P.V. TOTAL	19	914·85	144	243	3,139·75	762,689	32·6	0·134
Slide Valve 403	5	221·75	136	234	826·25	192,956	30·0	1·129
Slide Valve 406	5	228·80	132	229	826·25	188,734	31·0	0·136
Slide Valve 425	7	337·70	138	236	1,156·75	271,572	32·6	0·139
S.V. TOTAL	17	788·25	134	232	2,809·25	653,262	31·4	0·135

WATER

Water consumed was measured on 14 trips of the piston valve engines and on seven trips of the slide valve engines with these results:

Engines	No of trips	Coal Cwt	Ton-Miles	Water			
				Gallons	Lb used per lb coal	Lb per ton-mile	Lb per mile
Piston Valve	14	670·875	562,155	60,930	8·1	1·08	264
Slide Valve	7	338·675	270,872	30,030	7·9	1·11	248

their competitors on water consumption per ton-mile. Probably what the tests demonstrated most effectively, in the light of subsequent knowledge, was that the type of valve had far less influence on steam and water consumption than valve events.

The 4–4–2T engines were very solidly built, the later ones having a 20 ton coupled wheel axle load; they were still fitted with wedge blocks to the coupled axlebox horn faces and the springing of the coupled wheels was compensated, presumably a relic of the days when the LTSR permanent way was of somewhat dubious stability. Certainly the compensating beams in later days rarely seemed to get the opportunity to fulfil their function, for almost without exception they all became seized on the central fulcrum pin a short time after leaving the CME works, despite the application of grease under pressure as the lubricant; it never seemed, however, to get to the interfaces where it was wanted.

One aspect of the maintenance of these engines I found a little irksome was the frequent visits I had from Locomotive Inspector Jack Read. Having ridden on one of them, he would tell me that "She's down at the front end and so she won't steam like she ought to do". In my early days at Plaistow I changed a lot of bogie springs on the class on the strength of Read's allegations and employed a spirit level in the lifting shop to test the free stance of the locomotives on the rail in both transverse and longitudinal directions. I never had very much faith in this old Spanish custom, and even less after I had examined several hundred repair cards one day and found that almost the only occasions on which drivers reported a 4–4–2T not steaming was when Read had been riding with them! Thereafter bogie springs were changed only when the riding characteristics of the vehicle had deteriorated. I managed to avoid recriminations from Read, an extremely loyal and conscientious inspector, by telling him when I had changed springs (for other reasons!) and asking him to ride on the engine and let me know how it steamed.

It is amazing how many practices all over the country, started for some good reason and though invalidated decades earlier, continued to flourish and cost money in the locomotive maintenance world, particularly on lines like the 'Tilbury', where the staff continued to uphold a considerable tradition built on years of endeavour as a separate concern. Many traditional practices held good until the end of steam; many should have been exposed for what they were years earlier. On the other hand, that same loyalty to tradition which tended to perpetuate outmoded practices was often valuable in making acceptable to enginemen some classes of locomotives which otherwise would forever have appeared on the agenda at management/staff discussions.

When some of the 4-4-2T locomotives were drafted to other parts of the LMS after displacement by the Stanier locomotives there was an immediate outcry in some areas about the steam reversing gear, the lifting injectors and the driver's brake valve. Whilst it was true that if a leather wanted renewing or water adding in the cataract cylinder of the steam reverser the gear was difficult to hold up at short cut-offs, a little care and experimentation would soon reveal how to manage it. Acquisition of such titbits of knowhow was not without risk, as at least three Tilbury section drivers could testify who had lost a portion of finger in the process of acquisition. The lifting injectors would work very well provided one had a suitable piece of round section rod to hold internal components stationary until the suction pipe was filled and steam had started to be condensed by the water; yet when the engines moved away from their native haunts, it was found necessary to fit injector overflow pipes to convince their new masters that all the water was being picked up. At the same time a supplementary brake disc valve was fitted near the end of the rh side tank, as it was claimed that one could not buffer up to a train safely using the brake valve on the boiler backplate. Having said all this, I, for one, always treated the steam reverser with the greatest respect and always preferred, if I was going for a drive, to get on one of the ten Westinghouse-brake fitted engines in the series, Nos 2151 to 2160, because they also had screw reverse. The injectors did not bother me unduly, but here again one had to be able to accept with equanimity the spurt of very hot water which issued from the body of the injector when the human pressure on its entrails was released.

Mention of the Westinghouse brake recalls the reason for its retention long after any normal air braked stock of 'Tilbury' days or of any mainline company had been in evidence on the section. Every morning a train of coaches of ornate decor arrived at Barking Station about 11.00am from the western suburb of Ealing, having been hauled therefrom by two ugly double bogie electric locomotives of the former District Railway via Acton, Earls Court and Bow Road. At Barking the electric locomotives were replaced by a Westinghouse-fitted 4-4-2T Tilbury engine, which whisked the train to Southend. The train was heavy and had considerable time-keeping attention bestowed on it; indeed the passengers conveyed from the western suburbs always looked opulent, as though they could have afforded the trip every day of the week. Somehow the London Passenger

Transport Board and the LMS authorities never seemed able to contrive for long to achieve brake pipe and auxiliary reservoir pressures on their respective motive power units, which were sufficiently compatible to avoid the pulling of strings before this through train could depart. The working ceased shortly after the outbreak of war and thereafter the added complication of the Westinghouse equipment on the engines fitted was only justified by the length of service given by their flanged braked blocks. The air brake equipment on the engine could be coupled into the vacuum system in such a way that in passenger train working it was the train which stopped the engine; the engine brake rarely came into effective use except when running light or working a non-fitted train.

The flanged blocks fitted to the 4–4–2Ts had to be carefully adjusted to avoid binding on the wheel flanges on curves, as I have cause to remember. It was the practice for Sutton, whoever was the Running Foreman on the morning shift, and myself to attend a ceremony at 9.00am known as 'morning prayers' in Wood's office, at which current problems, shortages and hopes would be thoroughly discussed. We stood in front of Wood's desk and each made our contribution. When we left after 10–15 minutes of crisp dialogue each man knew his target for locomotive requirements to be met that day and the next.

One morning Wood glanced out of the window and, seeing a train stationary on the up fast line, phoned Inspector Read, who occupied a building in the loco yard, to find out why—quickly. Read arrived breathless with the news that 4–4–2T No 2115 was stuck fast on the sharp curve at Stepney East with an up train from Tilbury and there was a succession of trains blocked back behind it as far as East Ham. He could not yet say how the engine had failed. Wood surveyed the assembled company looking for a grain of comfort. Perhaps it was not the engine at fault, but a sticking brake piston on the train? Suddenly he roared at me: "Why aren't you on your way up there to get the bloody thing on the move?" I disappeared with alacrity, only to find on arrival at Stepney that the offending train had been dragged off the curve and things were moving again; but the delays were heavy and recorded in the evening newspapers. The brake on No 2115 had been adjusted the day before by a Grade 3 Fitter named Bethell, Ernest by name and earnest by nature, but who on this occasion had displayed rather less than his usual care. He had adjusted the brake blocks too close to the tyres to avoid rubbing them on a sharp 10mph curve such as existed at Stepney. However, Wood was all smiles later in the day. When Rudgard rang from Derby to enquire about the failure, he assured Wood that there was nothing new in this; he himself had experienced the same trouble in 1914, etc, etc; the thing was not to let it happen again. In those days little in the business of following up locomotive failures went by default; very senior people would frequently take a personal interest in them, often before the real facts could be established.

About this time use began to be made of the 4–4–2T engines to work loose-coupled freight trains during the night from the LTS section to sidings in the Cricklewood area via the Tottenham and Hampstead Junction joint line, the not inconsiderable gradients of which required almost continuous application of the engine brake in order to restrict speed to a figure at which the driver could retain control of the train. Braking at this slow speed caused a vibration of the blocks and hangers and a noise like a dozen brass bands at Kneller Hall competing with a violent thunderstorm. Public outcry was inevitable and the locomotives had to be removed from this duty, for which they were not suited in other respects.

An unusual failure occurred on 4-4-2T No 2157 in 1938, involving the collapse of the internal copper main steam pipe about $3\frac{1}{2}$in from the smokebox tubeplate. The collapse was a local one confined to a patch of a few square inches at one side of the pipe. In this region there had been severe internal corrosion and it was evident that there had been one or two tiny perforations caused by deep pitting before the final failure. Wall thickness was about 5/64in around the severely corroded patch and chemical analysis shewed the undermentioned results:

	Engine 2157	LMS Specification 27
Copper	99·59%	99·2% minimum
Arsenic	0·40%	0·30–0·50
Undetermined	0·01%	—

The metallurgist concluded that the development of the severely corroded patch was consistent with a local and abnormally high velocity of impingement of wet steam on a raised internal surface, caused by an external dent in the pipe.

Altogether work on the Tilbury section provided a feast of continuing interest. The work was made easier because of the *esprit de corps* still in abundant evidence on the section, and which owed its continued existence to comparative isolation from the main body of the LMSR. This feature allowed a large measure of independence of thought and action in all motive power matters, a feature which Wood was not slow to exploit, aided and abetted principally by George Sutton, George Fisher, the able Running Shed Foreman at Shoeburyness and myself.

Each year past and present motive power supervisors of the LTS section used to meet for a dinner at the London Tavern in the City, at which Wood would preside with Rudgard, Kinsman and Killingback, the District Controller, as the principal guests. They were riotous occasions, but no doubt was left in the minds of the 'present' team that they were going to improve performances even more next year—and they did. The 'Tilbury' made a substantial contribution to the efforts which secured the Byrom challenge cup for the Midland Division in the Express Passenger Train Punctuality Competition of 1938. In 1939 Wood received from Lord Stamp the challenge shield, which Plaistow won by attaining the premier position in the Motive Power League, obtaining the highest number of miles per engine casualty compared with other districts on the LMS.

Arguments still rage amongst old-timers as to the fairness of the principles of this competition, which placed no handicap on districts like Plaistow, whose locomotives rarely got into the hands of other people and whose longest non-stop run was less than 40 miles. Against these advantages, however, was the indisputable fact that the load factor at which most Plaistow locomotives operated was high compared with many on the trunk lines. If a failure did occur in traffic it was quite impossible for the event to escape notice at Derby headquarters because of the disruption to services which ensued. It is a fact, nevertheless, that during the first three four-weekly periods of 1939 there was not a single mechanical casualty on a Plaistow-based locomotive; the nearest thing to it was a ruptured Westinghouse flexible brake pipe which had just been coupled to its mate on the first coach of the Ealing-Southend through train at Barking. As 4-4-2T No 2156 eased slightly from the train after coupling up a piece of badly stacked coal fell from its bunker and fractured the brake pipe. Wood and I cogitated together and decided the failure was due either to to an act of God or mismanagement; it was coded under the latter heading, which the hierarchy found acceptable—and, I hope, the Almighty also.

A feature which was fitted to every Tilbury section locomotive, but not to many main-line engines, was the Hudd system of (so-called) automatic train control. This apparatus might seem an additional complication that risked additional failures; but in fact, because the apparatus was subjected to a mandatory daily test before any engine left the depot, it was quite often the means of finding a potential irregularity in the brake system of which it was virtually a part. The Hudd system had reached a high degree of reliability, the development work being pursued under the supervision of Andrew Rankin in a small laboratory in Bow works where I spent many happy hours. It was hoped to withdraw fog signalmen in 1939 and place reliance entirely on the audible warning given to the driver by the ATC apparatus if the next distant signal was at caution; but an alleged 'wrong-side' indication on Stanier No 2512 at Campbell Road Junction in that year delayed unreserved acceptance of the apparatus as a bona fide piece of signalling equipment until after the cessation of hostilities in 1946, despite the fact that only one irregularity—a 'right-side' failure—occurred during four weeks ending April 27th, 1940.

I attended my first meeting of senior Foremen Fitters in the London area of the Midland Division in 1938. It was held at Kentish Town Loco and although, regrettably, I never preserved the minutes, the agenda is sufficient indication of the then current topics of importance. There were the evergreen items of mechanical casualties, engines stopped for repairs, etc, for more than 24 hours, maintenance of stores stocks and a dozen other matters which never seemed to get settled once and for all to the satisfaction of our peers. On this occasion, however, there were two brand new items: 'Boilerwashing—use of variable cooling down nozzles'; and 'Micrometers for use at Motive Power Depots'. The reference to variable cooling-down nozzles was somewhat of a misnomer, as it was the method of use of a recently developed pressure and quantity regulating valve for the controlled cooling of boilers prior to washing out which was under discussion (Fig 36).

There were few hot water washing out plants on the LMS and the gradual cooling down of boilers had been the subject of considerable experiment for some months under the direction of E. E. A. Talbot of Kentish Town fame, who had been specially detached for this work. Formerly it had been the practice to empty a boiler and remove the washout plugs and mudhole doors some two to three hours after all the steam had been blown down prior to washout; the new drill required the hot water left in the boiler to be cooled down at a controlled rate by introducing cold water through a valve which regulated the quantity according to the pressure at the shed hydrant, and the setting of the valve which varied according to the size of the boiler; hot water displaced was led into the pit. By introducing the cooling water away from the firebox, too rapid cooling of the relatively hot firebox plates was avoided and the boiler and its contents was cooled at a controlled rate before being emptied preparatory to the washing out process (Fig 37). The same process of cooling down was applied to classes of locomotives which, under a recent decree had a firebox examination *without* the boiler being emptied at an interval halfway between successive washouts; but in this case the boiler water was cooled only to about 100 deg F—quite hot enough the ensure that the boilersmith would not linger unduly in the firebox!

Measures such as these, designed to promote a degree of sophistication in boiler maintenance practices hitherto unknown on the LMSR, coupled with the treatment of feed water and its concomitant, the removal of solids in suspension by the automatic blowing down process, did more in my view to contribute to the success of LMS motive power in the immediate pre-war years than any other campaigns conducted at running sheds. The other item of note I can recall was the issue by Urie to depots of micrometers with the stated object of enabling more precise measurements to be made of pistons, cylinders, valves and liners at periodical examinations based on mileage. When a piston was permitted more than $\frac{1}{8}$in clearance in a cylinder at a standard examination and liner wear measured at depots was as significant expressed in 64ths of an inch as in thousandths thereof, the intelligent use of accurately filed 'mets' and calipers really rendered the use of micrometers unnecessary, except possibly by the turner, in the circumstances of shed maintenance. Maintenance in the CME works, of course, called for entirely different standards, for here the aim was to turn out a locomotive in as nearly new condition as possible, necessitating the use of a highly developed system of limits and fits of which any engineering

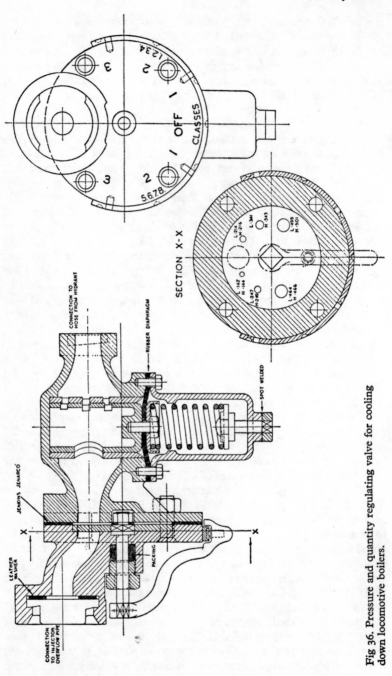

Fig 36. Pressure and quantity regulating valve for cooling down locomotive boilers.

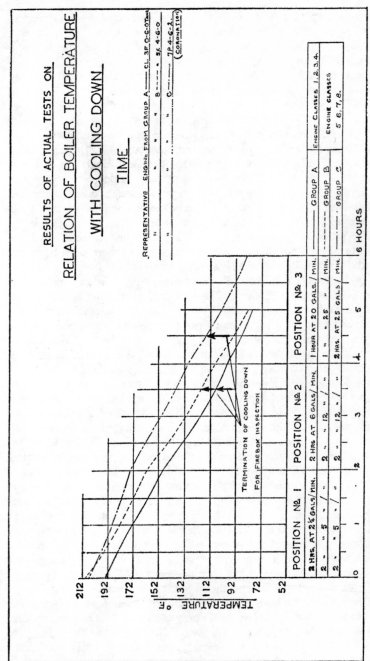

Fig 37. Graph shewing controlled rates of cooling down boilers.

shop could be proud. The art in shed maintenance—and it was a considerable one—was to determine what was fit to run with safety until the next examination and without accelerating undue wear of the machine as a whole or of its major components.

I kept in touch with the 'operating' side of the business by relieving Howard Peet, the Assistant Superintendent of the district, but located at Devons Road. It was during one of these spells that a trial was made of a Stanier Class 3P 2-6-2T No 105 on the Broad Street–Potters Bar passenger services, ostensibly to compare the coal consumption with that of a standard Class 3F 0-6-0T normally allocated to all the passenger services worked by Devons Road power. Not surprisingly the coal consumption of the 2-6-2T per ton-mile of train hauled was appreciably greater than that of the 0-6-0T. Even when the weight of the engine was included, the figure for the bigger superheated engine came out at 0.339lb per ton-mile compared with a corresponding figure of 0.334 for the smaller saturated locomotive. The trials were not extended and the 0-6-0Ts reigned supreme in the passenger train sphere until hostilities ended their exploits on the LNER main line.

Working at Devons Road allowed me to spend a lot of time in Bow Works. Adams, the Assistant Manager, had served his apprenticeship with the Stratford-on-Avon and Midland Junction Railway which began and ended nowhere and which, apparently, was so impecunious during most of its independent existence that the very best in the way of improvisation by its mechanical staff was exercised to keep its locomotives in service, an experience which stood Adams in good stead at Bow. The North London engines which still survived were limited to the crane engine No 27217 and the Class 1F 0-6-0T engines, extremely sturdy machines, some of which had cast iron slide valves fitted of great antiquity which nobody could remember having been changed. Cast iron slide valves were fitted on a standard Class 3F 0-6-0T at Devons Road, but damage to the port faces resulted and the experiment was soon terminated.

Many of the Tilbury 4-4-2T and 0-6-2T locomotives were shopped at Bow. I took every opportunity to see my own engines stripped and to acquire to a limited extent some of the experience which I had missed through my precipitate action in going to work at an outstation instead of a CME works a decade earlier. I was able also to continue on a more secure and regular basis technical studies at West Ham Municipal College from which I was frequently summoned in the evenings to take charge of a derailment somewhere. Altogether the years 1938 and 1939 up to the outbreak of war were amongst the happiest I can recall.

The period immediately following the declaration of war on September 3rd, 1939 was a difficult one for Tilbury section staff. Once the children and their mothers from London's East End suburbs and Essex had been loaded and despatched to the country, gas masks dangling pathetically around their necks, there was less than the normal amount of work to be performed due to a restricted passenger service and little change as yet in the freight situation. Everybody was united in wanting to make their contribution in a way that they never do in peacetime, but in the Plaistow district there was nothing extra for them to do. I suggested to the breakdown gang that we might find a knowledge of first aid useful in the months to come. None of us were qualified ambulance men, but I was able to say in my monthly personal report to Wood for January 1940 that seven of the 12 members of the gang and myself had gained the First Aid Certificate as indeed he had himself, although he said he would need to imbibe a half bottle of Scotch before tackling a gory incident.

An irritating difficulty which persisted throughout the war was the maintenance of anti-glare sheets, which festooned the cabs of locomotives. Footplate men in general never liked them and they certainly rendered the cabs stifling, on tank engines in particular. Although drawings had been issued for every class of locomotive, shewing the position of hooks and catalogue numbers of sheets to suit, the latter failed their designed purpose like the great majority of adjuncts to locomotives after they have been built, which were not incorporated in the general design. Maintenance costs of this humble item were out of all proportion to the use made of it, yet its continued provision was obviously a 'must'. (Plate 60.) Equally irritating were the restrictions which had to be enforced on the level of illumination at the scene of a breakdown, even though the sound of the air raid siren—the 'wailing banshee' as Winston Churchill once described it—may not have been heard for weeks.

The winter conditions experienced in January 1940 provided a challenge of their own. South-East Essex was badly affected by heavy falls of snow and intense frosts for which we were not properly prepared. Several 4-4-2Ts were shrouded in snow at Ockendon and had to be dug out by a company of soldiers. Wood insisted that I examined them before they were moved, although I protested that they would not be frozen up, having been protected by a snow drift; in fact they were not frozen. Less fortunate were five 4-4-2Ts which had been placed in store at Shoeburyness; on every one of them, ice which formed in the cylinders of the steam reversing gear fractured one or more cylinder covers.

In early April, Wood was promoted to be District Locomotive Superintendent at Nottingham and a rousing valedictory ceremony was held in the Labour Hall at East Ham one Saturday evening. It is amazing that a service on the Tilbury section was provided that night, for all the staff seemed to be there; although I have attended many similar functions since, I do not recall another like that one. Wood was succeeded by T. F. Mitchell, a quiet family man who hailed originally from the north where I believe he had spent some years on the LYR. Mitchell seemed content to accept things as he found them; indeed there was little point in making innovations which were not urgent at a time when it was now so evident that a violent upheaval was not far away.

One of the jobs falling to the lot of a foreman in charge of a breakdown crane was setting out, probably about 11.0pm on a Saturday night, to a bridge site where girders were to be renewed during Sunday and be ready once again for Monday morning's traffic. Such jobs were tiring because of the long hours involved and tedious because once the old girders had been removed and loaded there was often a long wait whilst preparations were made to receive the new ones. During the summer of 1940 I had such a job renewing the girders over a fairly narrow road bridge at Ockendon. Hooded lights were, of course, the order of the night and I had congratulated myself on extracting and loading the old girders with the leading wheels of the crane only 3in from the edge of the break in the rail and flanked on one side of the line by 40 to 50 communication wires, which I had skilfully avoided hitting with the jib of the crane. I dropped in the new girders to the satisfaction of the resident engineer and with a sigh of relief bade the crane driver make the crane right for travelling, which involved revolving the crane superstructure through 180deg with the jib raised. Both the crane driver and I completely forgot the wires we had successfully dodged all night. In a moment there was a noise like a modern Trinidadian steel band as the jib scythed through them like a combine harvester. I did not know at the time that most of them were GPO wires and it was afterwards alleged that part of Essex was without its air raid warning system until the linesmen had repaired the damage. I could say no more than I was sorry, but this did not prevent the development of a voluminous correspondence between the GPO and the LMSR, the outcome of which I never did hear.

Tension grew as the summer progressed towards a Sunday in August when the Luftwaffe decided to demolish the signalbox at Shoeburyness as an opening gambit in the general onslaught on the LTS section in general, and not the least its locomotives and staff. The full weight—or so it seemed to the hapless East-Enders involved—of Hitler's might in the air descended on an area bounded roughly by Stratford in the north and the Thames in the south and two to three miles wide. The raid began about 5.0pm on Saturday, September 7th and lasted for about an hour and a quarter.

When the 'all clear' sounded at about 6.15pm I left my wife in the care of neighbours and started out on my motorcycle for Plaistow shed, with which I had been unable to communicate by phone since the raid. A journey which normally occupied ten minutes was this time interrupted by dozens of fires and street blocks and it was about 7.0opm when I reached Plaistow station. This appeared completely deserted until, after walking the length of the up fast platform I met an extremely courageous PW ganger, I think named Ward but known to all as Gerry (later awarded the BEM), between Plaistow signalbox and the Northern Outfall Sewer bridge. He had walked his length from Bromley and had lost the toecap of one boot whilst diving for cover when a delayed action bomb, of which there were many, exploded en route. I told him I was bound for the motive power depot on the other side of the sewer bridge and he offered to accompany me, an offer which I accepted gladly since the scene was one of utter desolation and I dreaded what I was going to find.

The scene which confronted us en route to the depot is shown in Plates 65–68. An uncanny silence reigned. We found that the shed and lifting shop had been badly damaged and several engines were inclined at angles to the vertical. They had been lifted up by bomb blast and settled down again, not on the rails but wedged in the pit. A wagon load of boiler tubes had received a direct hit and the tubes, like broken, uncontrollable limbs, were perched amongst what was left of the roof principals. But there were no humans in sight. After trying unsuccessfully to re-establish telephone communication with Fenchurch Street Control Office from the Running Foreman's office, I decided to go home. As my ganger friend pointed out, even if I could have mustered a breakdown gang, both connections from the shed yard to the running lines were damaged and awaited attention from PW staff.

Arrived home in East Ham amidst further raid warnings, I succeeded finally in contacting Fenchurch Street Control about midnight and agreed with them that nothing could be done by motive power staff to commence line clearance that night. The railway was dead from Fenchurch Street to Barking and after a more complete appraisal had been made in daylight and some tracks had been mended we would know where to take the breakdown equipment and make a start. This may sound in retrospect like a policy of defeatism, but it was common sense. The railway and a vast area around it had been subjected to a bombardment the like of which few people could have preconceived and we were still a little incredulous that it had happened.

I arrived at the shed again at about 7.0am on Sunday morning to find some staff due on at 6.00am already beginning to clear up the mess. By 10.00am, 61 members of the repairing engines staff had arrived, many having stayed at home only long enough to see to the welfare of their families. We started rerailing the District train in West Ham up slow platform and at about 11.00am Rudgard arrived from Derby. He was the first senior motive power official I had seen that day and his appearance was a great morale booster for us all. He approved of what we were doing and impressed upon me that we were not to continue working during the hours of darkness unless it was to remove trapped people, since I should be denied any proper illumination. He ordered further that I was to see that the men were well fed and had a couple of bottles of beer every day; he would suitably instruct the catering authorities at St Pancras to meet my requirements. He then trotted off happily to peer down some mysterious holes which had appeared in the down side cutting and which proved later to contain delayed action bombs.

For the next five months I did little else but supervise the breakdown gang at docks and sidings all over the Tilbury and North London sections, where heavy damage by enemy action had occurred, punctuated by attending to day-to-day incidents on running lines whether or not caused by air raids. Within a short time such intensive and continuous clearance and rerailing work resulted in the formation of a first-class breakdown gang, which rarely found it necessary to summon help from another District despite the fact that the crane, a Cowans Sheldon, was only of 20 tons nominal capacity.

Earlier in the year I had impressed on the gang the need for the utmost care in rerailing, etc, operations so as to avoid personal injury. I had been guilty of lapses myself; on one occasion we had been called to Ilford Electrical Sidings to rerail LPTB motor coach No 4608. It was a wet night and after satisfying myself that the roads on either side of the derailed vehicle had been de-energised, I walked over to the yard foreman's office whilst the gang unloaded jacks and packing. The bottom of my mackintosh brushed the surface of a positive rail which was live when I stepped over it and I felt as though I had been poleaxed in the back of the neck.

A few weeks later we were called to the same place to rerail another motor coach, No 25981. As we were passing very slowly through East Ham Station the electrical ganger shouted to me that he had rendered all necessary roads dead. Having in mind my recent traumatic experience I asked Bill Hopwood, the only fitter in the gang, to put down a short circuiting bar to ensure that the adjacent road by the side of which we should be working *was* dead. He did so. A brilliant flash indicated that it was *not* dead, despite the ganger's assurances.

My self-righteous indignation was quickly dispelled when the LPTB foreman came running across from his office demanding to know who had stopped the entire morning peak electric service by causing the circuit breakers to operate in the substation at Heathway, east of Barking. London Transport remained unimpressed with my single-minded but untutored regard for safety during the correspondence which dragged on through many weary pages of foolscap during the following weeks. Then a load of incendiary bombs on the breakdown train mess van one night, where the papers reposed after I had added the latest episode to the epic story, put an end to it. A large number of bottles of Bass and Worthington also perished in the flames, a loss which was more keenly felt than my fall from grace.

Only once did I ask for help and that was later in September when the daylight raids had eased considerably. Stanier 2-6-4T No 2513 had run into a bomb crater at Warley and required to be lifted out in one piece—all 92 tons of it, which obviously implied the use of two cranes. I asked for the attendance of Kentish Town 36-ton crane, which did not arrive until late evening, accompanied by no less than A. W. F. Rogerson of Hasland fame, who was now the presiding genius at Kentish Town. I had already rerailed two coaches in difficult circumstances behind No 2513 and was brushing my teeth under an injector overflow pipe when Rogerson arrived slightly in advance of his cortège. I had attached lifting ropes to the bunker end of No 2513 in readiness for lifting and when Rogerson had approved the plan for joint action he announced that we would start as soon as his crane could be positioned. Whereupon I had to relate Colonel Rudgard's edict to me that we were not to continue working in the dark and point out further that my gang had been working 18 hours a day for the past fortnight; they needed rest and above all to ensure that their families were still intact. Bearing in mind all that I had heard of this remarkable man, I was amazed to hear him concur. So we lifted the engine out of the crater in quick time at first light next morning, both cranes being grossly overloaded but neither shewing signs of their maltreatment. I never favoured the gross overloading of cranes, but I knew what they could do and the sort of factors of safety built into their component parts and I never damaged one. In the case just described, however, there was nothing else available to lift the locomotive; one could only subject the equipment to the limit of its capacity with the object of avoiding a long wait for heavier tackle which was in great demand elsewhere on more important lines than the LTS section at that time.

If there was one instruction which I heeded with 100 per cent compliance in my railway career, it was that issued by Rudgard about feeding of men in severe conditions of working. Every morning Stanley Hopwood and another gang member took suitable containers and an indent to St Pancras refreshment rooms and collected the best food, either cold or capable of reheating, which was available that day together with appropriate supplies of bottled beer of the best quality. Such provision nowadays is normal routine, but prior to the last war breakdown gangs were expected to continue working for long hours on tinned beef, incompatible biscuits, Bovril and tea unless the job was likely to be a very long one. The attention now given to victualling arrangements paid handsome dividends in terms of work done and there were months of work to be done.

At locations like the Anglo American oil sidings at Purfleet, where row upon row of tank wagons had been bombed and burnt, it was possible to organise up to 30 men on salvage work with one crane by sending on ahead a team of acetylene cutters under Tom Riley, a boilersmith, who would prepare awkward cripples for lifting on to flat wagons. A common sight was a tank wagon, the solebars of which had been so hot that the weight of the buffers and the headstocks had caused the solebars to bend until the buffers touched the rails. It was often necessary to burn wheels from the rails to which they had become welded by the intense heat; the slag from the burning operation often set light to the ground, which was still soaked with oil from the bombing of weeks before.

Working in the London docks like Poplar and Millwall there was often a difficulty in hearing the air raid sirens due to the noise from the breakdown crane. In these circumstances, Ted Smallman, one of Sutton's tubers, used to climb the nearest eminence away from the site of work and armed with a bugle, he blew a blast like the Last Trump when enemy aircraft seemed liable to approach. In overcast weather the raid risk was usually less, although on one wet Sunday morning when we were working at Purfleet a Dornier flying very low appeared without warning in a gap in the clouds. We stood gaping at it until the guns of HMS *Cossack,* moored in the Thames nearby, fired at it but without success. On another occasion a similar intrusion was made at Purfleet, but this time the sirens sounded beforehand.

Terence Tandy, one of Urie's headquarters assistants, had been sent to the Tilbury section for the day to render any help he could. I do not know whether Mitchell passed him on to me or whether he had received over the grapevine a mention of the bacon and two-egg breakfasts we had to fortify ourselves for the morning's work. Whatever the truth of the matter, I extended to him the hospitality of the officer's end of the mess van, after which he descended to the scene of operations just as the sirens sounded. He asked me where we took cover and I replied that we didn't—not at that stage, anyway, even if there had been anywhere to take cover which there was not. Whereupon with great dignity and no evident alarm, Tandy removed his bowler hat, donned his helmet and laying a newspaper with delicacy on the rail, sat down under the headstock of a box van and watched us proceed with our salvage work. No visitors stayed very long in those early days of daylight raids; and there was little or nothing they could do anyway, however well intentioned they may have been, but the fact that they appeared assured us we were not forgotten. Rudgard was never far away after a particularly heavy raid and always appeared to be completely fearless. Charles Weston, another of Urie's assistants came to see us once, but if any other senior motive power officers visited the section during those fateful days of September, I never saw them. Wood was sent from Nottingham to help Mitchell for a couple of days, but was heartbroken at what he saw and realised that it was the job of the people in charge to get on with restoring a measure of normality. To the younger men, the excitement was stimulating while the work of clearance was in full swing, but during slack periods there was a tendency to fatalism. The common danger removed many so-called class barriers and unity of purpose was complete, but few of us planned beyond the next day.

Some peculiar things happened during air raids. A request was received at the depot one morning for us to remove a pair of wagon wheels from the cellar of a house *two* streets away from Barking Station. They had described a wide arc and penetrated the roof of the house, finishing in the cellar. The axle was bent, otherwise the set was intact. I sent for a couple of men and some gas and the wheelset was cut into small enough portions to remove through the domestic coal chute.

On February 4th, 1941, Mitchell received a letter from the Chief

Operating Manager which said that on February 13th I was to report to the District Locomotive Superintendent at Saltley, Birmingham, to which depot I was to be transferred and promoted, again in the position of Senior Foreman Fitter. I had no preliminary warning of this move and I accepted it eagerly but with mixed feelings. I had become very attached to the men at Plaistow, who like hundreds of thousands of others went to work in extremely difficult and often dangerous conditions but always with a lively sense of humour. I was about to find out whether similar bonds could be forged in a different setting.

Index